THE BATTLE OF THE SOMME

THE BATTLE OF THE SOMME

ALAN AXELROD

Guilford, Connecticut

An imprint of Rowman & Littlefield

Distributed by NATIONAL BOOK NETWORK

British Library Cataloguing in Publication Information Available

Library of Congress Cataloging-in-Publication Data Available

ISBN 978-1-4930-1861-1 (hardcover)
ISBN 978-1-4930-2209-0 (e-book)

♾™ The paper used in this publication meets the minimum requirements of American National Standard for Information Sciences—Permanence of Paper for Printed Library Materials, ANSI/ NISO Z39.48-1992.

For Anita and Ian

CONTENTS

CONTENTS

CHAPTER I

Chantilly Visions

SET LIKE A JEWEL IN THE CHANTILLY FOREST, THE COMMUNE OF Chantilly, traditional seat of the cousins to the kings, the princes of Condé, lies twenty-four miles northeast of Paris. It is known for Chantilly cream, Chantilly lace, and the racing and breeding of horses. The town is dominated by the conjoined Petit and Grand Châteaux de Chantilly, a vast Renaissance fairy-tale complex that was home to the Montmorency family and was, in the seventeenth century, one of the great nodes of French civilization. No less a figure than Madame de Sévigné reported that, when Louis XIV visited Chantilly in 1671, François Vatel, the maître d'hôtel to Louis de Bourbon, the Grand Condé, committed suicide for fear that the fish would be late to the banquet table.

The Grand Château was destroyed during the French Revolution, but completely rebuilt during the 1870s. It came under threat early in the Great War when German troops sweeping through northern France marched into Chantilly and, on September 3, 1914, occupied the château. The very thought of the Boche stomping their hobnail boots through the marble and parquet salons of the Grand Châteaux was at once humiliating and infuriating. Fortunately, with the eruption of the First Battle of the Marne to the south and the fatal faltering of the German juggernaut there, the soldiers did not stay long, and the château was not greatly harmed. On September 9, French troops returned to occupy the town, which became a military hospital center and home to a camouflage workshop. As of November 29, 1914, Chantilly also became the new seat of the Grand Quartier-Général (GQG), headquarters of the French army, presided over by Joseph Joffre, the army's well-fed and (at the time) much-loved senior commander.

The GQG did not take up residence in the château, but in the Hôtel du Grand Condé, a modern hotel built in 1908. For his part, "Papa" Joffre, as the French public affectionately called him, commandeered the nearby Villa Poiret as his own capacious private residence. A grand French villa with multiple high-peaked roofs, the residence spoke of quieter times and suited Joffre's notoriously inscrutable calm and studied attitude of taciturnity that might easily be taken for utter indifference. Generally imperturbable, fleshy, and slow moving, Joffre hardly looked the part of a supreme commander directing an army under imminent threat of anni-hilation in a country in the midst of deep invasion.

On July 7, 1915, Joffre hosted what became known as the First Chantilly Conference. One year into a war that the Allies—France, Brit-ain, Russia, Belgium, Serbia, and (since May 1915) Italy—were losing (each in their fashion), it was the very first time the commanders of the co-belligerent armies had come together to debate and decide strategy. The French principals in attendance were Commander-in-Chief Joffre and Alexandre Millerand, the war minister. Representing Britain were Commander-in-Chief Sir John French and the newly installed chief of the General Staff, William Robertson. The other nations—Belgium, Ser-bia, Russia, and Italy—each sent their senior military leaders.

Joffre took the lead in the conference. But all he delivered was a sin-gle message. It was that victory could be achieved only if the Allies fully coordinated their prosecution of the war. It was an astute proposition, but, unfortunately, Joffre was unprepared to flesh it out with a specific plan of action. Some plans were proposed and discussed, but none were passionately advocated, and the conference ended not in disagreement but without particular direction.

Five months later, from December 6 to December 8, 1915, the Sec-ond Chantilly Conference was convened. By this time, the war, at least on its main front, the Western Front, had congealed into a stalemate of slaughter along a line of opposing trenches running some 440 miles from the North Sea coast in the north to the border of neutral Switzerland in the south. At this point, some 1.6 million men had been killed, wounded, captured, or gone missing on all sides.

Although Joseph Joffre, general-in-chief of the French army, was technically on command par with Sir Douglas Haig, the British general invariably deferred to him as the senior partner in the Franco-British alliance. WIKIMEDIA

❧

Nobody expected things to turn out this way. Indeed, nobody expected, let alone wanted, a "world" war.

Franz Ferdinand von Österreich-Este was every inch the typical Hapsburg autocrat: elegant, bigoted, and quite out of touch with most of the empire whose throne he was set to inherit whenever his aged uncle, Emperor Franz Josef, happened to give up the ghost. On June 28, 1914, in company with his wife, the Grand Duchess Sophie, Franz Ferdinand arrived in Sarajevo, capital of Bosnia-Herzegovina, once a sovereign nation, now a mere province of the Austro-Hungarian Empire. The archduke had timed his visit deliberately. June 28 was St. Vitus' Day, the great Serbian national day of *Vidovdan*. Serbia wanted to pull Bosnia-Herzegovina out of Austria-Hungary's imperial clutches and incorporate it as part of an envisioned great Slavic state. The archduke was there to counteract this by asserting the Hapsburg brand.

Waiting for Ferdinand and Sophie on the streets of Sarajevo were five young would-be assassins, armed and trained not by the Serbian government but by the "Black Hand," a secret society of Serbian extremists. Fortunately for the archduke and grand duchess, the young killers were hardly professionals. The limousine route of the royal couple was no secret. On the contrary, it had been published in the local newspapers because Franz Ferdinand wanted to ensure an enthusiastic turnout along the capital's streets. The assassins deployed themselves along a three-hundred-yard stretch of the city's principal avenue, the Appel Quay. The first youngster, at the Cumuria Bridge, was armed with a bomb. The second, a few yards beyond him, had both a bomb and a Browning revolver. The third had a hand grenade. The fourth aspiring assassin was the least likely of the group, a dark, spindly, sickly looking youth with a Browning revolver, well concealed in the deep outer pocket of an overcoat much too big for his tubercular frame. At the end of this uncertain gauntlet was another man concealing a revolver.

That fourth youngster, the one who looked more dead than alive, was a twenty-year-old Bosnian Serb named Gavrilo Princip. He had every reason to expect that at least one of the other assassins would score a hit and that he would not be called on to act. But he showed up nonetheless.

Franz Ferdinand and Sophie rode in an open limousine that was perfect for displaying his lavish general's uniform, including a hat with green plumes, and for showing off his plumply pretty wife in her white silk dress with red sash, immense picture hat, and cape adorned with ermine tails. As the motorcade reached the Cumuria Bridge, the first assassin fumbled his bomb and failed to hurl it. The second managed to throw his bomb, but it bounced off the back of the archduke's car and rolled in front of the car following it. The explosion damaged that vehicle and sent shrapnel in all directions, injuring several spectators as well as members of the entourage. Poor Sophie's cheek was stung and bruised by a tiny metal fragment.

As the motorcade passed them, the last three killers were too stunned to do anything at all with their weapons. As the royal limousine drove on down the Appel Quay, Princip dejectedly stalked off, settling at an outdoor table belonging to Moritz Schiller's cafe. He consoled himself with a hot cup of coffee, the revolver still heavy in his coat pocket.

Franz Ferdinand and his wife attended a reception at the town hall as scheduled. But then the archduke called for a change of plan. He wanted to pay a visit at the local military hospital to look in on those who had been injured by the bomb blast. He did not want Sophie to accompany him. The city streets were clearly too dangerous. But she insisted, and he gave in.

The chauffeur had rehearsed the originally planned itinerary but was unfamiliar with the route to the military hospital. So, at the corner of the Appel Quay and Franz Josef Street, he suddenly turned. The archduke's military aide shouted to him.

Wrong way!

The driver spun the wheel but couldn't turn the large touring car around in the narrow, crowded street. So he began to back up—slowly, very slowly, because the crowds behind the car blocked his way. Finally, the chauffeur had to stop. Opposite the vehicle was Moritz Schiller's cafe and delicatessen. Just five feet away, Gavrilo Princip looked up from his coffee cup.

It was 11:15 in the morning. He recognized his target. He couldn't believe it. But there he was, Franz Ferdinand, archduke of Austria-Hungary, heir apparent to the Hapsburg throne. Princip fished for the Browning in his deep pocket, pulled back the hammer, withdrew the weapon, and leveled it. A vigilant policeman saw him and rushed to tackle him. Noting this, an out-of-work actor, apparently harboring nationalist sympathies, shoved the cop out of the way, giving Princip time to fire exactly three shots. One round penetrated the car door and hit Sophie in her stomach. The second drilled into the archduke's neck, neatly severing the carotid artery before lodging in his spine. The third shot went wild.

Those riding in the car with the stricken pair heard Sophie cry out to her husband, "For God's sake, what has happened to you?"

She then slumped against the archduke's chest and crumpled into his lap. The heir apparent cradled her head. "Soferl, Soferl, don't die! Stay alive for our children!"

But she was already dead. A certain Count Harrach climbed from the front seat into the back, took hold of the archduke, and asked him if he was suffering. The reply was a denial of reality truly worthy of a member of Hapsburg royalty in the twentieth century.

"It is nothing," he said. "It is nothing, it is nothing."

They were the final words of the heir apparent. Quickly apprehended, Gavrilo Princip immediately confessed to having pulled the trigger, so there was never any doubt of his guilt. There was not, however, a shred of evidence to implicate the Serbian government in the crime. And that was a problem for Count Leopold von Berchtold, Austria-Hungary's foreign minister, who was eager to find a cause for a war that would severely punish Serbia and serve as warning to any other nation that dared to challenge the empire. In the end, it was a problem the count simply ignored. Evidence or no evidence, he accused Serbia and decided to issue an ultimatum to its leaders.

Before he drew up the ultimatum, and even as he called for the immediate mobilization of the Austro-Hungarian army, Berchtold sent a message to the German government, asking if its support could be counted on. Kaiser Wilhelm II responded to the Austro-Hungarian ambassador over lunch in Berlin on July 5, 1914. In the middle of an agreeable meal, the kaiser announced that, yes, yes, he would back Austria-Hungary—even if it meant war with Russia.

It was a reckless knee-jerk response. Kaiser Wilhelm II always wore a military uniform, and he devoted a good deal of his empire's money to building an army and a navy. But he had no desire for war, not now, at least. Surely, Serbia would bow to whatever demands Berchtold made. The Serbian leadership knew it could not stand up against Austria-Hungary! The kaiser had every reason to believe that there would be no war.

Armed with the kaiser's promise, Berchtold sent ten demands to Belgrade on July 23 and gave the government forty-eight hours to reply to them. This sent the Serbian premier, Nicholas Pashich, to the bureaucrats who ran the Russian government for Czar Nicholas II. They promised that Russia would stand by Serbia, no matter what. Even so, Pashich quickly agreed to nine out of ten of Berchtold's demands. The only one at which he drew a line was the demand that Serbia give Austrian government officials the power to conduct police operations *inside* Serbia. To agree to this would be to cede Serbian sovereignty to the Austro-Hungarian crown.

Still, Berchtold had gained 90 percent of what he had asked for. No matter. Berchtold prevailed on his government to declare war on Serbia. In response, Russia ordered a partial mobilization of its forces near the Austrian border.

In the meantime, Kaiser Wilhelm II frantically tried to stop what he himself had put into motion. His chancellor, Theobald von Bethmann-Hollweg, telegraphed Austria's Berchtold: "Serbia has in fact met the Austrian demands in so wide-sweeping a manner that if the Austro-Hungarian government adopted a wholly uncompromising attitude, a gradual revulsion of public opinion against it in all of Europe would have to be reckoned with."[1]

Berchtold withheld any reply, thereby provoking another telegram from Bethmann-Hollweg. This one warned that Germany would refuse to be drawn into war if Austria "ignored our advice."[2] But it was too late. In the absence of conscious human will, events took on a will of their own. Even as he warned Austria-Hungary against counting on Germany's marching to war alongside it, Bethmann-Hollweg alienated British foreign secretary Sir Edward Grey by trying to force Britain into a secret pledge of neutrality. Remain neutral, he proposed, and Germany would not annex any of mainland France. Bethmann-Hollweg also denounced Russia's partial mobilization as provocative, and the kaiser ordered the mobilization of Germany's High Seas Fleet in the North Sea. This action provoked Winston Churchill, at the time Britain's first sea lord, to mobilize the British Grand Fleet.

All of this happened on a single day, July 29, 1914, the very day that Austrian river gunboats began to shell Belgrade, firing the first shots—discounting Princip's three—of the Great War.

Having partially mobilized on July 28, Russia commenced full mobilization on July 30. Hearing of this, Helmuth von Moltke, chief of staff of the German army, picked up a telephone and called Field Marshal Franz Conrad von Hötzendorf, his counterpart in the Austro-Hungarian army.

"Mobilize at once against Russia," Moltke ordered.

Imagine. A German general—not a head of state and without direction from a head of state—ordered a general commanding the army of a foreign country to take that country into war. Hötzendorf meekly complied. In the meantime, the German government issued an ultimatum to Russia, demanding that it rescind its general mobilization. Germany also issued an ultimatum to France, threatening it with war if it made any move to mobilize. Russia spurned the German ultimatum and continued to mobilize. The French government said nothing more than that it would consult its "own interests."[3]

On August 1, 1914, Germany ordered a general mobilization. On August 2, Germany demanded free passage through Belgium. By the time Belgium's King Albert angrily refused the demand, German divisions were already on the march through Flanders.

On August 3, at three in the afternoon, Edward Grey told the British Parliament that Britain was pledged to protect Belgian neutrality. "If . . . we run away from these obligations of honor and interest as regards the Belgian Treaty . . . I do not believe for a moment that, at the end of this war . . . we should be able . . . to prevent the whole of the West of Europe opposite us from falling under the domination of a single power . . . and we should, I believe, sacrifice our respect and good name and reputation before the world."[4]

Thus was Britain brought into the war. That evening, after Germany formally declared war on France, Sir Edward watched daylight dissolve into twilight and twilight into night. "The lamps are going out all over Europe," he remarked to a friend. "We shall not see them lit again in our lifetime."[5]

By dawn, having already invaded it, Germany declared war on Belgium, and England joined the other powers of Europe in a rush to deal death and to die. In fact, among most of the belligerent nations, people were thrilled by the prospect of what they believed would be a short, sharp, cheaply won war. They believed it because their leaders told them it would be so. The greatest anxiety many young men had in the summer of 1914 was that the war would end before they had a chance to join, let alone fight and win glory. Besides, labor at this point in the progress of the European Industrial Revolution was dull, dreary, and draining. Everywhere, men dropped their tools, threw down their picks and shovels, or closed their tedious ledger books, and dashed for the nearest recruiting office.

Germany entered the war with the famous Schlieffen Plan, drawn up, beginning in 1905–1906, by Count Alfred von Schlieffen, chief of the German General Staff. It called for a high-speed offensive thrust not simply from east to west, but in a "great wheel" arcing northwestward, westward, and then southwestward, swinging through Belgium and northern France so as to position for a coup de grâce attack against Paris from behind the principal armies defending it. While focusing on achieving a rapid victory in the west, the Germans would fight a defensive holding action in the east, keeping the big but bumbling Russians at bay until troops could be transferred after victory on the Western Front to triumph on the Eastern.

As for the French army, its plan bore a number, not a name. Plan XVII was more an article of faith than a plan of war. Founded on the idea of a certain French war spirit, a *furia francese* that was driven by what the great French philosopher Henri Bergson called *élan vital*, Plan XVII

9

called for an unremitting mass offensive that would arrest, turn back, or destroy any German advance. French ground was deemed sacred, and French forces were never to yield a single meter of territory, regardless of the cost in men. The principal objective of Plan XVII was to charge into the Alsace and Lorraine, the French provinces lost to Germany as a result of the humiliating defeat in the Franco-Prussian War of 1870–1871. In bold proclamation of their unstoppable élan, the French army went to war dressed in its traditional bright blue greatcoats, trousers of even brighter red, and soft cloth caps (*kepis*) instead of helmets. An ensemble designed to inspire courage, it created targets. By the end of 1914, French casualties numbered nearly a million, and Germany was firmly positioned to fight the entire Western Front war on French soil.

For that matter, during the first full month of the war, August 1914, it looked as if France would be forced to yield to Germany by early autumn. In August, the German armies defeated the French in encounter after encounter on the sacred ground of France. Simultaneously, German columns sliced through Belgium and then crossed into northern France through the virtually undefended Franco-Belgian frontier. In northern France, they encountered the British army, which, in the form of the British Expeditionary Force (BEF), had rushed to defend the neutrality of Belgium.

Germany went to war in 1914 with an army of 4.5 million, Austria-Hungary with three million, France with just over four million, and Russia with nearly six million. Throughout the nineteenth century and going into the Great War, British military power was founded largely on its navy, the magnificent instrument of imperial expansion and trade. The function of the ground forces, the British army, was to garrison the outposts of a global empire and to function as a small, highly mobile force to quell any developing unrest or conflict in the colonies. Fighting a new Napoleonic-style war, a great conflict on the Continent, was a scenario British military planners had failed to imagine, let alone seriously contemplate. In consequence, Great Britain was the only major combatant whose army consisted entirely of volunteers. There was no conscription. The army of August 1914 consisted of just four hundred thousand troops, more than half of them outside of

Europe, garrisoning outposts of the far-flung British Empire. Of the total, only about 120,000 were full-time professional soldiers. The rest were a mix of Regular Army reserve personnel and reservists serving in the Territorial Force, an all-volunteer ready reserve component that had been established by the so-called Haldane Reforms in 1908 for home defense. It is widely believed that, on August 19, 1914, Kaiser Wilhelm II personally issued his armies an order to "exterminate . . . the treacherous English and walk over General [Sir John] French's contemptible little army."[6] Although this order has never been located, the few who survived service in the British army of 1914 proudly called themselves "The Old Contemptibles."

Under Sir John French, the British Expeditionary Force (BEF) was deployed on the French army's left and thus constituted the northernmost flank of the Allied line on the Western Front. On August 23, 1914, outnumbered two to one, the BEF fought valiantly and inflicted heavy casualties on the Germans at the Battle of Mons, in Belgium, but was forced into a long retreat to the very outskirts of Paris. Here, French's army participated in the "miracle" of the Marne, the First Battle of the Marne (September 5–12, 1914), which succeeded in arresting Germany's monthlong juggernaut of conquest.

With Germany's forward momentum halted, the opposing armies began furiously and fruitlessly trying to outflank one another, sidestepping in what was soon called a "Race to the Sea." This resulted in a series of bloody battles, the costliest of which was the First Battle of Ypres (October 19–November 22, 1914) in Belgium. The BEF made up just 163,897 of the 4.4 million Allied troops who did battle against 5.4 million Germans. Strategically, the result of First Ypres was indecisive. In terms of casualties, it was catastrophic. The Germans suffered 46,765 killed, wounded, or missing. The French army lost between fifty thousand and eighty thousand (killed, wounded, or missing) out of nearly four million deployed. The Belgians, having fielded about 247,000 men, lost 21,562. But the British suffered 58,155 casualties out of 163,897. The First Battle of Ypres was essentially the end of the original BEF, which meant that it was nearly the end of the British professional army, which was the first of three armies Britain would commit to the war.

At the very outset of the conflict, Horatio Herbert Kitchener, 1st Earl Kitchener, Britain's magnificently mustachioed secretary of state for war and the most senior officer in the British army, had been the sole member of the Cabinet to predict that the war would not be over quickly. On the contrary, he was certain it would last at least three years and would "plumb the depths of [British] manpower to the last million," by which he meant that many would be killed or wounded.[7] The First Battle of Ypres was a compelling validation of this prediction, which had initially seemed outlandish. Accordingly, Kitchener was authorized to institute a massive recruitment campaign during 1914 and 1915. The enduring icon of this effort was a poster featuring an imposing head-on portrait of Lord Kitchener, his finger pointing from its gauntlet directly into the viewer's face. Above the image was the boldface headline "BRITONS." Below the image was

"wants
YOU"
JOIN YOUR COUNTRY'S ARMY!
GOD SAVE THE KING

So familiar was Kitchener's likeness that his name appeared nowhere on the poster. But hundreds of thousands answered Lord Kitchener's call. This became Britain's "second army," called Kitchener's Army, and it was assembled so rapidly that many recruits went months before receiving either a uniform or a rifle.

◆

After the First Battle of Ypres, the Western Front was doomed to stalemate. The sea put a geographical stop to the Dance of Death that was the flanking-outflanking maneuvers. Now there could be no further movement without one side or the other making a head-on, headlong breakthrough. But the awesome destructive technology of weapons available at this time favored defenders and doomed attackers. Two men manning a machine gun from a dugout or trench could kill hundreds of troops charging at them with bayonets and rifles. Heavy artillery could

Artist Alfred Leete's newspaper ad became the most famous recruitment poster of World War I. WIKIMEDIA

drive defenders out of their trenches, of course—but, then, both sides had artillery. And so, despite the defensive advantage provided by trenches, barbed wire, and machine guns, battle naturally tended toward strategic stalemate. Tactical victory or tactical defeat was measured strictly in casualties inflicted and casualties suffered.

By early 1915, both sides stubbornly tried to buck the odds against making a breakthrough. Both sides continued to squander men in attacks across no-man's-land—the fire-swept space between opposing trenches—that always ended badly for both sides, though typically worse for the attacker. Yet the big picture was this. Germany did not occupy anonymous no-man's-land. Its troops were dug into *French* territory. This was not only an intolerable assault upon French sovereignty, the lands occupied were some of the nation's richest and most productive in crops and coal. Stalemate was therefore hardest on the occupied nation. Realizing this, the Germans, who had been relentless aggressors in the first full month of the war, now assumed the defensive. They clung to the land like an infection, and, like an infection, they had to be driven out. For the Allies, defensive tactics did not seem a viable option. They felt they had no choice but to go on the attack.

It would be General Sir Douglas Haig, commanding the First Army, who would make the first determined British attempt at a major breakthrough on March 10, 1915, at the Battle of Neuve Chapelle in the Artois region of northern France. Haig was an impressive officer. In contrast to the rapidly aging, stocky, white-haired, white-mustachioed commander-in-chief of the BEF, Sir John French, Haig, ten years younger, appeared lean and fit. He also had a reputation for formidable intelligence. He had been educated at Clifton College and Brasenose College, Oxford, and then at the Royal Military College, Sandhurst. He rose quickly in colonial action in the Sudan and during the Second (Great) Boer War in South Africa. From the latter conflict, he emerged with an appointment as aide de camp to no less than King Edward VII. From this post, he became an officer of great influence in the army, first as inspector general of the cavalry and then as director of military training at the War Office. It was Haig, acting under the direction of Secretary of State for War Richard Haldane, who created the Territorial Army in 1908.

At the Somme, Sir Douglas Haig, commanding officer of the BEF, led the British army to the greatest single-day loss of life in its history. WIKIMEDIA

After serving next as chief of staff in India, Haig became, in 1912, commander-in-chief at Aldershot, the home of the regular British army. Here, he directed that force's training and preparation for war. Here, he laid down the basic principles of warfighting, as he saw them. He was convinced that every conflict invariably began with maneuvering for advantageous position, followed by the first big battle, and then played out through a long process of attrition leading up to an opportunity for one side or the other to deliver a decisive stroke: the breakthrough. This template would be used to justify much of the chaotic bloodletting of World War I.

For all his education, experience, and vaunted intellect, Douglas Haig was ultimately in tune with the unthinking French faith in the sovereign *spirit* of those fighting the war. Inculcate the proper spirit, the fire in the belly, and an army could overcome any adversary, even if that adversary were better trained, better armed, and blessed with larger numbers. Moreover, while strategic planning was important, Haig believed that tactics vigorously pursued were far more essential to victory than sound strategy. Thus, a good plan indifferently executed was far inferior to a bad plan applied with spirit. Much the same was true of decision making. Of course, it was always best to make the right decisions and then act on them. But there was something far worse than a bad decision, and that was no decision. As Haig saw it, the course of battle provided a chance to make up for bad decisions and inadequate or misguided strategy. Do *something*. Even if that something had little promise of success, do it, and you would find *some* opportunity.

At Neuve Chapelle, Haig was indeed able to achieve a breakthrough, but the British army suffered such heavy casualties that he was unable to exploit the breakthrough. It was, therefore, a short-term tactical victory rather than an enduring strategic triumph. It did, however, demonstrate that breaking through even very well-defended trench lines was possible, *provided that* surprise could be achieved and follow-through discipline maintained. The battle also persuaded the French that their British colleagues were actually capable of planning and executing an organized and vigorous attack. Finally, the scale and cost of the battle—eleven thousand British and Indian troops killed or wounded out of four divisions (about seventy thousand men)—began to accustom the British public to the high cost of a war that was far from approaching an end. Brigadier General John Charteris, who commanded a brigade in the battle, observed that England would "have to accustom herself to far greater losses than those of Neuve Chapelle before we finally crush the German army."[8]

General Sir Henry Rawlinson, one of Haig's corps commanders in the battle, drew his own valuable lesson when he sought to decisively "pinch out" the German salient at Neuve Chapelle using artillery rather than infantry. He said, "If the artillery cannot crush and demoralize the enemy's infantry by their fire effect, the enterprise will not succeed."[9]

General Henry Rawlinson, 1st Baron Rawlinson, was commanding officer of the Fourth Army, the principal British force at the Somme. LIBRARY OF CONGRESS

Unlike his commanding officer Haig, Rawlinson did not aspire to a sudden breakthrough, but to what he called an opportunity to "bite and hold." He believed that a piece of the enemy's line could be bitten off—the Neuve Chapelle salient, for example—and then held against counterattack. Do this systematically and patiently in as many places as possible along the line, and a breakthrough would eventually follow. Rawlinson believed that "biting" would not be terribly costly, and that the follow-on "holding" would compel the Germans to make counterattacks so costly that the enemy would suffer at least twice the casualties as the British troops assigned to hold the line.

It made some sense. At least, there was more strategy in the bite and hold approach than in a proposed breakthrough that relied entirely on spirit. Nevertheless, in 1915, even a relatively modest "bite and hold" strategy was beyond the capacity of the Allies, who had not invested sufficiently in the necessary heavy artillery.

Thus the First Chantilly Conference took place against a background of outright defeats, disappointments, and dull glimmers of mere possibility, which, however, a shortage of manpower and artillery prevented from fanning into full flame.

———— ✦ ————

The Second Chantilly Conference was convened on December 6, 1915, five months after the first. By this time, more battles had been fought in the northern portion of the Western Front, the greatest of which was at Loos from September 25 to October 14. Haig's First Army now had three corps, and it was the largest British battle of that year, pitting six British divisions against three German. Loos was only the British component in an ambitious Anglo-French offensive the French called the Third Battle of Artois. They expected the British to attack on a very wide front. Given the modest size of the British army, it was an unrealistic expectation, but Haig convinced himself that there was no alternative to fully cooperating with the French.

Keenly aware that First Army possessed insufficient artillery to deliver a crippling barrage against the German line, Haig decided to use a chlorine gas barrage to offset the deficiency in explosive firepower.

The Germans, after all, had used poison gas in April at the Second Battle of Ypres—and it proved highly effective, very nearly breaking the British lines. Rawlinson, commanding IV Corps in the First Army, did not believe that poison gas was in any way a substitute for adequate artillery, but did not feel entitled to object to his commanding officer. Haig further proposed to make up for the shortage of firepower by extending the duration of the barrage that would precede the infantry attack. There would be *four* days of shelling, followed by the gas barrage, and then the infantry attack. It would be brutal, but it would also sacrifice any element of surprise—the very element Rawlinson had deemed essential to a breakthrough.

Haig, like other British commanders, habitually overestimated the effect of artillery on German positions. That is because he based his assessment on the effect German artillery had on British trenches—which was devastating indeed. Haig and others failed to take into account the elaborate nature of German entrenchments, which were deeper than what the British dug and which also included deep dugouts, often reinforced with poured concrete. By 1915, in response to orders from Erich von Falkenhayn, chief of the German General Staff, German strategy had changed from an essentially offensive orientation to an essentially defensive one. The German idea was to occupy French territory, thereby forcing the Allies to attack—and to attack very hardened positions. Moreover, the Germans were developing defense in depth. They created at least two fortified entrenched lines behind their front line. In contrast to the French, who were under orders never to retreat, withdrawing from one line of defense to another was not only accepted in the German tactical playbook, it was a key aspect of German tactics. By retreating in one sector, the Germans could draw the French or British troops farther from their own trenches, and then attack, flank, isolate, and cut them off from their comrades. It is much easier to retreat when you are giving up enemy territory to the enemy, not the soil of your homeland.

Thus the British offensive at Loos was virtually set up to fail. It wasn't that the German soldiers were better than the British. It was that the German defenses were far, far better, the trenches deeper, the dugouts essentially shell-proof, and the barbed wire thicker and more extensively

A dead German soldier near the door of one of the elaborately constructed dugouts that were features of German entrenchments. The horror in the soldier's face and position is fresh, even though his body is partly skeletonized. IMPERIAL WAR MUSEUM PHOTOGRAPHIC ARCHIVE

deployed. Many of the French villages the Germans captured were hardened into fortified complexes, and lines of communication and support were robust. Most important of all was the Germans' positioning of artillery and machine guns to create lethal interlocking fields of fire. British and French positions were deliberately designed to discourage defensive thinking. If it was natural to seek safety in a deep trench, then encourage offensive action by making the trenches shallower. German defenses, in contrast, were designed to provide shelter, conserve manpower, and survive Allied attack in order to enhance German counterattack.

And so the British offensive at Loos failed and failed catastrophically. Of the roughly 108,000 British troops deployed at Loos, 59,247, nearly 60 percent, became casualties. On the German side, of some sixty thousand engaged, twenty-six thousand were killed or wounded.

The British public, politicians, and press demanded that someone be held responsible for the slaughter. When the Second Chantilly Conference convened on December 6, gathering together military representatives from France, Italy, Russia, and Britain, it was Sir John French who headed the British delegation. Surely, Sir John's mind could not have been entirely on the conference. Since October and the defeat at Loos, pressure had been mounting for the BEF commander-in-chief to fall on his sword and resign. He resisted, but on December 4, General French received a phone call from Walter Hulme Long, First Viscount Long and secretary of state for the colonies. Long conveyed the decision made by Prime Minister Herbert Henry Asquith: Sir John French *must* resign. Accordingly, the general sent his letter of resignation immediately, but it did not even reach the prime minister's desk until December 6. Having received no response from Asquith on the opening day of the conference, French attended. In the event, Asquith informed French that his resignation, while accepted, would not go into effect until December 18. So French was the lamest of lame ducks when he represented Britain in the meeting by which the Allies formulated their coordinated military agenda for 1916. General Sir Douglas Haig, the very man who had actually planned and directed the failed Loos offensive, was named to replace French as BEF commander-in-chief, but he was not even present at the conference.

General Joseph Joffre proposed that the Allies conduct a series of offensives in 1916 designed expressly to end the war. They were to be coordinated not only on the Western Front, but on the Italian Front and the Russian Front as well. Wherever possible, the offensives were to be conducted simultaneously. At the very least they were planned to be no more than a month apart. The objective was to make it impossible for the enemy to transport reserves from one front to another.

That was the vision of Chantilly: to hit the enemy hard and repeatedly from every direction, so that he could not build up reserves in any one place. Coordinate and maintain this offensive pressure, and Germany was sure to crack. Little wonder that the Second Chantilly Conference created a heady atmosphere among the Allies. The Germans could not be everywhere at once. Coordinate simultaneous offensives from the east

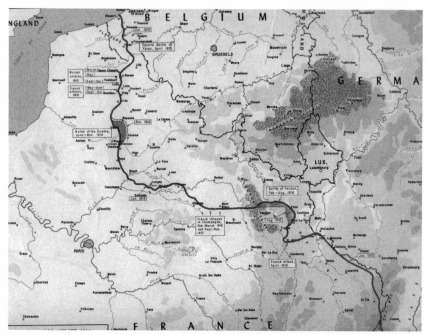

The Western Front in 1916. UNITED STATES MILITARY ACADEMY

(Russia), the south (Italy), and the west (France and Britain), and 1916 could hardly fail to be the year of Allied triumph.

Among the British, the optimism was strongest. "Kitchener's Armies" were rapidly filling up with bright, eager, spirited young men. Sir John French, thoroughly scapegoated for the fruitless slaughter at Loos, was out, and Douglas Haig was in as the new BEF commander-in-chief. In London, the Imperial General Staff also had a new chief, General Sir William Robertson.

Back in 1877, "Wully," as Robertson was affectionately called, had lied about his age to obtain enlistment in the army. He worked himself up from private through all the non-commissioned ranks and, after a dozen years as an enlisted trooper, he was promoted to second lieutenant of the 3rd Dragoon Guards. He served as an officer in India and India's North West Frontier with Afghanistan and then in the Second (Great) Boer War before entering into a series of high-level administrative posts. After serving as commandant of the Staff College, he was named Quartermaster General for the BEF at the outbreak of the Great War. It was from this important post that he was elevated to chief of the Imperial General Staff. Wully Robertson's combination of combat experience and ample administrative ability made him a welcome replacement for Sir Archibald Murray, in whom many had lost confidence after he suffered a physical collapse during the British retreat from Mons on August 23, 1914.

Yes, 1916 promised a fresh start in so many ways, and Douglas Haig, the newly minted commander-in-charge of the BEF, looked forward to a grand offensive with France in the Somme region, centered at the very place where the northern flank of the French army made contact with the southern flank of the British. A great and promising enterprise it would be. If only the four Allies could maintain the close collaboration, victory was surely within reach before the coming year was out.

CHAPTER 2

Chantilly Revisions

THE VISION OF THE FIRST CHANTILLY CONFERENCE, ON JULY 7, 1915, was one of grand coordination among the Allies, France, Britain, Russia, and Italy. The second conference, on December 6–8, sharpened this vision, specifying virtually simultaneous attacks by each of the Allies from every direction: France and Britain from the west, Russia from the east, and Italy from the south. The Germans were already strained by fighting a two-front war. Ensure simultaneous offensives on the Western and Eastern Fronts *and* add a third in the south. It seemed certain that Germany would break.

Sir Douglas Haig formally succeeded Sir John French as commander-in-chief of the BEF on December 19. In an obituary article published in *Pall Mall Magazine* in November 1928, Winston Churchill would write of Haig that he "does not appear to have had any original ideas" and had not even "a spark of that mysterious, visionary, often sinister genius which enabled the great captains of history to dominate the material factors, save slaughter and confront their foes with the triumph of novel apparitions." Haig's concept of strategy, Churchill believed, was limited to "Hurl [his armies] on and keep slogging at it. . . ."[1] But as Churchill saw it, lack of imagination was hardly the worst thing about Sir Douglas. The worst thing was the characteristic he shared with all of the other top commanders in the Great War, namely distance from the front lines.

Winston Churchill had been named first lord of the admiralty in October 1911. During the arms race with Germany that preceded the outbreak of the Great War, First Lord Churchill championed and led the rapid modernization of the Royal Navy, ensuring that it would remain superior to the quickly expanding German High Seas Fleet. Indeed, Churchill successfully lobbied for the largest naval expenditure in British history, so that the Royal Navy, far more than the army, was adequately prepared when World War I broke out in July 1914. Churchill entered the war with boundless confidence in the modern navy he had been instrumental in creating. This led him, early in 1915, to plan a daring amphibious assault on the strait dividing the Balkans from Asia Minor, the Dardanelles, which was held by German-allied Turkey. With the Western Front deadlocked, Churchill hoped that he could achieve a breakthrough on the Turkish front. Besides, he reasoned that if the Allies gained control of the Dardanelles, a vital supply line would be opened wide to Russia, the key ally on the Eastern Front. Bold though this grand strategy was, neither Churchill nor his naval commanders sufficiently pursued the tactical and logistical details necessary to execute it. World War I was fought on a vast scale that demanded sweeping strategic thought. Churchill and, for that matter, those who had attended the two Chantilly conferences were willing to paint strategy with the broadest of brushes. What they often could not do, however, was follow up with commensurate tactics. As a result, the naval assault on the Dardanelles was an abortive failure and resulted in Churchill's removal as first lord of the admiralty in May 1915.

His forced departure from office was a bitter defeat for Churchill. Worse yet, it did not save him from being associated with the Gallipoli Campaign, the land component of the assault. As the instigator of the naval offensive, he was also considered the architect of the land offensive, which failed catastrophically. Allied losses amounted to 252,000, including forty-six thousand battle deaths over eight agonizing months, long after Churchill was no longer in charge. Disgusted, Churchill severed all connection with the government in November 1915, believing his political career was at an end. He now sought and accepted command as colonel of the 6th Royal Scots Fusiliers, leading them in combat on the Western Front from January to May 1916. It was not his first experience of war—he had seen action in Cuba, India, Sudan, and South Africa—but the Western Front was unlike anything anyone had ever experienced, and it led him to criticize top generals of the Great War. Prior to the conflict of 1914–1918, generals were always in the thick of the battle. In the Great War, Churchill wrote, the generals worked "in calm surroundings, often beyond even the sound of the cannonade. There are no physical disturbances: there is no danger: there is no hurry." Indeed, Churchill continued, the "generalissimo of an army of two million men, already for ten days in desperate battle, has little or nothing to do except to keep himself fit and cool." That "generalissimo" had "no need . . . to wear boots and breeches," unless he wanted to "ride a horse . . . for the purposes of health." To the modern general, warfare is a matter of "staff [moving] flags upon his map, or perhaps one evening the Chief of the Staff himself will draw a blue line or a brown line or make a strong arrow upon it." As for "personal encounters," these "are limited to an unpleasant conversation with an Army commander who must be dismissed, an awkward explanation to a harassed Cabinet, or an interview with a representative of the neutral Press." There is no urgency, as "Time is measured at least by days and often by weeks. There is nearly always leisure for a conference even in the gravest crises."[2]

RESOLVE AND REALITY

The distance between those in command and those in the fight, Churchill believed, was responsible for much of the futility and much of the cost of the Great War. But it was even worse than Churchill thought. Douglas Haig actually had very little voice in deciding the precise role Britain would play in the planned joint offensive. The big decisions were made even farther from the front lines than Haig's headquarters at Montreuil, some ninety miles behind the Somme front lines. They were made by the War Committee of the Cabinet, meeting in London, 285 miles from the trenches. The decision there was to endorse the decisions of Chantilly and to focus British efforts on offensives in northern France and Flanders. The dissenting voice in this decision was that of Churchill's replacement as first lord of the admiralty, A. J. Balfour. He believed that the best chance for making a war-winning breakthrough was in the east and the other "peripheral" fronts, and he predicted that a major Western Front offensive was doomed to fail for the simple reason that the Germans had done and were still doing everything possible to "make their line impregnable." This prediction was not so much the product of fear or pessimism as it was of recent history. So far, Balfour held, neither the British nor the French had devised "sufficient reply to the obstacles provided by successive lines of trenches, the unlimited use of barbed wire, and the machine guns."[3]

Balfour's objection to the Chantilly proposal was really another way of saying what subsequent military historians would say of the whole of World War I. The technology of defense—trenches, barbed wire, machine guns, and (Balfour might have added) heavy artillery—far outpaced the technology of attack, which consisted (in 1916) mainly of bolt-action rifles, hand grenades, and chemical weapons. Balfour's objection also highlighted a key strategic difference between Germany and the Allies. After the First Battle of the Marne (September 5–12, 1914) ended more than a month of offensive in the form of German invasion and initiated the fruitless sidestepping maneuvers of the so-called Race to the Sea (September 17–October 19, 1914), the Germans dug into *French* soil and assumed not merely a defensive posture, but a posture of defense in depth. The Allies, in contrast, persisted in embracing all the technological disadvantages of an uncompromising offensive posture. In essence, they settled on a strategy of beating themselves to death against a deep defense that had plenty of room to retreat and still remain within France.

Balfour realistically asked the other members of the War Committee if the Allies were willing to fight an action in which they were likely to lose more men than the enemy did. He also expressed his belief that, in the end and after all that bloodshed, the Allies' strategic position would remain unchanged.

By letter, Lord Kitchener delivered a rebuttal to Balfour's position. He did not dispute any of the points Balfour made, any of the doubts he raised. Rather, he merely stated that Germany's objective was preeminence in Europe, which it intended to establish by crushing France, an outcome that would compel the other Allies to come to terms with Germany. This outcome could not be permitted, Kitchener argued. Although he did not give reasons why the offensive would succeed, he did say that the spring of 1916 was the best chance for its success. In essence,

Kitchener's rebuttal consisted of the assertion that the offensive had to take place because it had to take place.[4] In the end, the War Committee agreed on the offensive not because they were convinced it would succeed, but because failing to undertake it would produce an unacceptable outcome, a Europe dominated by Germany.

Armed with the less than confidence-inspiring mandate of the War Committee, Haig tasked the commanding generals of the three armies at his disposal with formulating, first, operations to wear down the enemy and, second, an offensive that would be a decisive attack "to pierce the enemy lines."[5]

To *pierce* the enemy *lines*. Those two words are significant. First, "pierce" implies a breakthrough over a narrow front. Second, "lines" is the plural of *line*, and in that plural is the nub of the problem the attackers faced. It would be difficult and costly to break through the first line of German trenches, but it could be done. In fact, the Germans habitually let this happen. Unlike the French and British, who were ordered to give up nothing and to hold everything, the Germans were quite willing to evacuate their front trenches—and, sometimes, even their second-line trenches. Their objective was to withdraw to the third line, get reinforced, and then envelop the Allied forces that had *pierced* a narrow breach in their lines. The German defenders could easily pinch off any narrow Allied salient, isolating the invaders and enfilading them on two flanks.

Haig insisted that, done right, the breakthrough would not be a trap, but, rather, would draw out the enemy, forcing him to "exhaust his reserves." Haig's plan was to wear down the Germans via the initial breach, and then follow up with mass attacks against the weakest points along the German line.[6]

It was more wishful thinking than anything else. One month into the Battle of the Somme, on August 1, Churchill would advocate withdrawing and renewing the attack in some different sector. His justification for doing this exposed the weaknesses in Haig's approach. After a month of fighting, Churchill wrote, penetration had been made on a front of only eight thousand to ten thousand yards across. "Penetration upon so narrow a front is quite useless for the purpose of breaking the line." The opening pierced was so narrow that "no large force could be put through."

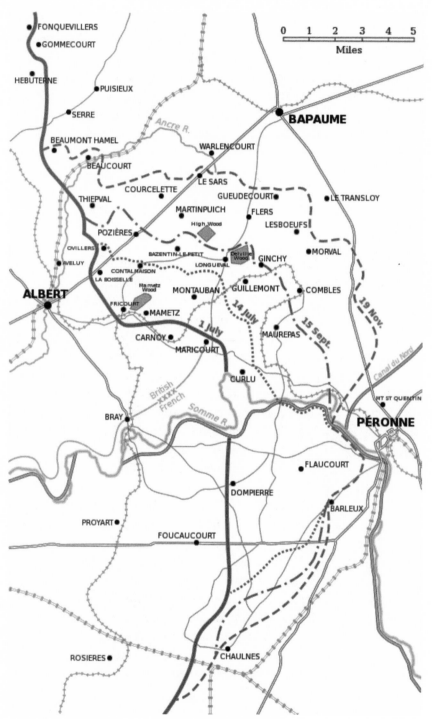

The Battle of the Somme on June 1, 1916. WIKIMEDIA

Moreover, Churchill pointed out the true meaning of German defense in depth. Even if a modest breakthrough were made, it would be made into very formidable backup defenses. Progress hitherto had been so slow that the Germans could "by now have converted the whole countryside in front of our attack into successive lines of defence and fortified posts." The men constituting the puny breakthrough would be quickly enfiladed and wiped out.[7]

And there was even worse, as far as Churchill was concerned. "The open country towards which we are struggling by inches is capable of entrenched defence at every step, *and is utterly devoid of military significance.*"[8]

THE VERDUN FACTOR

The War Committee should have seen the merit of Balfour's position, and they should also have recognized at the outset at least some of the conditions that Churchill pointed out one month into the battle. But they did neither, and so the offensive was ordered. Doubtless, the committee was encouraged by the knowledge that the BEF would not go it alone. The French promised to contribute forty divisions to the offensive—potentially 560,000 men, assuming divisions with fourteen thousand men each. That was critical, since the BEF was still very much in the process of building an army on the scale of the other combatants, both friendly and hostile. To realize the vision of Chantilly, very large armies capable of very large offensives were required on the Western Front just as they were on the Eastern and Southern Fronts. The only factor that would make the Somme operation effective, let alone decisive, was the sheer size of forces used. The vision articulated at Chantilly was one of overwhelming Germany with overwhelming attacks from three sides. This would stretch German resources to the breaking point, since high command, assailed from every direction, would not be able to shift resources from one front to another.

Winter intervened between the Second Chantilly Conference and spring, when weather conditions would be favorable for major offensives on all the fronts. Fighting did not stop in the winter—that is not the way modern warfare worked—but it was generally confined mainly to what contemporary commanders called "trench warfare," by which they meant holding actions, more or less desultory combat between the front lines without any intention of mounting a major operation aimed at a breakthrough.

One of the complaints Churchill lodged against Sir Douglas Haig was his myopic focus on the Western Front. The war created two strategic camps among the Allies, but in no ally more than the British. There were those who believed the war would be won on the Eastern Front and the other, more remote fronts: the Ottoman lands of Asia Minor and the Middle East, and the frontier region between Italy and Austria. And there were those who were absolutely convinced that the issue would be decided exclusively on the Western Front, compared to which everything else was quite properly a sideshow. Haig was one of the most extreme among this latter group.

In contrast to Haig was Erich von Falkenhayn, Prussian minister of war at the outbreak of the conflict and, since September 14, 1915, also chief of the German General Staff. Critics of Haig, who considered him an unimaginative plodder with a ready willingness to accept a high rate of "wastage" (the term Haig and others used in place of "casualties," let alone words like *killed* or *wounded* or *missing*), would have found in Falkenhayn the same characteristics. Indeed, since World War I, historians have been virtually unanimous in condemning both top commanders not so much as incompetent but as dim-witted. It is true that Falkenhayn's background was far from flamboyant, dashing, or brilliant. Falkenhayn wielded remarkable power early in the war, simultaneously holding the ostensibly civilian Cabinet post of minister of war *and* the highest office in the German military, chief of the German General Staff. Nevertheless, remarkably little is known about his personal life, and what *is* known is not particularly fascinating. Indeed, it contributes to the historical impression of his mental mediocrity.

Falkenhayn was born in 1861, married in 1886, and was accepted into the *Preussische Kriegsakademie* (Prussian War College) in 1887. Inasmuch as the Kriegsakademie was reserved for those young officers destined to positions on the German General Staff or other high command, Falkenhayn's few outright admirers had a hard time identifying any evidence of exceptional strategic or leadership talent in the young man. Indeed, he

Erich von Falkenhayn, chief of the German General Staff, presided over the battles of the Somme and Verdun before he was replaced by the team of Paul von Hindenburg and Erich Ludendorff. WIKIMEDIA

showed little interest in military theory, which was the principal subject taught at the Kriegsakademie. He did, however, gain a range of practical experience. From 1896 to 1903, he served in the German Military Mission to China both during the run-up to the Boxer Rebellion and at its height. Service in this limited but intense theater was conducive to promotion, and Falkenhayn moved from captain to major quickly and was even assigned a key role in the provisional government of Tientsin. No statesman, he governed with neither imagination nor humanity, but his superiors credited him with restoring order to a dangerous and confused situation. When he destroyed a large section of the ancient and sacred city wall of Peking (Beijing) to facilitate communications, supply, and reinforcement of German and other Western forces in the capital, his superiors did not object, let alone complain. They deemed the destruction evidence of military efficiency. Besides, Falkenhayn supplied Berlin with a steady stream of remarkably lucid reports from the front. Kaiser Wilhelm II found these good reading, and he became a champion of the officer who wrote them. When Falkenhayn returned to Germany in 1903, the kaiser saw to it that he was given command of an infantry battalion. Three years later, Falkenhayn was named chief of staff of the Sixteenth Army Corps at Metz. In this capacity, he served under General Maximilian von Prittwitz. That officer's eventual rise to full command of the Sixteenth was due less to Prittwitz's demonstrated ability than to Falkenhayn's efficiency. Unlike many underlings on whose good work a boss ascends, Falkenhayn was also (once again) recognized as an efficient officer. The kaiser had his eye on him.

By 1911, already a brigadier general, Falkenhayn was plucked for command of a prestigious Guards regiment. The next year, he was bumped up to major general and given another posting as a chief of staff, and in 1913, after promoting him to lieutenant general, Kaiser Wilhelm II named him Prussian minister of war. It was a meteoric rise without commensurately prodigious achievements propelling it. Most of Falkenhayn's colleagues were jealous rather than impressed, and Falkenhayn's demeanor—icy and remote—did nothing to ingratiate him with his fellow officers. But he had the approval and patronage of the one who mattered most, namely the emperor of Germany.

Little wonder, then, that so many took—and still take—a dim view of Erich von Falkenhayn. Yet, by early 1916, he had actually compiled a record arguably, maybe even clearly, superior to that of top command in any other combatant nation. To be sure, he had been among those who most enthusiastically urged a somewhat reluctant kaiser to go to war in the first place—on the assumption that the Schlieffen Plan would necessarily bring a speedy and relatively cheap victory. The advice proved catastrophic, and the assumption on which it was based proved wrong. Nevertheless, after the First Battle of the Marne (September 5–12, 1914) and the futility of the Race to the Sea (September 17–October 19, 1914), Falkenhayn was quick to see what neither Joseph Joffre nor Douglas Haig saw: that the course of the war no longer permitted a quick decisive victory or defeat. He also understood what this meant. *Vernichtunsstrategie, the* "strategy of annihilation" that the Schlieffen Plan was supposed to enable, now had to be exchanged for *Ermattunsstrategie,* a "strategy of attrition." This is something neither Joffre nor Haig recognized. They still thought that annihilation of the enemy was possible.

Embracing *Ermattunsstrategie,* Falkenhayn, as chief of the German General Staff, presided over several successes, including victory at Saint-Mihiel, the seizure of Antwerp and the English Channel ports, the triumphant offensive against the Russians in May 1915, the efficient neutralization of the Serbian army, and the heavy casualties inflicted upon the French in the Argonne. It was to these German victories that Joffre and Haig had decided to respond with the offensives agreed to at Chantilly.

Just wait for spring. But Falkenhayn moved first.

And he moved first because, in contrast to Haig, he looked beyond the Western Front and toward the wider war. Germany's war on the Eastern Front had not begun well. On August 17, 1914, the Russians invaded East Prussia, together with the Austro-Hungarian province of Galicia. But the Germans quickly turned defeat into overwhelming victory at the Battle of Tannenberg. Between August 26 and August 30, 1914, the German army inflicted on the 230,000-man Russian Second Army 170,000 casualties, killed, wounded, or captured. This triumph convinced Falkenhayn that there was great opportunity on the Eastern Front. Large forces were pulled out of the Western Front trenches and sent east to fight the

Second Battle of the Masurian Lakes (February 7–22, 1915) followed by the massive Gorlice-Tarnów Offensive in Galicia (May 2–June 10, 1915). By the end of 1915, Falkenhayn felt that the Russian threat to Germany's eastern frontier was largely ended, so he decided the time had come to bring a lot of men back to the Western Front.

What would he do with them? The short answer is that he decided to attack Verdun, a small city in Lorraine in northeastern France. Arguably, it was a good idea. France's humiliating defeat in the Franco-Prussian War (1870–1871) motivated development of a system of defensive fortifications along the Franco-German border that defeat had redrawn. Verdun was a major strongpoint in this system. Historically, this made sense. The Latin origin of the city's name is *Verodunum*, meaning "strong fort," and the town had been fortified first by the Gauls in their conflict against the forces of Rome during 58–50 BC. Geographically (at least in a macro sense), fortifying Verdun also made sense, since it served as a kind of gateway from the east into the French interior.

On a micro level, the town of Verdun was actually a very poor place for a fortress. The city has the Meuse River to the northeast and is otherwise surrounded by hills and ridges, high ground that gives the advantage to an attacker and the vulnerability to the defender. But after the Franco-Prussian War, it was not the *town* of Verdun that was the fortress. It was the military sector of which the town was only the anchor. By the time of World War I, the "Fortified Region of Verdun," as the sector was called, had thirty-four forts and *ouverages* (lesser fortifications). In fact, fortifications cropped up everywhere across the landscape, some of them huge and impressive, such as Fort Douaumont, at the time the largest concrete structure in the world. They were part of a greater fortification system initially designed by military engineer Adolphe Séré de Rivières, which ran from Dunkirk on the English Channel to Nice on the Riviera. From the 1870s to the outbreak of World War I, France built into this system 504 forts supplemented by 278 permanent artillery emplacements, including the forts and *ouverages* of Verdun.

In a conflict in which neither side would ever completely give up on searching for a breakthrough that would end the bloody stalemate of trench warfare, Verdun looked like a good place to use forces freed up from the east. What is more, in its adherence to a doctrine of attack to the exclusion of defense—a doctrine of "*attaque à outrance*," attack to the uttermost—French high command had stripped the fortifications of the Verdun sector of most of their heavy artillery and many of their soldiers, sending both commodities to other sectors, where they would be thrown away on hopeless offensives. In February of 1916, Verdun was therefore supremely vulnerable, and on February 21, 1916, Falkenhayn, with superior manpower and, even more important, overwhelmingly superior artillery presence, attacked.

LOWERED EXPECTATIONS

The German offensive against Verdun changed everything—but not as quickly as it might have. And this is where Falkenhayn's strategic rationale becomes dicey. Instead of throwing everything he had against the weakly held Verdun sector, Falkenhayn deployed his forces in a series of what some military historians have called "penny-packet" attacks. They had an effect, and it often looked as if the French would indeed lose the battle at Verdun, resulting in a German breakthrough. But, incredibly, the French line was bent, but it ultimately held, and what might have been a decisive German action at Verdun became yet another Western Front ordeal of futile sacrifice.

The Battle of Verdun would grind on from February 21, 1916, to December 20 of that year and would cost Falkenhayn his job as chief of the German General Staff. In a 1919 memoir and elsewhere, Erich von Falkenhayn argued that his objective had never been to force a breakthrough at Verdun. What he actually intended to do all along, he claimed, was to wage a campaign of attrition against the French army in order to—in a phrase that became infamous after the war—"bleed France white." In the 1919 memoir and an article on the war he published in a military magazine[9] the same year, he quoted a strategic memorandum he claimed to have sent to Kaiser Wilhelm II in December 1915. It has been known as the "Christmas Memorandum" ever since:

> *France has been weakened militarily and economically—almost to the limit of what it can stand—through the ongoing loss of coal fields*

in the northwest of the country. Russia's army has not yet been fully defeated, but its offensive ability has been so broken that it will not be able to regain anything like its old strength. Serbia's army can be considered destroyed. Italy has without a doubt recognized that it cannot count on its appetite for spoils being satisfied in the near future and would therefore probably be happy to escape from this adventure in any honorable way possible.

. . . There is only one matter—the most important one—that cannot be passed over. That is the incredible pressure that England still exerts on its allies. . . . Thus it is all the more important that all the means suitable for harming England in what is properly its own territory are simultaneously brought to ruthless application. These means are submarine warfare and laying the groundwork for a political and economic alliance not only between Germany and its allies, but also between Germany and all those states that are not yet fully constrained within England's sphere of influence. The formation of this alliance is not the topic of this exposition. Solving this task lies solely with the political leadership.

Submarine warfare, however, is a tool of war, just like any other tool. Those in charge of leading the war effort cannot avoid taking a position on this . . .

An advance against Moscow would lead us nowhere. We do not have enough strength for any of these enterprises. As a result, Russia is not a suitable object for attack. Only France remains. . . .

There are targets lying within reach behind the French section of the Western Front for which the French leadership would need to use their very last man. Should they do this, then France would bleed to death, *for there is no retreat, regardless* if we ourselves reach the target or not. *Should they not do this, and should these targets fall into our hands, then the effect on morale in France would be enormous. For these operations, which are limited in terms of territory, Germany will not be compelled to expend itself to a degree that would leave it seriously exposed on other fronts. Germany can confidently await the relief operations that can be expected at these fronts—and, indeed, hope to have enough forces available to meet the attacks with*

37

counterstrikes. For Germany can conduct the offensive quickly or slowly, break off the offensive for a period of time or strengthen the offensive, according to its objectives.

The targets being spoken of are Belfort and Verdun. What was said above applies to both of them. All the same, Verdun is to be preferred.[10]

It is a remarkable statement of war aims, which seems to amply demonstrate the great difference between Falkenhayn and Haig. Falkenhayn thought in terms of the biggest of big pictures, whereas Haig limited his gaze to the Western Front. In terms of battle doctrine, the Christmas Memorandum opposes Falkenhayn to Haig—and to Joffre, for that matter—even more starkly. Whereas Haig (and Joffre) could accept no doctrine other than attack, Falkenhayn's Christmas Memorandum argued that, after the collapse of the great German offensive of August 1914 at the First Battle of the Marne, attrition became the only viable approach to the war. Logically, this dictated that Germany shift from an offensive strategy to a defensive posture *upon French soil*. Against the entrenchments of a defense in depth, France would be obliged to bleed *itself* white.

Falkenhayn presents a cogent strategy here. There are just two problems with it. The first is that if the French government and military considered Verdun so important that they would defend it at unlimited cost, why did Joffre (with the approbation of most of his commanders) strip the sector of artillery and personnel, rendering it, defensively, an empty shell? The second problem is that the only place the Christmas Memorandum exists is in the postwar writings of Erich von Falkenhayn. Neither the original document nor any independent record of it has ever been found, which has led numerous historians to doubt that the document ever existed and to speculate that Falkenhayn had confabulated it after the war in an effort to exonerate himself for having failed to make the breakthrough at Verdun that might well have ended World War I in a German triumph or, at the very least, a negotiated settlement favorable to Germany.

As for the Chantilly plans for a massive offensive at the Somme, Verdun changed everything. Had Falkenhayn attacked all-out at Verdun and achieved a quick breakthrough, the change in plan would have been more profound because France would likely have been overrun and might therefore have solicited a negotiated peace with its enemy. Such an outcome would have, as Falkenhayn himself put it, "knocked the sword out of Britain's right hand," almost certainly obliging the British to withdraw from the war. But even the failure to break through changed everything nevertheless. It turned Verdun into yet another instance of Western Front mutual slaughter—a prolonged threat to France and its Allies.

As conceived following the Second Chantilly Conference, France and Britain were to attack on the Somme front with a combined strength of a spectacular ninety-five divisions. Although Falkenhayn had not made a quick breakthrough and, despite German advantages, was suffering heavy casualties, he refused to let up on Verdun. Both the French and British feared that Verdun would break.

They had good reason to. British and French political and military leaders met on March 28. The French confessed to very heavy losses at Verdun and told both Kitchener and Sir William Robertson, chief of staff of the Imperial General Staff, that it was time for the British to step up and take a larger role in the conduct of the war. When Kitchener called on Haig the next day, Haig told him, "I have not got an army in France really, but a collection of divisions untrained for the field."[11] In short, he did not feel ready to fight—but, of course, he would. It was not until May 10 that Robertson conveyed to the War Committee that the French now estimated their Verdun killed and wounded at 115,000—staggering losses that he believed were actually even heavier. Moreover, he thought the French were overestimating German losses. The committee had been digesting this information for a week—recall Churchill's comments on the leisure with which rear-echelon top command responded to urgent crisis—when Lord Kitchener warned them that Germany was winning at Verdun, and that the Germans would likely "wear through" the French there and "go on to Paris."[12] Compounding the problem of Haig's frank assessment of the readiness of his army was the fact that Joffre had decided to divert fifteen French divisions from the Somme to Verdun. He had promised Haig forty French divisions for the mighty offensive. Now he could afford to spare no more than twenty-five.

At the two Chantilly Conferences, the Allies had outlined a strategy for victory. By May, the vision of Chantilly had been radically revised. The new strategy—if that is what it can be called—was one of desperation. Deprived of fifteen French divisions on whose support it had depended, the partially trained British Expeditionary Force would assume the major burden for an offensive no longer designed to win the war but to avoid losing it. The objective of the great Anglo-French Somme offensive had been clear even if its prospects for success were questionable. It was to be one-third of a three-front assault on Germany intended to force Falkenhayn to allocate his forces to defend against simultaneous Allied offensives from the west, east, and south. Assuming (and it is a huge assumption) that all three would have taken place on time and effectively, this might well have been a war-winning action. Now, however, the objective of what would be a mostly British offensive on the Western Front was to do no more than relieve pressure on Verdun by compelling Falkenhayn to transfer resources from that sector to the Somme. This, it was hoped, would buy Joffre time to build up the Verdun defenses he himself had so heedlessly torn down and thereby prevent a German breakthrough that might well bring the war to a bad end for the Allies.

CHAPTER 3

The Men and Their Plans

IN 1914, BRITAIN WENT INTO THE GREAT WAR WITH A LAND FORCE
that was more police force than army. As an island, Britain had always
relied first and foremost on the Royal Navy for defense. For this reason,
its standing army was not only small, but consisted entirely of volunteers.
In 1914, Britain was the only major nation in Europe that did not popu-
late its armed forces through conscription. It was, at the outbreak of the
war, divided into five principal forces: the Regular Army (247,432 men
in 1914), a volunteer reserve called the Territorial Army (which rapidly
expanded from just two thousand men in August 1914, intended for
home defense), an Army Reserve (in 1914 consisting of 145,350 soldiers
retired from active duty but who committed to twelve days of annual
training), a Special Reserve (sixty-four thousand men who committed
to six months of full-time training, then three to four weeks of annual
training thereafter), and a National Reserve (215,000 men with military
experience, who were registered for call-up but who did not commit to
any training regimen).

BRITISH SOLDIERS
At the outbreak of the war, then, the British army had a paper strength
of nearly seven hundred thousand, of which only about 150,000 were
immediately available for mobilization as the British Expeditionary
Force (BEF). It was the proverbial drop in a bucket, compared with
1.65 million troops mobilized by France in 1914 and 1.85 million by
Germany. Before the Entente Cordiale signed by Britain and France in

1904, the English believed they had no good reason to create an army any larger than what was necessary to police the colonies. With regard to continental Europe, Britain maintained a policy it was pleased to call "splendid isolation." Guided by this diplomatic orientation, British military planners had no reason to think the nation would become entangled in a war against land powers with armies of much greater strength. Indeed, the principal object of the Entente was to end nearly a millennium of hostility between Britain and France mainly by reconciling the colonial interests of the two nations to avoid conflict. It was true that the Entente Cordiale also committed Britain to aiding France in the event of a *European* war, thereby necessarily ending the fiction of "splendid isolation." Yet the likelihood of a large continental war involving France seemed remote. Besides, the Entente obliged Britain to embark no more than six infantry divisions and five cavalry brigades.

Britain had another treaty obligation, much older than the Entente Cordiale, that had long threatened to undercut splendid isolation. By the 1839 Treaty of London, Britain committed itself to the protection of Belgian neutrality. Yet, as with the Entente, the likelihood of having to make good on the pledge seemed remote. Certainly, Belgium was not going to provoke a war with any of its European neighbors, and while Germany had already demonstrated aggression toward France in the Franco-German War of 1870–1871, it clearly coveted no territorial expansion at the expense of little Belgium. With a long border across which Germany might attack France, nobody in Britain dreamed that there would be reason to invade France via Belgium.

The Entente Cordiale and the 1839 Treaty of London were just two of many entangling alliances that bound the nations of Europe, and when what seemed impossible occurred in the summer of 1914, British leaders felt they had no choice but to go to war—and to do so with the army they had. When a nation commits a small force against much larger forces, the to-be-expected result is precisely what befell the Regular Army of Britain. By the opening of 1915, after the major battles of Mons (August 23, 1914), Le Cateau (August 26, 1914), the Aisne (September 12–15, 1914), and Ypres (October 19–22, 1914), that original army, the core of the profession of land arms in England, had been all but annihilated.

It was long popular among historians to portray this devastation as not only apocalyptic, but senseless—a slaughter. In fact, although it was indeed a slaughter, it was not futile. The small British army was instrumental in slowing and then halting the German advance. The bloody actions of 1914 bought time for the French to stave off the complete conquest of their country and for Lord Kitchener to recruit young (and some not-so-young) patriots and adventure-seekers into a far more substantial army. The net result, by December 1914, was an expansion of the BEF, even as the Regular Army—now referred to as the "Old Army"—wasted away. First came the Territorial Army and then the "New Army," popularly called "Kitchener's Army." By the end of the first year of the war, the BEF consisted of a First and a Second Army. In July 1915, a Third Army came into existence, followed by a Fourth Army and the "Reserve Army," which, in 1916, became the Fifth Army. The Third consisted of a large proportion of Territorials and some Kitchener's Army men. The Fourth and the Fifth were mostly staffed by Kitchener's Army troops.

What Kitchener's Army lacked in training and seasoning, it made up for in spirit. The New Army emphasized the so-called Pals battalions, units made up of groups of men who had grown up together in the same towns or in the same neighborhoods of larger cities or who worked in the same industries and professions or went to the same schools. Some were teammates on football (soccer) and cricket teams. They were indeed pals—sometimes even family.

The Pals battalions were a great recruiting tool, adding the incentive of peer example, encouragement, and pressure and lending ready-made cohesiveness to many units. On the other hand, when the butcher's bills came due during 1915 and 1916, the young male population of entire villages, neighborhoods, families, and vocational communities was wiped out. The losses in 1915 were staggering in themselves, but those in the Pals battalions hit hardest because the sons, brothers, and fathers of so many in so many towns and neighborhoods were killed, often in a single battle, sometimes in one action in a single battle. World War I is often described as history's first conflict in which death and devastation were created on an industrial scale. The carnage was such that many casualties remained unidentified, giving the war an air of anonymity. In fact, institutions such as the Pals battalions made the war less anonymous and far more painfully personal, magnifying individual loss through a multitude of intimate connections.

Although voluntary enlistment during 1914–1915 was encouraging—some 2.6 million men by January 1916—the unremitting death toll, magnified by the Pals battalions, slowed the pace by the end of 1915. The Battle of the Somme (July 1–November 18, 1916) is often cited as the reason for passage of a conscription law; the toll of combat in this battle was so heavy that voluntary enlistment all but dried up. In fact, conscription for unmarried men was introduced in January 1916 and for all men, aged eighteen to forty-one, in May. Both laws were enacted before the Somme battle.

The more than one hundred thousand British, Commonwealth, and colonial troops (thirteen divisions of the Third and Fourth Armies) on the Somme front on the first day of the battle, July 1, 1916, were mostly volunteers. By this time, the true veterans, the members of Old Army, the majority of whom had served for years, were dead or severely enough wounded to be unfit for further service. Many units still had a core of old hands, including Canadian, Australian, New Zealand, and Anglo-Indian troops. These were invaluable in breaking in the newcomers. Wherever possible, reservists—who were at least partially trained—were poured into units stiffened with the remnants of the Old Army. The objective was to accelerate at least something resembling Regular Army training. In the "Old Army" 1st Somerset Light Infantry, for example, four hundred reservists were completely clothed and equipped in the space of four days and then put through intensive training for a few more days before shipping out to France. This was typical. Some units drew more heavily on Territorials to fill out their ranks. These men had rather more training than most other reservists. During peacetime, they regularly reported to the local drill hall on some evenings and most weekends. During several weeks in the summer, all the local units in a county would meet at a camp for full-scale training. Territorials came into regular service with a fair amount of training time under their belts, but many regarded membership in the Territorial Army as more a social than a military enterprise.

The Territorials entered the war legally immune from non-voluntary service abroad. Those who were driven by patriotism, social pressure, or a desire for adventure could sign a "General Service Obligation," by which they waived the domestic service limitation. Overwhelmingly, after the outbreak of war, Territorials signed it. Still, although they formed cohesive units, which, like the Pals battalions, were usually locally raised and trained, that training was expressly for service as a home defense force. Even after the war was well under way, Territorial units whose soldiers had agreed to overseas service were promised a full six months of combat training before being shipped to France. As the Regular Army was melted away in the summer and fall of 1914, however, His Majesty's government asked the members of the Territorial Army to volunteer for immediate service overseas. The response was a resounding yes. The handful of individual soldiers who refused were left at home, officially unmolested until the advent of conscription.

As Territorials and other reservists were rushed into action, Lord Kitchener began the recruiting campaign described in chapter 1. Through 1915, the response to his call was overwhelming. Kitchener believed that *private citizens* could be quickly converted into *army privates*. For non-commissioned and commissioned officers to lead them, however, Kitchener raided the ranks of reservists and regular units. The result was that Kitchener's Army, a citizen army, was led mostly by non-coms and officers who had at least some military experience. Yet their numbers were insufficient, and many units had an insufficient complement of sergeants and an even thinner supply of company-grade officers (lieutenants and captains). For this reason, Old Army detractors referred to the New Army not as Kitchener's Army but as Kitchener's Mob. It was not a nickname born of affection.

BRITISH OFFICERS

We have already met Field Marshal Sir John French and General Sir Douglas Haig. These were academy trained, highly experienced commanders, but they had never envisioned commanding forces the size of those deployed on the Western Front, especially at the Somme. Both French and his replacement Haig were and continue to be criticized as dull and unimaginative. In fact, probably no one in the British army at the time— a force diminutive by European standards—could have performed much better than they, for the simple reason that no one had any experience handling a quarter-million, half-million, or even more men. Throughout the British army of the period, conceptions of strategy had been built on colonial conflicts, such as the Second ("Great") Boer War, in which most battles were fought between relatively small units or with small units against insurgents. Strategy on a scale suitable to a *world* war did not exist in fact or even, really, in imagination.

Haig would initially have two numbered armies on the Somme front, the Third and Fourth, in addition to a unit designated the Reserve Army. When this was later renamed the Fifth Army, it constituted the third numbered army on the front. The Fourth Army, which would be the principal force at the commencement of the battle, was commanded by General Henry Rawlinson, 1st Baron Rawlinson, who had been its commanding officer (CO) since January 24, 1916. This force was manned largely by men of Kitchener's Army, and, during the run-up to the first day of the Somme battle, July 1, 1916, Rawlinson harbored persistent doubts about their readiness. Still, he confided proudly to his diary, "It is not the lot of many men to command an army of over half a million men."[1]

It is a telling comment. None of Rawlinson's military education or experience—none of Kitchener's, French's, or Haig's, either—even contemplated command on such a scale. Like both French and Haig, Rawlinson had an impressive intellectual and military pedigree. The son of a polymath military officer who essentially created the archaeological field of Assyriology, Rawlinson was the product of Eton and Sandhurst. After serving in India, he transferred to the elite Coldstream Guards and subsequently served on Kitchener's staff in Sudan. A field-grade officer during the Second ("Great") Boer War (1899–1902), Rawlinson was made commandant of the Army Staff College when he returned to Britain, and by 1909 was a major general. At the outbreak of the Great War, he was given command of the 4th Division in France and then, promoted to temporary lieutenant general, became commander of IV Corps.

On July 1, 1916, day one of the Battle of the Somme, the cream of British high command would lead their enormous forces into what still stands as the greatest one-day loss in British military history, discounting only the abject surrender of Singapore in World War II, in which eighty thousand out of a British garrison of eighty-five thousand became prisoners of war.

In the "Old Army," the entire officer corps, from lowly subaltern (roughly equivalent in World War I to a US Army second lieutenant) to general, was drawn almost exclusively from candidates who had attended one of the public (that is, elite private) schools and then received training at either of the British military academies, Sandhurst or Woolwich. This process produced an adequate number of officers to serve prewar needs, but the Great War quickly outstripped the supply. In part, this was due to astronomical casualty rates, and in part it was simply a function of the exploding size of the British wartime military. During the period of the Battle of the Somme, a typical British division needed fifty new officers each month. Consider that the Fourth Army fought at the Somme with *twenty-five* divisions.

General Haig was loath to abandon the public school as a source of supply. Because the military academies were working beyond capacity, he called on Oxford and Cambridge to "send out young . . . men as officers," reasoning that "They understand the crisis in which the British empire is involved."[2] Indeed, when Viscount Richard Haldane, as secretary of war, introduced the reforms that created the Territorial Army in 1907, he also introduced the Officers' Training Corps (OTC), a kind of ROTC program instituted in Oxford, Cambridge, and several other UK universities. Haig didn't limit his call to OTC men, however. As he saw it, any university graduate potentially possessed the pedigree fit for a British officer. As the demand for officers exceeded what the universities, with or without the OTCs, could supply, the public schools began sending young officer candidates directly into the army, bypassing the universities and the OTCs altogether.

During the first year of the war and well into the second, leaders like Haig stubbornly clung to the public school as the ultimate source of officers. The point, really, was that training in the military vocation was less important in a British military leader than maintaining an elite class of officers. Haig and most others of the Old Army believed that officers should invariably be of higher socioeconomic class than enlisted ranks. Above all other things, membership in this class was certified by a public school pedigree.

Before 1915 was at an end, casualty rates, coupled with the expansion of the New Army, outstripped even the supply of officers flowing directly from the public schools. The Old Army old guard had no choice but to look beyond the traditional class-defined sources of command. Before the Battle of the Somme ended in November 1916, only about a third of army officers had come from private schools (what Americans would call public) and universities, with or without OTC programs. During the battle, many enlisted men were given field promotions as officers. In the battles that followed the Somme, field commissions became nearly commonplace. By the end of 1916, it was clear that the Great War was both killing *and* democratizing the British Empire.

In the course of the Battle of the Somme, many of the "Old Army" officers continued to be less troubled by the killing than by the democratizing. They criticized the enlisted ranks as "Kitchener's Mob," but they often excoriated the junior officer corps as the "Kitchener subalterns." Lieutenant Colonel John F. Lucy complained that, by the end of 1915, "the civilians took over. They were undersized, they slouched, they were bespectacled. They wore their uniform in a careless way and had a deadly earnestness which took the place of our *esprit de corps*. They saluted awkwardly and were clumsy with their weapons. Their marching was a pain to look at. . . ."[3] Max Plowman, author of the memoir *Subaltern on the Somme*, recalled how his colonel addressed him and his fellow subalterns on their arrival at the Somme: "The discipline of the battalion is damnable. Some of you officers don't know your job at all. You think the men will respect you just because you wear a belt. They won't, and I don't blame them. . . . I see officers talking to men as their equals. I won't have that. . . . You think you've come to France to loaf about. You'll find your mistake. There's got to be a drastic alteration, or back you go. I'll not allow the men to be under the command of inefficient officers."[4]

Plowman was dumbfounded by this greeting. "Why should we be cursed by a man who has never set eyes on us? We are volunteers; most of us joined in '14, and our prospects of dying for our grateful country are the brightest in the world. Is this the way the modern commander spurs his men on to victory?"[5]

Plowman and the other members of Kitchener's Army had a lot to prove, and, in fact, they would prove it at the Somme. But transforming enlisted men into officers was not simply a matter of military training. At the commencement of the battle, the rigid class system imposed even on the modern British army discouraged—even barred—initiative among the enlisted ranks. Their lot in the military was the same as their lot in civilian life. It was to stay in their places, to obey orders from the class of men above them, and to do neither more nor less than that. To convert a culturally ingrained mindset of obedience—of the execution of the will of others—into a mindset of command was a tall order indeed.

GERMAN SOLDIERS AND OFFICERS

In both its constitution and its character, the German army was very different from the British. At the outbreak of the war, the most dramatic difference, of course, was size. In 1914, Germany mobilized 1.85 million men. This was possible thanks to conscription. German males were obligated to three years of active service and an additional four years in the reserve. The regular standing army was essentially a training formation for conscripts. It was built around a small, elite cadre of professional non-commissioned and commissioned officers who continuously brought new recruits up to highly disciplined fighting standards. At the end of three years of active service, training continued on a part-time basis for four years in the reserves. In this way, a large standing army— active and reserve—was maintained along with a huge body of former soldiers who had had extensive military experience and were subject to call-up in time of war. The German army could thus very rapidly mobilize very large numbers.

The German system was based on the system long operative in the Prussian army before the Franco-Prussian War of 1870–1871 spawned the unified German Empire. Although, after 1871, the German army was legally a unified force, its four constituents—from Prussia, Bavaria, Saxony, and Württemberg—retained internal homogeneity and a regional character. Although there was no equivalent of the British Pals battalions, the German army generally emulated the Prussian practice of dividing national territory into army-corps districts. This had the effect of localizing corps and attaching them to geographical districts. The practice enhanced cohesiveness and esprit.

By law, men were drafted into the army at eighteen. As in the British service, the upper class became officers; however, whereas "upper class" in the UK could be a matter of membership in the peerage or simply the possession of wealth, in the Prussian and German armies of the nineteenth century, officers were almost exclusively drawn from the so-called Junker class, young noblemen, most of whom had the noble "von" prefixed to their surname. During World War I, the western democracies, including Britain, frequently denounced Germany as a brutally militarized autocracy dominated by the Junkers. In fact, even before the war, by the end of the nineteenth century, the German military increasingly opened its officer corps to talented commoners, mostly volunteers. There was actually little of the kind of disparagement of officers promoted from the ranks that was found throughout the British army.

Probably no army was better trained or better commanded at the outbreak of World War I than the British Regular Army; however, the German system produced a much larger body of at least *adequately* trained soldiers. This was due, first and foremost, to the maintenance of a core of professional officers supported by a large cadre of career non-commissioned officers. It wasn't that training was of a higher quality in the German army than in the British, but that it was more efficient. Ultimately as well, there was probably less active class prejudice in the "autocratic" German army than in the "democratic" British one. In Germany, a noble military class had long been recognized, which led to a reduction in friction and resentment between the so-called Junkers and the enlisted ranks. Indeed, when a commoner proved his merit and earned promotion to the officer corps, he was generally welcomed and admired. The point is that, yes, compared with Britain and the other Allies, Germany was a significantly militarized state. This being the case, the transition from civilian to military life in the German army was less abrupt and more thorough than it was in the armies of the western democracies.

DOCTRINE

In terms of combat skills, the soldiers of Britain and Germany were probably equally matched, yet neither was particularly well suited to fighting a war of attrition—at least not at the outbreak of the conflict. Germany came into the war having enjoyed a great triumph against France in 1870–1871. The British had honed their combat skills not on European battlefields, but during the Second ("Great") Boer War of 1899–1902.

Both armies had learned valuable lessons about what long-range rifles could and could not do, about the advantages of marching fire (fire while advancing), and about the use of artillery to support infantry attacks. Thanks to the experience of the Boer War, the British army developed advanced doctrine concerning infantry marksmanship as well as tactics of fire and movement. British rifle marksmanship was more highly developed than what prevailed among the Germans; however, German defensive tactics emphasized the use of machine guns, which proved extremely formidable. Still, neither the German experience in a contest between great armies in 1870–1871 nor the British experience in fighting what was largely an insurgency in South Africa had much to teach commanders and soldiers about the nature of trench warfare in a contest of attrition. On balance, the Germans proved more flexible in shifting from a predominantly offensive orientation during the first month of the war to a generally defensive posture during most of the rest of the conflict.

In the field, the most visible differences between the British and the Germans were found in the far more elaborate defensive preparations the Germans made, as compared to both the French and the British. The Germans created stronger, deeper, more sophisticated trench systems, complete with poured concrete dugouts and "bombproofs" (covered and reinforced dugouts, usually furnished with basic rations and other provisions, designed to provide shelter during prolonged artillery bombardment). They also devoted inordinate amounts of labor to create defenses in depth.

Going into the Battle of the Somme, the British, like the French, spurned defense and espoused attack. The Germans, in contrast, were defensively oriented, determined to make the most out of weapons—machine guns and heavy artillery—that favored the defense. Both sides had an understanding that the Great War had become a war of attrition, yet only the Germans truly embraced that concept, and this acceptance gave them a doctrinal and strategic advantage in the coming contest.

PLANS

The original plan for an Anglo-French offensive at the Somme front, in which British and French forces would take equal part, invigorated Sir Douglas Haig. It gave the BEF an opportunity to fully do its bit, even as it bolstered, with a large experienced French force, a British army that was still being built and combat trained. Haig shared some of his "Old Army" officers' doubts about the "New Army" soldiers. At the very least, they lacked combat experience. (Of course, on the Western Front, part of the "combat experience" was, often, death.) Attacking alongside the French—the British taking the line from just north of the River Somme, and the French taking it from the Somme southward—would give the BEF some experience to lean on.

At Chantilly in December 1915, British prospects in a "big push" on the Somme looked reasonably bright. In the early spring of 1915, however, because of the dire situation at Verdun, those prospects turned black. Haig and the BEF were put in the worst possible situation. Joffre ranted to Haig. He demanded, cajoled, and finally pleaded. Joffre leaned on Haig to deliver a powerful British effort on the Somme front to take pressure off of the French armies at Verdun—to save Verdun, save Paris, save France, and save all Europe from German domination. And he needed Haig to deliver victory pretty much on his own. Circumstances had changed since the Second Chantilly Conference. Joffre had to transfer French divisions from the Somme front to Verdun. For if Verdun fell, Joffre explained, nothing done on the Somme would convert ultimate defeat into final victory.

Haig was in a terrible position. Joffre was demanding pretty much the impossible, Yet, Haig believed, in view of the crisis at Verdun, Joffre had no choice but to make that costly demand. Haig therefore revised his original plan as best he could to give Joffre as much as he possibly could. No longer could he promise to break through the German lines to decisive victory. The best he could commit to was forcing Germany to transfer substantial numbers of men from Verdun to the Somme, thereby saving Verdun, Paris, France, and Europe. The cost to the BEF, Haig knew, would be heavy. Just how heavy, however, he had as yet no inkling.

Originally planned was a joint advance across a broad front of twenty-five miles. Haig's idea had been to punch through with infantry over much of that front and then follow up by exploiting the gap with a massive cavalry attack of fast-moving horsemen. He believed—or he imagined—that, once on open ground, the cavalry could wreak havoc on the German rear lines. Unlikely that it really could have, but Haig, an old cavalryman, had a weakness for cavalry and was perpetually frustrated by fighting a trench war in which his favored arm had so far played virtually no role.

But now the twenty-five miles had been crushed down to just eight—an eight-mile front, along which the BEF would act pretty much alone. Given the 440-mile extent of the Western Front, this was somewhat more than a pinprick, but not much more. The risk of attacking over such a narrow front is being sucked into enemy territory, exposed to flanking attacks, and deprived of any room to maneuver and any avenue of survivable retreat. The risk was marching your army into a sack, only to have the narrow opening of the sack tied off. The risk was losing your army.

So Haig turned to his subordinate commanders to manage their expectations. What he had originally presented as a plan to do no less than *win* the war on the Western Front was now reduced to an operation with three modest objectives. First and foremost, the BEF would attack on the Somme front to relieve pressure on the French at Verdun. Second, the BEF would inflict as heavy a loss on the Germans as possible. Finally, the hope was to at least position the BEF for bigger and better things—not in 1916, certainly, but in 1917. Save the French now, and they could join in then on *that* breakthrough attack—later, later.

It was a modest proposal that made no mention of a major break-through. The problem with modest proposals is that they can result in obscene losses. But the French needed something to be done, and they needed it by July 1, 1916. Beyond that date, Joffre protested, France could no longer promise to hold at Verdun.

So Haig assigned General Rawlinson, now in command of the Fourth Army—mostly an army of Kitchener's Mob—to execute the main part of the attack. On his right (south), Rawlinson was in contact with the French. From this point of contact, the Fourth Army was deployed northwesterly, with its left flank (in contact with the British Third Army) just south of the village of Gommecourt. Rawlinson was to attack the German positions on the Pozières Ridge along a ten-mile front, which ran from his southern (right) anchor at Mountauban to the River Ancre between Thiepval on the south and Beaumont-Hamel to the north. Haig instructed Rawlinson to reserve one corps north of the River Ancre to overrun the German trenches just south of Beaumont-Hamel in order to create a flank to protect the main attack.

The ruins of this German bunker so impressed the British troops passing through the western edge of Pozières that they dubbed it Gibraltar. British troops were invariably impressed with German field fortifications, which were much better constructed than anything the Allies built. The photograph is from August 28, 1916. AUSTRALIAN WAR MEMORIAL

It was not a complex attack at all, consisting, as it did, of just one main push across ten miles and one flanking attack across three. But it did represent an expansion from an eight-mile front to one that was now sixteen miles in length. Haig might be spreading his forces a bit thin, but there was a lot to be said for simplicity.

If only Haig had been able to leave it at that. But his earlier ambitions of a cavalry attack unaccountably revived. Haig suddenly wrote his five cavalry divisions into the plan. Apparently unable to reconcile himself to merely relieving pressure on Verdun, Haig reverted to the optimistic ambition of Chantilly—yet without the commitment of forces France had made on that occasion. Maybe there still was a possibility of breaking through! Break through with infantry, gallop into the open with cavalry, and bring to the congealed Western Front a war of movement at last. Maybe this could be done.

Unfortunately, the addition of the cavalry component complicated what had been an admirably straightforward plan of attack by putting inordinate focus on the cavalry—an element that, depending on how the infantry fared, might very well never even get into the fight. Holding back two of his five cavalry divisions, Haig assigned three to Lieutenant General Sir Hubert Gough, a dashing cavalry commander who was by far Haig's favorite subordinate. He also assigned Gough some infantry divisions—and he specified that this mixed command, designated the Reserve Army, would be entirely independent of Fourth Army. Under Haig's plan, Gough's mission was to wait for the infantry to punch a gap into the German lines, ride through it, and capture the village of Bapaume. Leaving a small force to hold that prize, Gough was next to advance into the open, far behind the German lines, riding toward Arras. All of this involved many moving parts and even more speculation. The plan contained a great many *whens* and *shalls*—all depending on even more *ifs*. And what made those *ifs* even more iffy was the fact that, while Gough was entrusted with an independent command, he was not promoted to a rank equivalent to that of Rawlinson. Thus, while nominally independent, Gough was ultimately and actually subordinate, with limited authority as to the on-the-fly decisions he could make.

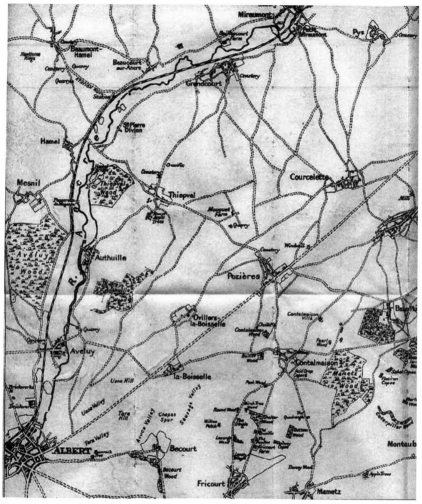

Pozières and vicinity. WWW.CMHG-PHMC.GC.CA

The complexity of Gough's orders, together with the ambiguity of his independent-yet-inferior position, did not bode well. Worse, Haig's infatuation with cavalry actually subordinated the main Fourth Army attack to Gough's exploitation of the breakthrough. Assuming Rawlinson's infantry achieved a breakthrough, the infantry was then immediately to support Gough's cavalry as they rode through that breakthrough.

Lieutenant General Hubert Gough (left) explains the combat situation to King Albert I of Belgium during the Battle of Mons, Belgium, August 23, 1914. "Goughy" was a cavalry commander much admired by General Sir Douglas Haig, who gave him command of the Reserve Army (subsequently designated the Fifth Army) at the Somme. WIKIMEDIA

This required the Fourth Army to redeploy in concentration on the German trenches alongside Gough's line of march while the much-reduced French presence at the front was to be used to hold the right (southern) flank against a German counterattack. That is, the main attack, if it succeeded, was to subordinate itself to the cavalry's moment of glory—even though the cavalry commander, Gough, was ultimately subordinate to the infantry commander, Rawlinson. In truth, Haig's plan was fatally flawed strategically, tactically, and even in the inept and ambiguous assignment of command authority. Much as Haig was hedging his bets by giving Gough independence from the Fourth Army while preserving his subordinate rank, so he bifurcated the objective of his plan. In part, it was a fairly broad assault on the German line. Yet it was also a cavalry breach exploitation, which would require the diversion of some of the forces responsible for making the overall breakthrough. Both hedges had the effect of creating dilution rather than adding leverage.

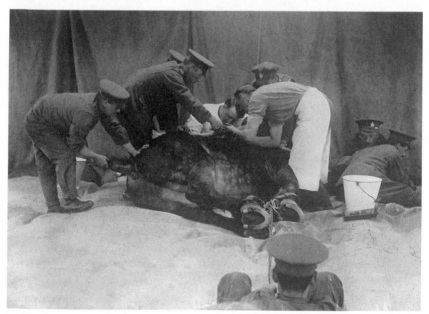

Britain lost 480,000 horses in World War I combat, one animal for every two men killed. The Royal Veterinary Corps did its best to treat sick and wounded animals, like this one, which is at a frontline veterinary hospital in 1916. BIBLIOTHÈQUE NATIONALE DE FRANCE

And Haig had yet one more misbegotten trick up his sleeve.

While the Fourth Army bore the brunt of the main attack, and the Reserve Army waited in the wings, the First Army, also deployed along the Somme front but not committed to the main battle, was tasked with carrying out a series of feints to put the Germans off guard and tie down their reserves.[6] The Third Army, under Sir Edmund Allenby, which held the line on the left (northern) flank of the Fourth Army, was to carry out a special diversion by attacking Gommecourt, a strongly held German salient. The First Army's action was nothing more than a *feint*—something extra that did not figure centrally in the plan. The Third Army's assignment was to do more. It was to create a *diversion* that Haig also wanted to leverage as a serious assault essential to the plan. As Haig saw it, using the Third Army against Gommecourt combined the virtues of a diversionary assault with the necessity of destroying an important German position.

As the proverbial attempt to kill two birds with a single stone, there was an appealing economy about the assignment Haig handed the Third Army. In truth, however, it was yet another divided objective. Mounting a

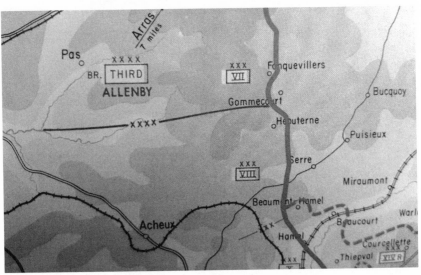

The Third Army position near Gommecourt, objective of a "diversionary" attack.
UNITED STATES MILITARY ACADEMY

Edmund Allenby, who commanded Third Army at the Somme, poses here early in the war with Nicholas I of Montenegro. NATIONAL ARCHIVES AND RECORDS ADMINISTRATION

mere diversionary attack against a position that might well wipe you out is a very dangerous bet, and Allenby did not like the odds.

Sir Edmund Allenby would earn his World War I fame not on the Western Front but, later in the conflict, as commanding officer of the British Empire's Egyptian Expeditionary Force, in which his most celebrated subordinate was the exuberantly insubordinate T. E. Lawrence—Lawrence of Arabia. Part of Allenby's eventual fame would rest, of course, on his connection with Lawrence, but, in his own right, he was also highly effective in the Middle Eastern theater, dealing significant blows against the Ottoman Empire on this front. Yet, unlike other top British commanders, he had not embarked on a military career with any great display of promise. His youthful ambition had been to climb the ladder of success and influence in the Indian Civil Service, but, failing to pass the entrance exam required for this career channel, he settled on the army instead. He did well enough at Sandhurst, but when he sought a route to higher command via the Staff College, he once again came up short on the entrance exam. Undaunted, he gave it a second try the following year—and passed. This put him in the same Staff College class as then-Captain Douglas Haig. The two took an instant dislike to one another, and they seem to have competed shamelessly for the admiration and loyalty of their classmates. In the end, Allenby was judged to be Haig's intellectual inferior, but was nevertheless far more popular with his fellow officers.

In the Second ("Great") Boer War, Allenby distinguished himself both by his bravery in the face of the enemy and by his efficiency. He ended the war in 1902 as a brevet colonel and, by 1909, was a major general. The combination of his combat performance, his imposing physical presence, and his explosive temper earned him the nickname of "The Bull" or, sometimes, "Bloody Bull." He seems to have done nothing to discourage either appellation.

Early in World War I, Allenby distinguished himself as commander of a cavalry division, earning promotion to temporary lieutenant general and given command of the BEF's Cavalry Corps. Allenby gave up this position, however, to accept command of V Corps at the Second Battle of Ypres (April 22–May 25, 1915). Had Haig been offered the same choice, it is doubtful that his love of the cavalry would have permitted him to

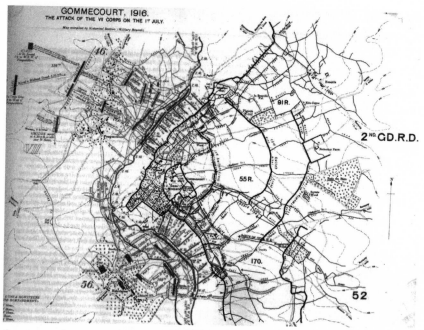

Gommecourt. BRITISH ARMY HISTORICAL SECTION

make the same sacrifice in rank. As it is, although Allenby succeeded in turning back massive German assaults at Second Ypres, his insistence on retaking the offensive by repeated counterattacks resulted in casualty levels so high as to create controversy not only among fellow officers, but among the British public as well. Despite this, in October 1915, he was named to command the British Third Army, which, like the Fourth, was heavily manned by soldiers of the "New Army."

The Staff College rivalry between him and Haig had by 1916 evolved into a permanent state of mutual disdain. Allenby was therefore constitutionally inclined to dislike Haig's plan for the Third Army's attack on the German salient at Gommecourt. That is, he would have faulted the plan even if it had been a very good plan. It was, however, no such thing. To begin with, as a combination of sideshow and major undertaking, its odds for success were slim to none. The plan's ambiguous status created a specific tactical defect. Looking to ensure the flexibility of his main assault, Haig left a mile-wide gap between the Third Army assault on Gommecourt and what should have been the point of contact between the Third and Fourth Armies at the latter's northern flank. If the Third and Fourth Armies were to move together, Allenby wanted them to move seamlessly, without a gap. This would afford Allenby's troops at Gommecourt much-needed flank protection. If, however, Haig did not want the Fourth Army's advance to be tied to that of the Third Army, then it would be far better for the Third Army to make its diversionary attack at a much greater distance from the main attack. In this way, Allenby's right flank would not be exposed to German soldiers advancing against the main British attack. Apparently unable to overcome his personal dislike of Haig, however, Allenby did not press the issue of his vulnerable right flank. Instead, he uncharacteristically dumped the matter on the commander of the corps that formed Third Army's right flank, Lieutenant General Thomas D'Oyly Snow, whose surname and girth earned him the nicknames of "Polar Bear" (affectionate) and "Slush" (not).

If anything, Snow disliked the plan to attack Gommecourt even more than Allenby did. He believed that the German response to a diversion might well be a devastating counterattack. Yet while "Slush" made his feelings known to Allenby, he did not press his argument with vigor. It has been said that he feared Allenby more than he feared the Germans.[7] To make Snow's predicament even more acute, Allenby allotted him just two divisions for the attack. As Snow saw it, this parsimony definitively ruled out a simple frontal attack. Instead, he assigned one division to one shoulder of the salient and the other to the opposite shoulder. Moreover, Snow had so little expectation that these attacks would make good progress that he instructed his division commanders to devote a limited number of battalions to them. If the attacks succeeded, these battalions were to link up behind Gommecourt, at the base of the salient, pinching it off. If both attacks failed, they would have to withdraw. That was bad enough, but the consequences of one failure and one success were even worse. If one division's battalions succeeded, but the other division's battalions failed, the men of the successful division would have no comrades with whom to link up and would suddenly find themselves utterly isolated deep behind enemy lines. They could be cut off completely.

Lieutenant General Thomas D'Oyly Snow, affectionately known as the "Polar Bear" and also—more contemptuously—as "Slush," commanded the right wing of Allenby's Third Army at the Somme. It was his unhappy lot to attempt the execution of Allenby's doomed plan to attack and capture Gommecourt. WIKIMEDIA

It seemed that prospects could not possibly get worse for the Third Army. But get worse they did, as Snow advised his divisional commanders that they were embarking on a limited diversionary action. There would be no reserve forces behind them to exploit any breakthrough; therefore, he instructed them to refrain from advancing until German defenses had been neutralized by British artillery. Essentially, Snow nullified the very diversionary effect on which Haig was counting.

THE RAWLINSON DISCONNECT

And what of the main instrument of attack, the Fourth Army? Haig saw its role as creating a breakthrough sufficient for cavalry to exploit, disrupt the German rear, and restore movement to the Western Front. Henry Rawlinson, the commander of the Fourth Army assigned to execute this improbable martial miracle, had a very different vision. He believed that a cavalry exploitation was a pipe dream. He believed there would be no breakthrough to exploit. He believed that the very most that could be hoped for—the most that could feasibly be achieved—was a painful biting through each enemy line, one trench at a time.

The teeth that would do the biting were neither foot soldiers nor horse soldiers, Rawlinson decided, but artillerymen and their weapons. His intention was to precede the attack with a full five days of intensive artillery preparation. His plan was to destroy one enemy trench line after another. Following the intensive five-day general bombardment focused on the German first line, he would send in his infantry, whose job would be no more than to mop up whatever Germans were left in the trenches, occupy those trenches, and, from them, fight off the anticipated German counterattack. That counterattack would come as British artillery focused on the second and third lines of German trenches. Thus the Germans would be caught between the British infantry, now occupying what had been the first German line of defense, and a second British artillery bombardment landing ahead of that infantry. When the second line had been sufficiently depleted by shelling, Rawlinson planned to reinforce the first wave of British attackers and advance to the second German position, from which they would attack the third German line—which, by that time, would also have been softened up by artillery bombardment.

Rarely has an army commander been so strategically disconnected from a theater commander. The latter envisioned a grand cavalry charge through an infantry-created breach. The former envisioned nothing at all grand. His guns and his men were to chomp their way through the German defenses, one layer of tough sinew and stubborn gristle at a time.

THE GERMAN POSITION

At its inception, the Battle of the Somme was a *British* battle. The French took a minor role, vastly scaled down from the star turn originally planned. And the Germans had a part to play that was pretty well dictated by whatever the British might do or fail to do.

During the first five weeks of the war, Germany had been a juggernaut, continually on the attack and on the move. After the First Battle of the Marne (September 5–12, 1914), Erich von Falkenhayn dictated a radical shift from offense to defense. The offensive phase had already bought—and cheaply at that—a great deal of French territory. Falkenhayn intended not merely to occupy or *hold* this ground, but to *use* it as a great defensive machine designed to grind down everything thrown at it. He understood that the French could not passively tolerate foreign occupation of their homeland. While *he* could afford to take time to establish a second massive line of defense behind the first and then a third line behind the second, *Joffre* was under intolerable pressure to push the enemy out, whatever the cost. Falkenhayn intended to exploit that pressure to draw in the British and feed them to his German guns.

By the time of the Battle of the Somme, the German forces were arrayed in a first line, a second line, and a third line all across the front. The heaviest German artillery, the artillery with the greatest range, was arrayed mostly behind the third line. It was deployed in so-called barrage sectors (*sperrfeuerstreifen*), each sector assigned to cover a portion of the front line. The barrage sectors were also interlocked, their fields of fire overlapping each other, so that attackers would be enfiladed by artillery fire.

Among the British and the French, both of whom embraced a doctrine of attack, defensive entrenchments were hastily conceived, hastily executed earthworks intended to be very temporary, nothing more than stepping off points for pressing forward the attack. In contrast, the Germans had been patiently developing their Somme defenses since the fall of 1915. This system was designed not as a mere springboard to advance, but as a formidable means of enduring barrages so that, after the enemy had lifted its preparatory barrage, German infantry could emerge from well-constructed dugouts and bombproofs to kill the incoming British and French—those, that is, who had survived the interlocking fields of artillery fire raking no-man's-land.

In theory, it was a diabolically powerful means of waging war. First, on the Somme sector, as elsewhere along the Western Front, German soldiers were fighting on, not for, French soil. Whereas the British and French had only one favorable or even permissible direction in which to move—forward—the Germans could stand fast in position or, if the situation favored it, advance. If the battle went against them, they could also withdraw, from the first line to the second line and even to the third line. All of these motions, after all, were in France, not the German homeland. The Allies were being forced to repurchase French soil with their blood. The Germans were not obliged to defend that soil with theirs. For them, at least as Falkenhayn saw it, French soil was not to be defended at all, but to be maneuvered upon in whatever direction would cost the most Allied lives. France was not territory to be conquered. It was ground on which to kill.

In theory, the German position was nearly unassailable. In practice, fighting from defense was much harder than Falkenhayn made it out to be. It was partly about dealing death to exposed attackers. But it was mostly about passively, helplessly, miserably, enduring attack, especially artillery bombardment. German soldiers came to know the pounding squalor of deep trenches and concrete-reinforced dugouts. Moreover, although defense in depth was designed as a killing machine, drawing the enemy in to be ground up, it relied on the inviting vulnerability of the first line of trenches. These were inevitably the main targets of the initial barrage followed by the initial attack across no-man's-land. The lot of the men in these positions was to exact as many casualties against the attackers as possible before finally withdrawing to the next line. Timing and leadership were everything. Remaining in place without ever falling back was suicide. Falling back too soon was failure or even cowardice. At its best, the German strategy on the Somme—and until 1917, throughout the Western Front—was a slaughter of attrition executed with a patience that *might* someday be rewarded with victory. Allied propaganda portrayed the German military as "the Hun," embodiment of the cruelest sadism. In fact, the German war plan, as put into practice at the Somme and elsewhere on the Western Front, was better described as the deadliest masochism deployed on a mass scale.

Chapter 4

Breaking Ground

From the perspective of Douglas Haig, the coming battle was nothing that he wanted—not now and not under these conditions. He believed his armies needed more training, more preparation, more front-line experience. At Chantilly, he was sold on the idea of being part of the Western Front action against Germany, even as Russia attacked from the east and Italy from the south. *That*, he believed, would truly be the "Big Push" the newspapers were clamoring for: the fully coordinated Allied action that would break Germany and at long last end the war.

But then Verdun happened. France was in danger of collapse, and Haig, who had taken such pride in being assigned to lead half a million men, was being pushed and elbowed by the rotund form of Joseph Joffre. Of the British, Joffre demanded nothing less than salvation—or was it simply sacrifice? Either way, he cudgeled Haig into action—premature and with nothing approaching a sufficient French contribution, since so many French divisions had to be rushed to Verdun. Of course, Joffre wanted Haig to win at the Somme. For him, a British breakthrough would be thrilling. Yet Haig must also have realized that, as Joffre saw it, a *British* triumph was not absolutely necessary. Anything the BEF could do to force the Germans to move men and guns from Verdun to the Somme would take pressure off the French at Verdun. That was the only boon that truly mattered to Joffre.

The cost? In terms of *British* casualties, Joffre was willing to fight on the Somme at any and all costs. British troops, after all, were not French troops. Their loss would necessarily have less impact on France than the loss of French sons, brothers, and fathers. But even more important, the Somme meant far less than the Meuse, if only because it was farther from Paris. To be sure, the war could be lost at either place. At Verdun, it could be lost very quickly. At the Somme, it would take longer. And that was a big difference.

Verdun had a degree of symbolic value, which French politicians and the French press had, in the past few weeks, pumped up into something quasi-mythological. There was talk about Verdun as the heart and soul of France. In truth, it was a region with terrible weather and boggy land, a region French high command had largely ignored. But, now that it was threatened, it took on the air of irreplaceable value, second only to Paris itself. Verdun also had a modicum of actual strategic importance. It was an obvious point of entry into the French interior targeted precisely on Paris. It was, in fact, so obvious that the Schlieffen Plan had *avoided* it, opting instead for a grand counterclockwise wheel that took the advancing German armies northwestward, through Belgium, all the way to the English Channel coast, and then down upon the French left flank and rear. With the collapse of the Schlieffen Plan at the First Battle of the Marne in early September 1914, German high command saw real value in returning to the obvious. With the rear door now barred to the German armies, they were tempted to try the front door after all.

Joffre needed to defend—and to counterattack—at Verdun. That was the current imperative. The Somme? The Somme never had more symbolic value than any other tract of French real estate—and it actually had little enough strategic significance. There was nothing special about it. A German breakthrough here would be bad. A German breakthrough at Verdun would be far worse. The only significance of the Somme River was as a landmark denoting the place where the right flank of the BEF made contact with the left flank of the French army.

THE LAST BATTLE

Haig understood all this, and his enthusiasm for the coming battle must have been heavily tempered by that understanding. What disappointment and doubt he must have felt, he kept to himself. Certainly, nothing was shared with his subordinates, including Fourth Army commander Henry

Rawlinson. In the weeks leading up to the attack, the Tommies—as British soldiers were called—were deployed to a large tract of land in the rear, near Amiens. Rawlinson had chosen it on the advice of the French, who assured him that it was very similar to the sector along which his troops would be fighting. Work parties carefully laid out tapes to indicate the position of German trenches. Dugouts, strongpoints, redoubts, and fortified villages were identified with neatly painted signs. Troops were assembled, ordered "over the top" (the British trenches marked with more tape) and sent at a walking march toward the German "trenches." Invariably, they captured their objective and successfully consolidated behind it. Except for the occasional case of heat exhaustion—it was a sunny June, and the men were loaded down in full kit, about sixty pounds' worth—there was nary a casualty.

The troops were led by company-grade officers—captains down to subalterns—and non-coms, but field-grade officers, from major to general, including no less than Sir Douglas Haig, mounted on his very large black horse, observed. Obviously, they couldn't judge the behavior of the troops under fire, but they could assure themselves that the men at least knew how to advance in good order and respond to commands. They could also take note that they were in very good spirits. Certainly, the soldiers were hearing that phrase "Big Push" bandied about, and day after day of "rehearsal" (that was what their sergeants and subalterns called it) persuaded them they were about to make history. Many believed this would be the last battle of the war. Ending the war was, after all, the objective of the "Big Push." Among the believers was Private E. C. Stanley of the 1/8th Royal Warwicks. "I thought this would be the last battle of the war," he later recalled, "and I didn't want to miss it. I remember writing to my mother, telling her I would be home for the August Bank Holiday."[1] Anything, it seemed, would be better than another cold, wet winter in the trenches of northern France and Flanders.

Doubtless, many of the men were nervous, some even terrified. But, for most, the greatest source of apprehension was not the prospect of being wounded or killed, but of showing cowardice, of failing to put on a proper, manly show. No one wanted to let their "pals" down, and no one wanted to be humiliated in their presence. As for the possibility of defeat or death, what they saw around them, in the vicinity of Amiens, were seemingly endless columns of British artillery being hauled into position: massive firepower. Their commanders repeatedly told them that this war, this "Great War," was above all an artillery war. That meant that the job of infantry—the men rehearsing right now—would be little more than mopping up, because they believed the artillery would kill just about every German soldier before a single Tommy began his advance toward the German trenches. Yes, there would be the occasional Jerry survivor and holdout to tangle with, but, mostly, it would be an advance over a dead or dying foe.

Of course, this assessment turned out to be tragically mistaken. But it was a sincere belief, not some fairy tale fabricated to build morale. The years 1914 and 1915 were chiefly years of defeat for the Allies. First there was the long retreat through the entire first full month of the war. After the German advance was arrested at the First Battle of the Marne at the beginning of the war's second month and then the so-called Race to the Sea that followed—the frantic dance of the two adversaries fruitlessly sidestepping one another in a fruitless effort to gain access to a flank—the war on the Western Front quickly settled into a bloody standoff fought from trenches protected by mile upon mile of barbed wire. The Allies mounted one offensive after another, none of which achieved appreciable gains in terms of territory and each of which resulted in terrible losses in terms of human beings. Almost always, the Allied losses were greater than those of the enemy.

There is a persistent mythology about the course of the war after 1915, a mythology so stubborn that it even drives the writing of some historians. It is that, after two years of unproductive bloodletting, the Allies embarked on another two years, knowing that they would be just as bloody and just as unproductive. The fact is that, by the middle of 1915, the Allies realized that the strategy and tactics of the Napoleonic era would never end the stalemate on the Western Front. Trenches, machine guns, and barbed wire ultimately doomed any infantry attack. The Allies, like the Germans, therefore began looking to artillery for a breakthrough. The French, it is true, were slower to resort to artillery than either the Germans or the British, but they came around well before the end of the war, and as of Armistice Day, November 11, 1918, the French artillery park was bigger than that of Germany or Britain.

But British firepower by 1916 had already become formidable. British industry was enlisted to produce an endless stream of artillery. Indeed, by the end of the war, the Royal Artillery alone was bigger than the entire BEF fielded in 1914. The reason for this firepower was the unshakeable belief that massive shelling by heavy guns would achieve three things. It would obliterate the enemy trenches and most of those who occupied them. It would destroy the barbed-wire obstacles in no-man's-land between the opposing lines of trenches. And it would disrupt the enemy's rear echelon, blasting routes of supply and reinforcement as well as avenues of retreat. Anyone in and around Amiens, which included the Tommies rehearsing for the "Big Push," would have been thoroughly impressed by the sight of the guns being pulled into position mostly by horse teams but also by a handful of primitive tracked vehicles, motorized tractors called caterpillars. Equally impressive were the seemingly endless cargoes of shells—a million of which would be fired from 1,010 pieces of field artillery (18-pounders and 4.5-inch howitzers) and 427 "heavies" (4.7-inch guns to 15-inch howitzers) during the week before the artillery attack. Who could possibly believe that the British would *not* prevail— and quickly, too? Who could not be persuaded that here, at last, were the makings of the final battle of the war?

NEW URGENCY

Before it erupted into the bustling, laborious preparation for battle and the battle itself, the slice of Picardy between the winding River Somme and the Ancre River, which branches off from the Somme to the northeast, was a quiet place, isolated and inland. Few of the British gathered here late in May and early in June had any reason to think about the war at sea—until two pieces of news suddenly stormed through their ranks.

On May 31, 151 combat ships of the Royal Navy's Grand Fleet began a battle with ninety-nine ships of the Imperial German Navy's High Seas Fleet in the North Sea off the coast of Denmark's Jutland Peninsula. In a war deadlocked at land on the western European front, both sides were looking to make a naval breakthrough. Britain's naval blockade of Germany was having an impact on both the German civilian population and the military. In the years leading up to the war, Germany and Britain were in a naval arms race. By the outbreak of the war, the Royal Navy was still too large for Germany's High Seas Fleet to take on head-to-head, but the German commander, Vice Admiral Reinhard Scheer, believed he could draw out, cut off, and destroy a significant portion of the Grand Fleet—enough of it to break the blockade. For his part, the British commander, Admiral Sir John Jellicoe, saw an opportunity to engage the High Seas Fleet and destroy a large portion of it. At the very least, Jellicoe believed he could bottle up the German fleet, confining it to German-controlled waters and keeping it out of the principal Atlantic shipping lanes. For two days, the largest naval battle of World War I was fought. On both sides, commanders, politicians, and the public were anticipating something new in this war: a decisive battle. What they got instead was a seagoing version of the Western Front. The clash was costly—6,094 British sailors killed, 2,551 German sailors killed; fourteen British vessels and eleven German vessels lost. In tactical terms, neither side was victorious. Generations of scholars and armchair admirals have debated the reasons for this. Both sides, certainly, made their share of errors, but probably the biggest reason for the tactical draw was the fact that, despite British superiority in numbers and tonnage, the major German warships were newer, with more and heavier guns, marginally greater speed, and better maneuverability. Each side's advantage cancelled out that of the other. As was true of the land war, the naval war was, more than anything, a question of material rather than men. *Abundance* of technology could not decisively overcome the *latest* in technology—and vice versa.

As the men preparing to fight at the Somme interpreted it, the news from Jutland was this: The Royal Navy had lost fourteen ships—without beating the Germans. In time, it would become clear that what the Royal Navy *had* achieved was the intimidation of the German admiralty, which, following Jutland, kept the High Seas Fleet close to home and out of the "high seas" for the remainder of the war. (This, of course, applied only to surface ships. German U-boats would continue to prey on Allied commercial shipping.) This outcome was a significant, if hardly triumphal, strategic victory. But the Tommies did not see it as such. Somewhat dejectedly, they concluded that turning the tide of war now rested entirely on their shoulders. They accordingly committed themselves to the Somme with a mixture of gloom and resolve—a feeling that, yes, the war really was riding on them now.

As this sentiment settled in on the troops, another piece of news exploded among them. At 7:30 in the evening of June 5, the armored cruiser HMS *Hampshire* was caught in a Force 9 gale while setting off on the long voyage to the Russian port of Arkhangelsk. The winds and seas drove the vessel into a mine that had just been laid by the German U-boat U-75. The *Hampshire* sank west of the Orkney Islands with the loss of all aboard, among them Horatio Herbert Kitchener, 1st Earl Kitchener, who was on a diplomatic mission to the czar.

From across no-man's-land, Private J. Sutherland of the 1st Edinburgh City Battalion heard a German shout out in English "that Kitchener was drowned and he would go to Hell."[2] Kitchener! His was the mustachioed visage, his was the pointing finger, floating above the words "WANTS **YOU**" in the most famous recruiting poster any country has ever produced. Kitchener was the father of the New Army—Kitchener's Army—the army to which almost all of the men at the Somme belonged, having answered the summons of that poster. The ambiguous result of Jutland had stirred disappointment into the excitement that prevailed in anticipation of the Battle of the Somme. Now the death of Lord Kitchener stirred gloom into the mix. But both events were perceived as adding to the already high stakes of the impending battle.

THE SHOVEL WAR

To all appearances, the nations of Europe stumbled into a war no one wanted. The whole, horrible thing had the air of an accident—a stupid, terrible accident. Never mind that the conditions for war had actually been in preparation since the Franco-Prussian War of 1870–1871. The Europe Otto von Bismarck and other European statesmen had created, a continent in which the appearance of stability was maintained through a complex net of alliances and treaties, some public, some secret, was the script, the platform, the predicate, and the prescription for an all-engulfing war. Like a meticulously choreographed ballet, there was nothing accidental or even spontaneous about any of it, yet it all had the appearance of accident and spontaneity.

After Germany's initial invasion of France and Belgium, the "Battle of the Frontiers" in August and September of 1914, and the frenzied, futile Race to the Sea that followed in September and October, the Western Front settled into the kind of trench warfare that became an icon of the entire 1914–1918 conflict. From this point on, major battles were never random clashes. Each was fought from trenches, a system of fortifications that became increasingly elaborate as the war progressed. Each major battle, therefore, began as a construction project. The fighting started with shovels, not cannon or rifles.

Trenches were hardly new to combat. They were as old as siege warfare. Advancing armies dug in to protect themselves from the arrows or bullets of the besieged. In siege warfare, by the seventeenth century, trenches became something more than improvised cover—"hasty field fortification," as modern military writers term it. Trenches were carefully designed by commanders and by engineers. Armies advanced toward their objective via "saps," trenches dug perpendicular to the enemy. At night, they would excavate trenches perpendicular to the saps and parallel to the enemy. From these, the attackers could deploy along a front rather than attempt a penetration at a single point. The triumphal Yorktown Campaign (January–October 1781) of the American Revolution consisted mostly of a patient, systematic Franco-American siege waged from the cover of trenches against the army of Lord Charles Cornwallis on Virginia's Yorktown Peninsula. Even the American Civil War (1861–1865), which we usually think of as a series of highly dynamic encounters between armies fighting in the open, included large-scale trench warfare. The Siege of Vicksburg (May 18–July 4, 1863) and the Siege of Petersburg (June 9, 1864–March 25, 1865) were long operations fought from elaborate trench systems. For any World War I commander who had studied or personally witnessed operations during the Russo-Japanese War, the Siege of Port Arthur (August 1, 1904–January 2, 1905) must have loomed as an especially deadly lesson in trench warfare.

But in all the history of warfare, trenches had never been employed on so vast a geographic scale as they were on the Western Front, when they defined a battle line running from the English Channel in the north to the frontier of neutral Switzerland in the south.

After having failed to swiftly conquer France in August-September 1914, the Germans were quicker to embrace the full implications of trench warfare than the Allies. This is not surprising, since Germany had come into the war with strategic doctrines very different from those of either the French or the British. Germany's first resort was to overwhelming force. After that failed at the First Battle of the Marne (September 5–12, 1914), the German army shifted to a defensive posture. Fighting from entrenched positions on the ground they had conquered from France, the German armies learned to rely heavily on artillery and machine guns. In contrast, despite one failed offensive after another, the French were loath to abandon their doctrine, of "attaque à outrance" (attack to the uttermost), the doctrine with which they had entered the war. As for the British, they had never formally embraced any doctrine at all; however, British commanders universally believed that trenches were bad for morale because they discouraged an aggressive orientation. For this reason, they, like the French, never developed their trenches as elaborately as the Germans.

Even as late as 1916, neither the French nor the British devoted much attention to defense in depth, a system of entrenchments that allowed for orderly withdrawal as necessary, providing strong backup defense systems to resist breakthrough by the enemy. In contrast, German defensive entrenchments provided for multiple lines of defense in depth. This is what made it virtually impossible for the Allies to exploit any breach they might tear in the German front trenches. When a portion of the German line was in danger of collapse, commanders would order a withdrawal to the next line of defense. The attackers would enter the abandoned first line of trenches, only to be flanked, swallowed up, and cut off by the second or third lines. Defense in depth repeatedly foiled French and British attempts to wipe out the German line with artillery bombardment alone. Having built elaborate dugouts and bombproofs,

German troops could shelter in place as the shells rained down. When the opportunity presented itself, they could strategically withdraw to their second or third line, wait for the enemy infantry to advance, and then envelop the attackers.

On both sides, the earliest trenches were rudimentary. They were conceived as nothing more than holding positions from which to launch attacks. Trenches were not intended as positions from which the battle itself would be fought. The early trenches might consist of a single line of trench, or, if there was a backup trench line, it featured very few "communication trenches" connecting it to the front line. Instead, troops were closely packed shoulder to shoulder into a single rudimentary trench, there to await the order to go "over the top." For both the French and the British, making the trench basic, crowded, and uncomfortable was not merely an expedient, it was an intentional design feature. Commanders *wanted* their men to be uncomfortable. They did not want soldiers to think of the trench as their home. They therefore built them not as places to stay, but as places to leave—and the faster the better.

The early trenches created heavy casualties, mostly from artillery shelling. Unable to move or seek shelter, the closely packed troops were annihilated in bombardments. Those the artillery spared were vulnerable to follow-up infantry attacks. On the Allied side, the initial response to heavy losses in inadequate entrenchments was to put fewer men in the trench. This, however, had the effect of slowing offensive actions while also rendering the line more vulnerable to being overrun. To compensate for a thin defense, the Allies deployed generous amounts of barbed wire to protect the trench. An American innovation commercially elaborated in the 1870s from early mid-nineteenth-century British and French precursors, barbed wire transformed the vast plains of the American West from wide-open spaces to confined pasturage conforming to the property lines of ranchers. If barbed wire was adequate to restrain bulls and buffalo on the prairie, surely it could keep an enemy from invading one's trench. And so, on both sides, "wiring parties" ventured out by night into no-man's-land to lay new wire and to repair breaches in existing wire defenses.

As the war continued, both sides rapidly expanded and elaborated their trenches. Expansion was matched on one side by expansion on the other. Neither side could afford any gaps the enemy could exploit. Nevertheless, the Germans lavished more time and effort on their trenches than either the French or British devoted to theirs. Whenever *poilus* or Tommies overran a German trench, they were invariably astounded at how much more spacious, well-constructed, secure, and livable the German trenches were than theirs. Conversely, when German soldiers entered an Allied trench, they were appalled by the conditions they found there. The French trenches were filthy, with inadequate drainage and sanitation. The British trenches were hastily dug and perpetually crumbling away. Both the French and British trenches were often clogged with the wounded and the dead because communication trenches—the trenches that connected with the rear—were relatively few and far between. Nevertheless, among all combatants in 1916, trenches were far more extensive and complex than they had been in 1914 and even most of 1915.

Today, the phrase "trench warfare" conjures up combat conducted from two opposing ditches. In fact, by the time of the Somme campaign, Western Front trenches were elaborately developed interlocking defensive works. At its most basic, a line of trench, vintage 1916, consisted of four principal, parallel trenches behind relatively short lengths of trenches most immediately fronting no-man's-land. The short trenches either held the advance line of defenders and observers or were so-called dummy trenches, intended to trap an attacker. Both of these forward entrenchments were protected by thick rows of barbed wire. The advance trench might be connected to the principal frontline trench, called the main fire trench or main fighting trench, by a simple communication trench or via a "sap," a short tunnel.

Located behind its own row or multiple rows of barbed wire, the main fire trench was dug about twelve feet deep—although some Allied trenches were shallower. They were not simple straight ditches, but, viewed from above, appeared either zigzagged or stepped. Early French and British trenches were dug in a wavy zigzag pattern, but, by 1916, they followed the German stepped pattern. In a plan view, the "line" of a stepped trench resembled a row of widely spaced teeth or the crenelated profile of the parapet of a medieval castle. The portion of each crenellation that projected out toward the enemy was called a fire bay. It was from the fire bays that riflemen fired at the approaching enemy. By 1916, German trenches added another element to the fighting trench, forward traverses, which projected out beyond even the firing bays, providing a position to create crossfire across the front of the trench. Later in the war, this feature became standard for French, British, and American trenches as well.

Building crenelated trenches was extremely labor intensive, at least doubling the length of a simple straight excavation. The labor was essential, however, because the 90-degree corners of the crenelated trench served two vital functions. First, if a straight-line trench were overrun by the enemy, the invaders could simply enfilade the trench, opening fire down its length and knocking down the trapped soldiers like dominoes. The sharp corners yielded to raiders or invaders no extended line of fire, while also providing cover from which defenders could return the fire of any infiltrators. Second, and even more important in an "artillery war," the 90-degree turns in the trench created a series of earthen blast walls that were highly effective at containing the destructive shock and fireball of even a direct artillery hit. If a high explosive shell impacted a straight-line trench, the blast wave and the fireball would be conducted in two directions through the earthen corridor of the trench. The crenelated design, in contrast, absorbed a great deal of the blast energy and also provided firewall protection, thereby containing the damage and limiting casualties.

Often, a narrow "supervision trench" was dug immediately behind the fighting trench. From here, officers and non-coms could direct the fighting. The supervision trench also provided a quick means for moving across the length of the fighting trench without disturbing soldiers busy in delivering fire or returning enemy fire.

Located at least twenty-five to thirty-five yards behind both the main fighting trench and supervision trench was the support trench, which held troops performing support functions, troops rotated out of the front trench, and the wounded. This trench was also a position to which troops in the fighting trench could withdraw, if they were being overrun. If supervision trenches had been dug, the support trench was connected to them via communication trenches. If not, the support trenches were connected directly to the fighting trench.

Some ninety to three hundred yards behind the support trench was the reserve trench, which held the reserve line. The reserve trench communicated with the support trench via long communication trenches. Although the reserve trench served as the "last ditch" fighting position of the front trench system, true defense in depth required a minimum of two additional trench systems a mile or more to the rear of the front system. These provided fighting positions for any portions of the front line that needed to make an orderly, fighting withdrawal. At the Somme, the British rear trenches were poorly developed. In contrast, the Germans created not one but two fully developed trench systems behind their front system. This was not conceived as an emergency measure, but as an essential tactical feature. For the French and the British, fighting on French soil, any retreat meant yielding precious national territory. For this reason, retreat was seen as yielding to an invader. It represented defeat. For the Germans, however, who were fighting exclusively on conquered soil, withdrawal was not defeat, but a legitimate and useful tactical option. If the enemy troops broke through the front trench system, they could be flanked, cut off, and destroyed by defenders who had withdrawn to the second or third trench system. Ultimate breakthrough was therefore virtually impossible.

In the front system of trenches, various strongpoints, shelters, and dugouts were built, mostly intended to provide additional cover for forward command posts and supplies. Dugouts, or bombproofs, which were fully covered underground shelters, served as places to sleep and eat. In the case of German trenches, these were often reinforced with poured concrete and were used to shelter all of the occupants of a trench during the prolonged artillery barrages that customarily preceded an attack. The presence of especially well-built dugouts in the German trenches enabled most soldiers to survive the initial artillery attacks by which the British hoped to annihilate most of the enemy *before* the infantry was sent in to attack. Sited at the rear of the support trench, British dugouts were excavated to a depth of eight to sixteen feet. The German dugouts, similarly sited, were at least twelve feet deep. Some were large cellars, at least three stories in depth—with each "story" a separate floor, accessed via concrete stairways. British soldiers who beheld these were astonished. Wherever possible, the Germans incorporated villages into their support-line trench system, using the deep cellars of existing buildings as ready-made dugouts. The extraordinary quality of German trenches was the source of many a British tragedy.

The Germans based their ideas of entrenchment on what German observers had witnessed in 1905 during the Siege of Port Arthur in the Russo-Japanese War. From these examples, they borrowed construction techniques using reinforced concrete and ventilation systems. The objective was to render survivable the kind of prolonged artillery bombardments considered invariably lethal. In attacking German trenches, neither French nor British infantry ever enjoyed the "walk over" their commanders repeatedly predicted or even promised.

Having looked at the Western Front trenches from an overhead perspective, in a plan view, we now switch to a cross-section. This perspective provides an even greater appreciation of how far the Western Front trench differed from a mere ditch.

In front of the main fighting trench was no-man's-land, the territory between the opposing trenches. Each side would construct barbed-wire obstacles in no-man's-land, doing so most densely directly in front of its own trenches. These constructions were specifically referred to as "wire tangle defenses," and were designed to slow down any infantry attack, thereby making the incoming troops vulnerable to raking machine gun fire.

Just behind the last wire tangle was the parapet, a rising slope that ended in a more sharply banked quantity of earth forming the lip of the trench facing the enemy. Often, this lip was additionally built up with sandbags, which served to provide cover against rifle fire and a degree of protection against the blast wave from exploding shells.

Trenches are dug into earth, and earth readily becomes mud in the rain. For this reason, the sides of the trenches were typically "revetted," or reinforced, using sandbags or gabions ("cages" made of wood and/or wire mesh and filled with soil, sand, rocks, or concrete) to give the trench walls stability. The revetted wall at the front of the trench sloped inward a few degrees and was footed on a step called the firing step. This step allowed soldiers to sight their rifles over the lip of the trench, fire, and then step down below the level of the lip to reload or to avoid incoming fire. The top of the firing step was covered with wooden boards called duckboards, which provided drained flooring. Duckboards also ran along the floor of the trench, which, otherwise, would quickly be churned into a quagmire. Below the duckboards was a sump designed to carry off water that drained between the boards of the duckboard.

The wall at the rear of the trench sloped upward to an earthen berm usually topped with sandbags and backed up by a wire tangle, which was built on a depression between the berm and the higher ground behind the trench. Called the parados, this depression, with its barbed wire, was designed to foil any attempt at infiltration from the rear. The berm and sandbags were intended mainly to absorb blast waves from any shells falling behind the front trench. At various intervals behind the parados, a machine gun nest might be dug out. World War I machine guns were large, tripod-mounted weapons usually served by a crew of two—one man who aimed and fired the weapon, the other who fed it its belt of ammunition and reloaded as necessary. Positioning the machine gun behind the trench enabled troops in the trench to better defend the emplacement, and the slightly elevated position gave the machine-gunner a significant advantage in raking the ranks of approaching attackers.

The simplest way of firing rifles from a trench was to mount the firing step, peek above the lip of the trench, and fire. This, however, was also the most dangerous manner of firing, since it exposed the rifleman to enemy return fire. Often, therefore, loopholes were built into the parapet portion of the trench, allowing the rifleman to see ahead and fire without exposing his face and head. If the parapet had a sandbag wall, the loophole might be no more elaborate than a space pushed in between the sandbags. Sometimes steel plates were fitted into the sandbag apertures to provide greater protection. German snipers circumvented this defense with special armor-piercing rounds. Binocular periscopes were another means of observing and shooting at the enemy without lifting one's head above the lip of the trench.

As this description makes evident, trench warfare was part battle and part construction project. Moreover, these two parts were not neatly separated. It was not as if the opposing armies had the luxury of showing up at a place, building their trenches, and then and only then beginning to shoot. While military historians divide the action on the Western Front into discrete battles, combat was in fact continuous all along the front. Even when no major battle was taking place, the opposing sides fired on one another, with rifles, hand grenades, and artillery. Much of trench life consisted of boredom and the misery of rain, snow, ice, and mud. But the monotony and physical suffering were always—and frequently—punctuated by fighting. In varying degrees, soldiers learned to accept the high probability of death in battle. More difficult to accommodate, however, was the perpetual awareness of sudden, random death in the form of a carefully aimed sniper's bullet or the round casually fired by some enemy soldier seeking nothing more than a break in his own monotony. Most of the time, the great objective of trench life was to avoid making oneself a target. The soldier who allowed his vigilance to lapse, who carelessly struck an unguarded flame to light a cigarette, or who walked from one part of the trench to another without bending his knees deeply enough— he frequently became a casualty, even during quiet times.

Subaltern Max Plowman recalled that any time spent out of the trenches was, for a soldier, "like being born again." For life in the trenches, even between major fights, was lived in a "cloud of uncertainty." Plowman recalled that the simple phrase "In an hour's time" could not be uttered in a trench "without challenging Fate." Trench life was life without hope—or even the right to hope. "To be deprived of reasonable expectation—even of the next moment—is the real strain" of trench life. "It is the perpetual uncertainty that makes life in the trenches endurance all the time."[3]

Trench construction was, by definition, construction under fire. It was hard work, and it was dangerous work. In terms of time and labor, the most expedient method of digging a trench was simply to dig—to "entrench." Typically, a large entrenching party would work together to excavate one whole length of a trench at a time. The downside of this was the exposure of the working party, who could be picked off by enemy

Writing and receiving letters from home was the soldier's chief source of morale. Privacy was eked out in cubbyholes dug into the earthen back wall of the trench.
NETHERLANDS NATIONAAL ARCHIEF

snipers. For this reason, entrenchment close to no-man's-land was usually carried out under cover of darkness. British manuals specified that 270 yards of fighting trench could be excavated in six hours of nighttime work by a party of 450 men.

Two alternatives to entrenching, sapping and tunneling, required far less exposure. In sapping, a trench was extended by digging away at its end face. Diggers could keep their heads below the lip of the trench they were extending, but no more than two men could dig in these narrow confines at any one time. Progress was therefore slow. Another version of sapping, tunneling, also dug at the end face of the trench, but left a roof of soil overhead, resulting in a covered tunnel rather than an open trench. If a trench and not a tunnel was the required end product, diggers would open the "roof" when each section of the extension was completed, thereby transforming the tunnel into a trench. Work on trenches was never really completed, since the weather and shelling took a continual toll. Maintenance was therefore continuous.

At the Somme, in addition to working on the main trenches, parties were dispatched to excavate "assembly trenches" just behind the main fighting trench. These accommodated soldiers about to be launched into the attack. Also on the Somme, additional labor parties were required in areas where no-man's-land was particularly large. The standing British order governing the impending battle was that no attack was to begin more than two hundred yards from the enemy. To traverse more of no-man's-land than this was deemed suicidal because of the prolonged exposure to enemy machine gun fire. In many places, however, the British front trenches were much farther from the German lines than two hundred yards. Opposite Gommecourt, for instance, the distance was eight hundred yards. So, by night, working parties covered by patrols were dispatched to dig twenty-nine hundred yards of new trench, which was connected with the existing entrenchments by fifteen hundred yards of communication trenches. The work was completed in three days with casualties characterized as minimal: eight killed, fifty-five wounded.[4]

In the run-up to the battle, soldiers wielded their shovels to another purpose as well. At the Somme, the British had taken over many sections of trench originally excavated by the French, who had also begun digging mines—tunnels, perpendicular to the French trenches, that passed under no-man's-land to positions under the German trenches. General Rawlinson ordered the French tunnels to be extended, and he directed that some new tunnels be dug as well. By the day of battle, seven large mines were either extended or excavated from scratch, and several smaller mines were also dug. The objective was to dig to points adjacent to or beneath German dugouts and other strongpoints. Once these had been reached, the end of the mine was packed with explosives and remotely detonated. The idea was to detonate these mines immediately before the advance of the British infantry, thereby creating death, confusion, and panic just as the infantry was beginning their attack. Detonating a mine under the enemy's trenches blew some men to bits and buried others alive. This sent survivors scurrying to dig out their comrades. Soldiers engaged in such desperate work were in no position to fire on approaching attackers.

Although miners, working underground, were concealed from enemy bullets and shells, the work was perilous in more than a few ways. It was inherently dangerous, since the prospect of cave-in was always present, especially on ground that was being continually pounded by artillery. Countermining was another hazard. Since the earliest days of siege warfare, mines were challenged by countermines—mines dug by the enemy in the hope of intercepting the incoming attack mine. A "gallery" at the end of the countermine was packed with high explosives and detonated near the incoming mine. The aim was to cause the incoming mine to cave in, killing all the enemy miners. While digging, both the French miners and German counterminers used listening devices—some electronic, some no more sophisticated than a doctor's stethoscope—in an effort to detect one another's presence. Surprisingly, no German countermine ever made contact with the incoming tunnels; however, one British tunneling party was shocked when they broke through into a *German* dugout. Fortunately for them, it was unmanned at the time, and the digging party was able to quickly conceal evidence of the breakthrough.

BEHIND THE TRENCHES

While the front lines were being prepared and the German lines undermined at various points, the rear areas bustled with activity as supplies, provisions—food for humans, fodder for draft horses—were laid in and positioned as close to the front as seemed prudent. The trick was to determine the sweet spot for storage of vital materiel: far enough back to be out of range of the enemy's heavy guns, but close enough to save precious minutes and expose fewer lives in transportation to the front lines.

The area chosen for the offensive, the point at which the French and British lines made contact, was a provincial backwater, agricultural country with few roads and fewer rail lines. Suddenly, in preparation for battle, it was being transformed into the equivalent of a thriving metropolis. Accordingly, British engineers set about building new roads and new railways while also widening and extending existing roads and adding spur lines and sidings to existing railroad main lines. The roads and the railway roadbeds required a great deal of stone—a commodity virtually lacking in this portion of Picardy, where the subsoil consisted mostly of

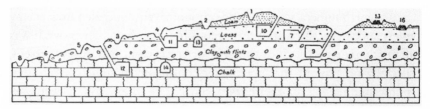

This geological cross-section of a typical hill in the Somme sector shows the chalk basis of the soil. Exposing this bright white chalk made the German trenches highly visible to British artillery. DOUGLAS WILSON JOHNSON, *WORLD WAR, 1914–1918* (NEW YORK, HENRY HOLT, 1919

crumbling chalk. Not to be daunted, the British engineers ordered stone to be hauled in from wherever it could be found, even as far away as Jersey in the English Channel off the coast of Normandy, and more distant Cornwall at the southern tip of England itself. Telephone lines also had to be installed. As these got closer to the front, the cables were buried in trenches eight feet deep in the hope that they could be made to survive enemy artillery bombardment. (They rarely survived for long.)

An army requires massive amounts of water, far more than the sleepy countryside had available. Well-digging parties were dispatched to sink new wells and to lay pipe from them to designated watering stations. The rear was also the area in which air bases were built to accommodate ten Royal Flying Corps (RFC) squadrons, 185 aircraft in all. These would be vital for intelligence, reconnaissance, and artillery spotting.

PREPARING FOR THE INEVITABLE

Despite the disappointment of the reduced scope of the coming battle—from a war-ending "Big Push" to a mere gambit intended to relieve pressure on Verdun—Douglas Haig clung to the hope that he could make the Somme something bigger, a true offensive, one capable of achieving a major breakthrough.

Would the battle bring victory? Haig could only hope. What he and everyone else knew for a certainty, however, was that the battle *would* produce casualties. Douglas Haig is typically portrayed as a commander who had no problem committing large numbers of men to hopeless and all-but-hopeless battle. To some degree, this grim reputation is deserved.

However, he was also intensely concerned to provide adequate medical facilities in the rear to treat the wounded.

To transport the wounded to the hospitals, Henry Rawlinson, commanding Fourth Army, ordered motor ambulances and special ambulance trains as well as ambulance barges, which could transport wounded men down the Somme. He wrote to the British quartermaster general, specifying a need to evacuate from the front a minimum of ten thousand wounded per day. This, Rawlinson wrote, would require "12 ambulance trains and 6 improvised ambulance trains" to operate daily.[5]

Even as the hospitals were being built and ambulance service by road, barge, and rail prepared, more men with shovels began their work right alongside the rising medical facilities. They were excavating mass graves, under orders to have them ready well before zero hour.

THE BARRAGE

None of the armies of World War I went into combat in 1914 with enough high-explosive artillery shells. At the outbreak of the war, nobody anticipated that the next four years on the Western Front would be of necessity an artillery duel. The belief was that it would be yet another contest fought on open battlefields. The principal role of artillery would therefore be to support the infantry. Field guns, not relatively immobile heavy artillery, would be required, and they would fire chiefly antipersonnel rounds—shrapnel shells rather than high-explosive shells intended to destroy concrete fortresses and strongpoints as well as deep entrenchments.

The shortage of high-explosive shells was especially acute among the British. To give Lord Kitchener his due, as early as the fall of 1914, he recognized that the Western Front was congealing into trench warfare, which called for high-explosive shells. He raised the alarm, but it took a covert collaboration between David Lloyd George, at the time chancellor of the exchequer, and the *Times* of London to create the climate of crisis necessary to spur production of the needed ammunition. When the BEF was defeated at the Battle of Aubers Ridge on May 9, 1915, Colonel Charles à Court Repington, serving as the *Times* war correspondent, sent a telegram to his editors blaming the failure on an acute shortage of shells. This resulted in a May 14 story headlined NEED FOR

SHELLS: BRITISH ATTACKS CHECKED. LIMITED SUPPLY THE CAUSE.[6] The story, which had the blessing of Lloyd George, prompted Liberal Party prime minister H. H. Asquith to dismiss his Cabinet ministers and form a coalition government. At the request of Lloyd George, Asquith created a new Cabinet ministry, the Ministry of Munitions, and named Lloyd George its first minister. He performed heroically in the task, ordering the construction of new munitions factories and also converting existing railroad and locomotive manufacturing facilities to the production of munitions. By June 6, 1916, Lloyd George's success in his new role earned him appointment as secretary of state for war on the death of Kitchener. For the first month, Lloyd George held this position while also continuing to serve as minister of munitions. By December 1916, Lloyd George would replace Asquith as prime minister.

While making the transition from munitions to war secretary, Lloyd George promised the men gathered on the Somme that they would be supported by heavy artillery standing wheel to wheel. Unlike most political promises, this one was not far from the truth. Along the front staked out for attack, there was one howitzer or mortar—heavy artillery that fired at a high trajectory intended to obliterate trenches and other fortifications—every seventeen feet. The plan was to direct these in a five-day bombardment to precede the infantry attack, which would mark the commencement of the battle proper. A million shells would be lobbed in that span, more rounds in the space of five days than had been fired in the first twelve months of the Great War.

For all the soldiers set to digging during June, no troops worked harder than those of the Royal Artillery. They prepared emplacements and then, working by night to avoid detection by the enemy, they brought the guns into position. The next task was to "register" (aim) the weapons. This was done by firing individual rounds toward the enemy while observers in the front line of trenches, or flying over enemy lines in fixed-wing aircraft, or rising aloft from British lines in tethered observation balloons reported on their impact. From the trenches, the reports came via field telephone. From the airplanes, information was either reported after landing or, in some cases, transmitted in real time via wireless in Morse code. From the balloons, telephone cable ran along the tether. In this way, the guns were aimed to do maximum damage to the German trenches. In World War I, the heavy artillery tactics were static rather than dynamic. They depended on careful preparation. The heaviest guns were carefully registered (aimed) and then moved in carefully prescribed patterns. They assumed the presence of an enemy in place, an enemy that did not move.

The bombardment commenced on June 24 because, at this point, the infantry attack was scheduled to step off on June 29. Every morning began with an eighty-minute barrage from every gun. This was followed by a lesser but continuous barrage for the rest of each day. After nightfall, half of the guns were silent while half continued the bombardment, which was accompanied by heavy machine gun fire directed against the rear trenches. The intention was to prevent the beleaguered garrisons huddled in their trenches and shelters from receiving provisions and other supplies.

Tommies who witnessed the continuous bombardment found themselves almost feeling sorry for the Germans. Who could survive such a pounding?

British artillery ejected mountains of brass shell casings at the Somme. This dump is not far from Fricourt. IMPERIAL WAR MUSEUM PHOTOGRAPHIC ARCHIVE

CHAPTER 5

Into the Fire

WHO COULD SURVIVE THE BRITISH BARRAGE THAT BEGAN ON JUNE 24? Lieutenant William Bloor, of the 149th Brigade, Royal Field Artillery, 30th Division, recalled a "whole countryside" transformed into "just one mass of flame, smoke and earth thrown up sky high." As he watched, he "could not resist feeling sorry for the wretched atoms of humanity crouching behind their ruined parapets. . . . the awful ordeal of those poor devils, even though they *are* Boches, must be impossible to describe."[1] One of those "poor devils" was a Private Eversmann of the German 26th Reserve Division. He spoke of two of his comrades getting killed while fetching dinner and of how the "uncertainty" of sudden death "is hard to bear." After thirty-six hours of barrage, Eversmann asked himself how long it would go on. He spoke of "drum fire"—artillery fire that was continuous, like the ceaseless beating of a drum. "In twelve hours shelling they estimate that 60,000 shells have fallen on our battalion sector. Every communication with the rear has been cut. . . ." As the second day of continuous barrage continued, no food reached the front lines, and the men dug into their "iron rations"—nonperishables they kept with them, mostly bread.[2] By the third day, Lieutenant F. L. Cassel, of the 26th Reserve, concluded that the British intention was "first to starve us and then to shoot us out of our positions." For water, the men in his battalion resorted to wells that had been "prohibited for drinking as they were suspected to be contaminated."

Who could survive? Men like Eversmann and Cassel lived to write their recollections of the barrage. To be sure, it was terrible, but, for the majority, not fatal. From David Lloyd George down through every level of military command, the British sincerely believed that their new ability to deliver a massive, prolonged barrage would destroy the German trenches and kill pretty much everyone in them. The job of the infantry would be merely to "mop up" what little was left.

But this proved not to be the case at the Somme. For one thing, the shells that Lloyd George's crash production program was turning out contained a high percentage of duds or partial duds. Worse, most of the shells were fused to detonate on impact. Where the ground was muddy, the detonation was attenuated or did not happen at all. Still, the sheer volume of shells fired should—it seemed—have been sufficient to kill many, many of the enemy. From the vantage point of the Tommies who witnessed the shelling, this certainly looked like what was happening, but even the 1.5 million shells lobbed in a week of bombardment would not, in the end, have been sufficient to kill anything approaching the entire German front line, not across a front that extended for some sixteen miles to an average depth of three miles. General Rawlinson could not but imagine that a million and a half shells would kill an incredible number of the enemy. Yet had he, Haig, Lloyd George, and the others in charge actually worked the math, they would have concluded that too few shells were falling on each square yard to be lethal at anywhere near the levels they anticipated.

And there was yet another miscalculation, one far more grave. When the Tommies left their positions to advance against the German line on July 1, 1916, they did not look back at the trenches they had left. Why should they? They were hastily excavated and miserable to occupy. At just about eight feet deep, they were hardly deep enough to give much protection. You were reasonably safe from rifle fire if you crouched down, but stand up, and you risked a shot through the head. Everyone, from private to top commander, assumed that the German trenches on the Somme were similar to the British. A ditch, after all, was a ditch. Only later, when British troops actually entered some frontline German trenches, did the attackers learn the awful truth.

As Lieutenant Lionel Ferguson, of the 13th Battalion, Cheshire Regiment, wrote, the typical German trench at the Somme was *fifteen* feet deep—"We must have gone through a mile of this, which was just wonderful"—and each fire bay (the portion of the trench that projected toward no-man's-land and from which concentrated rifle fire was directed) had a ladder, "also a deep dugout quite near." Ferguson realized that "after all our bombardment the trench [he entered] was little damaged." When Ferguson's company set up to occupy this section of trench, they "selected a dugout for company headquarters; the best thing in dugouts I have ever seen. It had two entrances being about 40 feet deep, extending underground about 30 yards. The inside room was fitted up with glass doored cupboards, these contained detonators and mining implements. A large stove was fitted, also a periscope looking over the old British line. In an anteroom at one end was an engine for working the electric light of the trench system. At the opposite end was a tunnel large enough to place about 100 men."[3]

By 1916, the major combatants in Europe had concluded that the Great War was an artillery war. The Germans had responded not only by manufacturing more artillery and ammunition, just as the other combatants were doing, but also by building defenses against artillery. Neither the British nor the French had thought of doing this. They could not—or did not want to—think outside of their cherished doctrine of attack. The soldiers' purpose was to attack. Trenches, therefore, were places to leave. They were to be built just adequately enough to provide shelter prior to launching an attack against the enemy. They were not to be perceived as an alternative to perpetual offensive. They were not to be made *too* safe or *too* comfortable.

In fact, the German concept of defense in depth, which was present at the Somme and elsewhere along the Western Front, went beyond the front complex of trenches. German planners saw entrenchment as only one aspect of so-called trench warfare. They integrated the trenches into a system of modern fortification that tied into full-scale redoubts—small concrete-reinforced fortresses built into the trench system—and fortified villages. German engineers laid out their trench lines so as to incorporate many of the villages in the French territory they occupied. They did this in the knowledge that French houses typically included deep earth-fast cellars. These the Germans reinforced with sandbags and, sometimes, concrete to use as rear firing positions, machine gun nests, aid stations, command posts, and simply places to hole up during even a prolonged barrage.

There is no doubt that German troops suffered mightily under fire. Shell shock and other symptoms of mental and physical stress took their toll. Transport of supplies, including food and water, was certainly disrupted. Soldiers did die under bombardment. Yet, when the barrage was lifted, many—most—survived to gun down the advancing attackers in no-man's-land and, even more, as they attempted to invade their front trenches. More than a million shells could not destroy reinforced dugouts and the soldiers within them. Like everyone else in the chain of command, Sir Henry Rawlinson was wholly ignorant of the nature of German defenses. His confidence in the efficacy of his artillery was absolute. When Haig himself challenged Rawlinson to lose no time between the lifting of the barrage and the commencement of the infantry attack, suggesting that he advance his infantry to within forty yards of the German line *before* the barrage lifted, the Fourth Army commander refused. He believed that positioning his men at one hundred yards' distance from the enemy trenches was safer, even though it prolonged the time between the lifting of the barrage and the infantry's contact with the enemy. Haig knew that this interval was sufficient for the Germans to bring men into position to defend their trenches, but Rawlinson expressed his complete confidence that no great rush was necessary. He was certain that no one could be alive in the trenches after the long bombardment.

To a great extent, as men like Lieutenant Lionel Ferguson watched the barrage their side had unleashed—a bombardment of sufficient magnitude to elicit pity for the enemy—they witnessed an illusion of destruction. Or, rather, they witnessed a spectacle of destruction that presaged the fate of thousands of British soldiers far more than it told of death among the Germans.

TRENCH RAIDS AND GAS ATTACKS

Many historical discussions of the Battle of the Somme—and, for that matter, other major Western Front battles—make it appear that the infantry sat on its hands during a long artillery preparation. At the Somme, the infantry was kept busy, dangerously busy, during the period of the barrage. During predetermined intervals in the bombardment, under orders from General Rawlinson, small parties ventured out at night to raid the German trenches. These forays served three purposes. First, they were intended to further harass the enemy, wearing down whatever morale the artillery pounding had left intact. Second, the raiders were to assess the level of damage done by the bombardment. Third, the harassing raids were meant to ensure that the Germans would keep their front lines manned throughout the barrage. The British did not want large numbers of the enemy sitting out the barrage in the rear.

Whatever the raids did to the Germans, they were certainly very hard on the Tommies assigned to carry them out. As Private J. S. Kidd, 1st Edinburgh City Battalion, reported, conducting trench raids "was a frightening experience, a matter of dodging from one shell hole to the next and, very often, finding that your companion in the shell hole was a partially decomposed body. . . ."[4] Often, the Germans beat off the raids, usually inflicting heavy losses in the process. This did not impress the British commanders, however, who persisted in sending more raiders.

The intelligence the parties brought back was mostly misleading. They tended to report that the German front line was badly chewed up from the attack—yet also void of troops. Instead of concluding that a great many German soldiers had been ordered to the rear during the barrage and were hunkering down in deep dugouts, the British commanders believed that the bombardment had simply sent the Germans running. It was, to be sure, a comforting thought, but it left open the question of where the occupants of those trenches had gone. There was no way to pursue an answer, since the raiding parties could not penetrate to the reserve trenches to find out if the men from the front had simply withdrawn to the rear. What should have been apparent to everyone was the relative paucity of dead bodies shattered by the detonation of high-explosive shells. If the front trenches were empty, not only of the living but of the dead as well, the obvious conclusion was that a lot of men had found shelter during the barrage and were very much alive. But neither Rawlinson nor his subordinates admitted this possibility.

A small number of raids served yet another purpose, namely to mislead the Germans into thinking that, despite the barrage, the impending infantry attack would be made farther north. To create this impression, Haig ordered portions of those of his armies that were not directly involved in the Somme operation to march as far north as Belgium, where they dug new lines of trenches and scratched out dummy gun emplacements. To add seeming substance to the illusion, small collections of artillery were directed to lob fire against the Germans in these northerly positions, and raiding parties were dispatched nightly. These raids—though mere feints and deceptions—proved especially costly, and it is highly doubtful that the Germans were deceived as to where the attack was actually going to take place. The build-up along the Somme was unmistakable.

In addition to launching harassing raids, the British periodically deployed poison gas. At the Somme, they did not fire chemical-weapon artillery shells before the attack, but instead released chlorine gas from cylinders brought forward and attached to long hoses stretched into

French soldier in a gas mask. French gas masks were primitive compared with those used by the English and Germans. BIBLIOTHÈQUE NATIONALE DE FRANCE

no-man's-land. The releases could be made only when the prevailing wind was from the west. If the wind suddenly changed direction, it was the attackers who were gassed—and the wind often changed direction. Moreover, the gas cylinders were large, and, not infrequently, German fire found them. When an enemy shell hit a cylinder, a massive amount of gas was suddenly released within the British lines.

UNCERTAINTY AND ORDER

On June 27, even as the barrage was under way, Lieutenant General Sir Hubert Gough, the cavalryman selected to command the Reserve Army, a mix of cavalry and infantry divisions, met with Haig to complain that he was rather in the dark concerning both his position and his objectives for the attack. Sir Henry Rawlinson, he said, repeatedly failed to make either of these clear.

It was a staggering confession of ignorance, seeing that the infantry attack was (at this point) scheduled to step off on June 29. So, just two days before the biggest operation the BEF had yet launched in this war, the commander of one of its armies was unsure of what, exactly, was expected of him. Moreover, instead of hashing this out with his direct commanding officer, Rawlinson, Gough overleaped the chain of command and instead sought enlightenment from the commander of the entire BEF.

It turned out that he had come to the wrong man. All Haig managed was to repeat the vague outlines of the grandiose assignment he had originally given to him. If the coming attack created a gap, Gough was to exploit it with cavalry. If possible, he was to take the village of Bapaume, and then shift north toward the city of Arras. Gough nodded, but he made clear to Haig that Rawlinson had assumed control of *his* infantry units, so he was, two days before battle, quite uncertain of whether he would have any infantry to coordinate with his cavalry. Haig responded to this not by convening a meeting between his two subordinates, but by dispatching his chief of staff to Rawlinson for the purpose of laying out a procedure for turning over control of the Reserve Army's infantry to Gough, the Reserve Army commander—assuming the progress of the battle permitted.

Hubert Gough as a dashing young cavalry officer. He was responsible for the aggressive offensive late in the Battle of the Somme, which achieved an incomplete success. WIKIMEDIA

If the top commanders had questions about what they were supposed to do come June 29, the rank-and-file troops and their officers did not even know the date set for zero hour. They knew only that the attack was imminent, and battalion-level commanders were issued orders detailing how they were to advance their men—when the order came to attack.

The one thing it would *not* be is a wild charge. Each battalion—some seven hundred men led by twenty-five officers—consisted of four companies. The first two companies to advance, typically A and B companies, each consisted of four "fighting platoons." Two Company A platoons constituted the first wave, and two, behind them, were designated the second wave. The two lead platoons of Company B were the third wave, and they were followed by two more platoons assigned as the fourth wave. The Company C lead platoons were called mopping-up platoons. These were followed by two support platoons.

Advancing with each company were the men of its headquarters. They moved forward between the lead and trailing platoons. Behind C Company, which made up the fifth and sixth waves of the attack, were the constituents of battalion headquarters. This group included the signalers, the battalion commander, and the battalion adjutant and was designated as the seventh wave of the attack.

Behind battalion headquarters was D Company, a logistical organization consisting of four so-called carrying platoons. The two lead carrying platoons were the eighth wave, the two trailing platoons the ninth wave. Behind D Company was the tenth wave, the battalion stretcher bearers.

On paper, the organization of the battalions in their advance was rigid. A distance of five yards was to be strictly maintained between each man in a wave, and 100 yards was to separate one wave from another. This was calculated to ensure that the advancing battalion would cover a rectangle four hundred yards wide by nine hundred yards long. The pace of the advance was to be stately, not rushed—not to exceed one hundred yards every two minutes, a walk of somewhat less than two miles per hour. There was to be no cheering, no shouting, not even any loud talking—for fear that the enemy would hear their approach before they saw them coming. Should they encounter fire, they were forbidden to run until they were within twenty yards of the enemy. The officers explained that running too soon did nothing but create exhaustion. Besides, they assured the men, rifle fire was not accurate at distances greater than twenty yards, so there was no use rushing. Furthermore, the trenches to which they were advancing would be so devastated by the long barrage that it was highly unlikely there would be anyone left to fire against them.

In prior battles—and in battles in previous wars—a British advance was usually conducted in short rushes. General Rawlinson forbade this. The slow, steady, orderly pace would keep the battalion massed for more effective fire and would prevent small groups from being enveloped and cut off, he believed. Besides—and to repeat the obvious—the intense barrage would have left few of the enemy to offer resistance. The best tactic, therefore, was to roll over the vastly depleted German positions in parade strength.

The idea, really, was to create a slow-moving juggernaut. The Western Allies called the czar's huge army the "Russian steamroller." Rawlinson wanted to do his best to convey the impression of just such a steamroller with the men assigned to him. They were to advance in order and at a stately pace, but they were to be unstoppable. This meant never pausing—not to take prisoners, and not to aid wounded comrades. (The stretcher bearers in the last wave would take care of them.) The issue of prisoners was delicate, since the accepted conventions of "civilized warfare," to say nothing of the generally agreed-upon concepts of military honor, dictated that if an enemy soldier surrendered to you, he was to be disarmed and taken prisoner. A surrendering man was not to be shot. Little wonder that orders to take no prisoners were never put in writing. They were delivered verbally. For the benefit of those who were plagued by conscience, it was pointed out that getting food up front to the attacking troops might not always be easy. It would be best, therefore, to avoid taking on any new mouths to feed.

Most officers were sincerely convinced that the infantry assault would be pretty much of a cakewalk, courtesy of the Royal Artillery. "You will be able to go over the top with a walking stick," the Newcastle Commercials (a typical Pals battalion) were told. "You will not need rifles. When you get to Thiepval you will find the Germans all dead, not even a rat will have survived." Others were told that "Success is assured and casualties are expected to be ten per cent" and that, going over the top, "you can slope arms"—carry the rifle comfortably on the left shoulder—"light up your pipes and cigarettes, and march all the way to Pozières [the village that was a first-day objective in the German rear lines] before meeting any live Germans."[5] Typically, senior officers encouraged junior officers and the men under their command to treat the attack as an opportunity for adventure, distinction, and the gratifying knowledge that they had served their king and country while protecting their families at home. In *Subaltern on the Somme*, Max Plowman spoke of comradeship as "the very basic test of manhood," adding that courage "is a social quality. Out here I see it means caring for your pals more than yourself. For me it has no meaning apart from some degree of friendship."[6] Many men felt this way—but just in case fear should overcome comradeship, the Tommies were made aware that military police were prepared to shoot anyone who refused an order to "go over the top."

In this photograph from August 1, 1916, British or Australian soldiers walk along a line of trenches excavated during the German advance beside the road to Pozières. Visible in the distance is the village of Contalmaison, under bombardment by the Germans. On the far left horizon is "High Wood," stubbornly held by the Germans. The ruins of Pozières were the focus of some nineteen Anglo-Australian attacks between July 23 and early September. During this period, the Australians suffered their highest casualties in history. AUSTRALIAN WAR MEMORIAL

Each man in the first wave would go into combat loaded down with at least sixty-six pounds of gear, including his packs, a rifle with fixed bayonet, 170–220 rounds of ammunition, two gas "helmets," tear gas goggles, two empty sandbags, a rolled-up waterproof cape, first-aid kit (consisting of a field dressing and a bottle of iodine), a spade, wire cutters, and a signal flare. In addition, these men carried a pair of hand grenades (called Mills bombs), but, incredibly enough, were instructed not to use them, but to hand them off to specially trained "bombers" for throwing. The troops in the rear waves had even more to carry, including duckboards, which were intended to be used as "bridges" to cross over any intact wire entanglements that might be encountered. They also carried rolls of barbed wire and stakes to erect barbed-wire obstacles around captured trenches. Selected troops toted a long pole with attached pennant to be used as a marker to direct artillery fire. Some men carried as much as seventy-six pounds into combat. Troops at the head of each wave had tin triangles affixed to the backs of their uniforms, so that observers could better track the progress of the attack. (When these men would strike out across no-man's-land, the tin would often catch the sunlight and, if they turned the wrong way, mark them as targets for German snipers.) Each wave included men with carrier pigeons for signaling, and some signalmen were given bags full of pieces of paper, with which they were to sow a trail for fellow signalmen to follow when they laid telephone cable. It is difficult to believe that anyone with common sense would think that the paper scraps would remain undisturbed in the course of the battle.

As the barrage continued, some raiding parties began returning with disquieting news. First, in many places, the shelling had failed to destroy the barbed-wire entanglements. Second, some parties observed German soldiers emerge from even the most intensively targeted trenches to repair damaged wire. On the face of it, the second observation should have been the more disturbing of the two, since it put the lie to claims that practically everyone in the frontline trenches would be dead. But British officers were actually more worried about reports that so many wire entanglements remained intact. Those who pointed this out to their superiors, however, were accused of exaggerating. Tired of hearing such reports, General Rawlinson himself finally put a stop to all expressions of doubt preceding the attack. "All criticism by subordinates," he warned, "will . . . recoil on the heads of the critics."[7] At least one field-grade officer, a major, quietly confided to his diary that the corps commander assured everyone that the wire in their sector "had been blown away, although we could see it standing strong and well. . . ."[8]

SUMMER STORMS

During June 26–27, a series of violent summer thunderstorms broke out, bringing torrential rains. At this point, only the senior commanders knew that June 29 had been set as the day of the attack. Among them now there was talk of postponement. Attacking through mud and terrain pocked by waterlogged shell holes would be suicidal. Men stuck in mud and water were no longer soldiers. They were targets.

The rain continued during the predawn hours of the 28th and let up some time after sunrise. The clouds broke, and the sun even emerged from behind them. But, by this time, no-man's-land was a bog. After considerable debate, at eleven o'clock in the morning—less than twenty-four hours before zero hour—upper command decided. The attack would be postponed until July 1, with zero hour fixed at 7:30 that morning. By then, they believed no-man's-land would be reasonably dry.

The biggest problem was that ammunition had been laid in for a barrage of five days. Now it was to be extended to a total of seven. Quick calculations were made, and orders dispatched to artillery commanders to reduce their rate of fire. This could not have gone unnoticed by the Germans, who must have correctly concluded that the attack, which had been impending, was now to be delayed.

As for the Tommies, those who had been sent to the front trenches, packed in closely together, surely knew they were about to go over the top. Now they were ordered back to the nearby villages where they were billeted. Troops still advancing from the rear were ordered to turn back. Even though most of the rank and file had not been told precisely when zero hour would come, they were aware it was imminent. Now they knew, without having to be told, that the attack was postponed. The letdown was not good for morale. Indeed, the waiting was just too much for some, and incidents of self-inflicted wounds spiked between June 29 and July 1.

"Wishing All Ranks Good Luck"

Spending two more nights in their billets was preferable to time spent in the trenches—but the billets were far from luxurious. Subaltern Plowman confessed himself "ashamed to see [his] men in the hovel they've got. In England a tramp wouldn't sleep in it. . . ." Junior officers didn't get much better. Plowman slept in a stable. Most of the French residents in the rear of the Somme front resented having to billet British soldiers, and the accommodations they provided were the shabbiest rooms and outbuildings they could offer.[9]

On the afternoon of June 30, the men were ordered back to the front trenches. Once again, they marched through the artillery lines. By the time the barrage would lift, at 7:30 the next morning, 1,437 guns would have fired 1,508,652 shells. Evidence of that rate of fire was on exhibit to the passing infantrymen, who took no end of comfort in seeing the

Sleep was a precious commodity in frontline trenches. Compare the hasty construction of this narrow British trench with the elaborate construction of the German trench pictured on page 112. NATIONAL LIBRARY OF SCOTLAND

members of the Royal Artillery diligently serving their weapons. Some had blood running from their ears after six days of round-the-clock firing. Sweating and shirtless as they were, many of the artillerymen paused to extend a hand to the passing infantry. One lad headed to the front recalled an artillery major's greeting: "Goodbye, boys. Sorry I can't come with you." The infantryman deemed that remark "Joke number one."[10]

Each infantry unit had been assigned a place in the trenches. These, however, were poorly marked, and there was much confusion as men fumbled their way through the maze of communication trenches and side trenches. As it was, the troops were packed into very tight spaces, and few would find it possible to doze, let alone sleep, before the battle. At 10:17 p.m., General Rawlinson sent out a message to the entire Fourth Army, most of which was wide awake:

> *In wishing all ranks good luck, the Army Commander desires to impress on all infantry units the supreme importance of helping one another and holding on tight to every yard of ground gained. The accurate and sustained fire of the artillery during the bombardment should greatly assist the task of the infantry.*[11]

The morale-building effect of this dull, impersonal verbiage, absent all trace of the first-person pronoun, must have been nil or close to it. Worse, one of Rawlinson's staff officers, concerned that the precious words of his superior would not reach the front trenches in time, transmitted the message, in the clear, via field telephone. This was a serious violation of security protocol, which assumed that the telephone lines, exposed in so many places, had been tapped by the enemy.

THE FIRST HERO

At about four in the morning, July 1, a light rain began to fall. Would the attack be postponed—again? The men speculated, but they also took advantage of the increasing downpour by taking out their "dixies" (tin mess pots) to catch the fresh rainwater. This was a sweet improvement over the sad rations of water, redolent of gasoline, that were doled out from recycled "petrol tins." But the rain stopped before five, which was about the time most of the men were finally told that zero hour was at 7:30.

By the time they were told, the sun was already rising, and many were convinced that the attack was indeed going to be postponed. The assumption was that any attack would step off just before dawn, not in full daylight. The news of the "late" start elicited some grumbling. On the other hand, for units fortunate enough to have alert culinary personnel, the 7:30 zero hour provided sufficient time for preparation and distribution of a decent breakfast. In some units, the food was hot. But even in those that got nothing more than cold rations, hot coffee arrived in the ubiquitous petrol tins. Better yet, the beverage was well laced with rum. Rum, long a staple of British military life on land and sea alike, was doled out liberally in advance of the battle. In some units, the rum ration was take-all-you-want, and it was not uncommon for men to drink themselves tipsy, if not frankly drunk, then stagger out of the trench at the sound of the officers' whistles.

By 5:30, German artillery fire intensified. Many men speculated that the Germans suspected an attack was imminent and were determined to hit trenches that were thick with troops assembled for the attack. Perhaps the enemy had tapped the field telephones after all.

The repeated impacts of the German bombardment shook off its ledge a crate of hand grenades, which suddenly fell onto the duckboards of a trench occupied by the Ulster Division. Someone noticed that, on impact, the pins had fallen out of two of the grenades, which, now armed, would detonate within four seconds. A soldier named Billy McFadzean elbowed his way through a knot of his comrades in the jammed trench and threw himself bodily over the spilled grenades. He took the full forces of at least two detonations, maybe even more, and was killed instantly. No one else was seriously injured. It was the first act of heroism in the British assault on the Somme.

THE BRITISH MINES

At 6:25, as it had every day of the past six, the Royal Artillery commenced its bombardment. There would, however, be one difference today. Today, instead of lifting at 7:45, the barrage would halt at 7:30. The hope was that the Germans, grown accustomed to the precise 6:25-to-7:45 schedule, would adhere to it this morning, remaining in their dugouts for at least the first several minutes of the British advance.

As zero hour neared, many men fell to their knees in spontaneous prayer. Others hastily completed the Last Will and Testament forms the army had thoughtfully provided in advance of the attack. Some swapped stories of family and home. And some—only a few—went crazy. Driven by panic, they became catatonic, or they shook violently, or they stormed and raved and had to be restrained by their comrades in arms. Most men, however, made a credible show of eagerness to fight—to "bring the war to Jerry."

At 7:20—zero minus ten—the British barrage suddenly increased in tempo and intensity. Within a few minutes of this intensification, some battalion commanders gave the order for the first wave to advance. It was not an accident. The idea was to get an early start, get across a good distance of no-man's-land, and then lie down flat—out in the open. The object of this was to create a leading edge for the first wave by positioning some men very close to the German frontline trenches.

The early starts were also intended to throw the Germans off-balance, and to draw them out of their shelters and dugouts. The British wanted them out in the open when their mines, which had been so laboriously excavated in the weeks and days leading up to this moment and that were now packed with tons of high explosives, were detonated. There were three major mines and seven smaller ones. The large mine under a German redoubt near the village of Beaumont-Hamel was detonated at 7:20 in an effort to neutralize that redoubt. The others were detonated as close to simultaneously as possible eight minutes later, at 7:28.

But the early detonation of the mine near Beaumont-Hamel proved to be a tactical error. The Germans apparently took it as a signal to intensify their own artillery barrage, just before the British attack stepped off in earnest. Many Tommies were killed or injured before they could even begin to go over the top.

When the two other major mines, both at La Boisselle, went off at 7:28, the impact was almost as hard on the Tommies as it was on the enemy. Each mine was packed with twenty-four tons of high explosives, making these excavations by far the most powerful thus far detonated on the Western Front. "The whole world seemed to be moving," recalled Corporal H. Beaumont of the 1st Edinburgh City Battalion. As he lay prone in no-man's-land, awaiting the order to continue the advance, he watched "the debris rise hundreds of feet into the air" and buried his head underneath his washbasin helmet. A Royal Flying Corps pilot who observed the detonations reported seeing the "whole earth" heave and flash before "a tremendous and magnificent column rose up into the sky," reaching, he estimated, an altitude of four thousand feet."[12]

0730, 1 JULY 1916

Packed into trenches along sixteen miles between the Somme on the south and the area opposite the village of Gommecourt in the north were sixty thousand British soldiers of the BEF's Fourth Army. Company officers focused on their wristwatches. As minute hands closed in on the six and second hands patiently traversed the 180 degrees from six to twelve, they clamped their whistles between their teeth. At zero hour precisely, the seemingly eternal British barrage ceased. The ears of sixty thousand men suddenly decompressed, and for some seconds or fractions of seconds, the silence was deafening—until it was torn by the shrill of all those whistles. Across sixteen miles of northern France, they screamed.

And then there was the rumble and scrape of men scrambling up the ladders leaned against the front walls of the trenches. Yet it was still quiet enough to hear birds crying through what had become an almost cloudless morning. The explosive sounds of battle having suddenly ceased, Lieutenant M. Asquith of the 1st Barnsley Pals led his men out of the trench by announcing to them "It's a walk-over." At that moment, he believed it. "I had almost a feeling of disappointment," he wrote later, adding, "It was short lived."[13]

ON PARADE

As men overtopped their trenches, they saw ahead of them those troops who had been sent earlier into no-man's-land. They had been lying out there, many as close as forty yards from the German front trenches. They now rose, as from sleep or death itself. But they did not spring forward in the kind of fierce charge many of these young men would have read about just a few years earlier in some classroom lesson on the Napoleonic Wars. They were, after all, soldiers who had been tediously drilled in formation and parade, and, on this occasion, they had been told to march at a stately two-mile-an-hour walking pace so as not to exhaust themselves prior to contact with the enemy. Having risen, then, they looked left to right, formed up, and quietly advanced.

The men who were starting from the trenches struggled up the ladders with their sixty-plus pounds of bulky gear. Officers, unencumbered by packs and not even carrying rifles, appeared more keen. Gesturing with their canes, the homely scepters of their authority, they sidestepped quickly along the lip of the trench, urging their men on, encouraging them, even giving some a hand up before pushing them toward the enemy.

Unlike those who had lain out in no-man's-land prior to the attack, the men who went over the top did not immediately form into orderly waves. The first priority was to get clear of the ground directly in front of the trench, to make way for the others, and then to advance beyond their own wire entanglements. During the night, spaces between these had been prepared, but the men assigned to carry duckboards now laid these over areas of uncut "friendly" wire. Only after a company was beyond the wire did their officers and non-coms form them up in neat waves and then start them going, abreast, toward the enemy in something resembling parade order.

In at least one company, consisting of four platoons of the 8th East Surreys, the commander found a novel way to begin the attack. As his men waited in the trenches, Captain W. P. Nevill distributed footballs (soccer balls) to the lieutenants commanding each platoon. Whoever was first to kick their ball into the German trenches would receive the "commander's prize." At zero hour, Nevill himself kicked off the first ball. This inspired an infantryman to ascend the ladder and kick his football toward the German line. The others kicked theirs, and so the men began their advance. It was great good sport.[14]

A SOUND OF BUGLES

From German trenches near Gommecourt came a call of bugles. It was a strange musical note injected into a world of detonations, impacts, and rifle fire. The advancing Tommies could hear it as well as the enemy could. It was the alarm, the summons to emerge from dugouts, to man the trenches, to defend the trenches, and, most immediately, to start the machine guns on their deadly harvest.

In the staccato ratchet of fire from machine gun emplacements positioned to rake bullet streams across no-man's-land at intersecting angles, the vision of a cakewalk or walkover and 10 percent casualties yielded to the thousand scythes of industrialized warfare. Private W. H. T. Carter of the 1st Bradford Pals saw his regimental colonel fall back into the trench after having taken only a few steps along its lip. Carter, still in the trench, rose to prop the stricken officer against the trench wall. "I had not reached my full height," he recalled, "when a machine-gun bullet smacked into my steel helmet. I felt as if I had been hit with a sledge hammer." The helmet was torn from his head. Carter "caught a glimpse of it . . . it was completely smashed in."[15]

The German machine-gunners began targeting the gaps that the British had made in their wire during the night before the attack. These, they knew, would be the avenues of advance as soldiers formed into waves. At every gap, it seemed, machine gun fire from at least two angles converged. Each gap became a strait more lethal than Thermopylae.

As more machine-gunners emerged from dugouts and took to their weapons, the rate and volume of fire steadily increased, sweeping the British wire and the rest of no-man's-land. This fire was joined by German artillery lobbing antipersonnel rounds the British called whizz-bangs. While the artillery shells used against trenches were fired from heavy, high-trajectory howitzers and mortars, whizz-bangs were fired from medium 130-mm artillery at close to flat trajectories, which were intended to mow down closely massed bodies of advancing troops. Whereas the shells falling from the arc of a high trajectory screamed loud and long, whizz-bangs were all but silent until it was too late to duck or run. Then it was a *whizz* followed immediately by a *bang.*

German soldiers pose for the camera with a Maschinengewehr 08 (MG 08) heavy machine gun. Capable of firing six hundred rounds per minute at a muzzle velocity of nearly three thousand feet per second to a maximum range of 3,828 yards, the massive weapon required a crew of four to operate. It took a terrible toll at the Somme and Verdun and was used through the end of the *Second* World War as well as in the Korean War and the Vietnam War. Note the elaborate construction of this German trench. The soldier at the right uses a periscope to observe the enemy. The canister hanging from his shoulder holds his gas mask. The helmeted soldier is about to throw a "stick grenade," also known as a potato masher. Note the steel plate blocking the notch in the trench wall. This plate would be removed for firing. The officer at the left sits with his symbol of command authority, a wooden cane, slung over his knee. LIBRARY OF CONGRESS

As more British soldiers advanced beyond their own wire, the machine-gunners searched for relatively open areas in no-man's-land, knowing that the incoming waves would seek these. They did—and there they were cut down in their impeccably well-ordered ranks. A private from the Cambridge Battalion watched a "long line of men" as they "came forward, rifles at the port as ordered. Now Gerry started. His machine-guns let fly. Down they all went. I could see them dropping one after another as the gun swept along them. The officer went down at exactly the same time as the man behind him." After a minute, "another wave came forward. Gerry was ready this time and this lot did not get so far as the others."[16]

Then the German artillery began to bombard no-man's-land in earnest. Not just the whizz-bangs, but everything—everything that, before the attack, had been directed as counterbattery fire against artillery positions behind the British trenches was now aimed at the advancing infantry. The first waves, though badly mauled by machine gun fire, were mostly spared the artillery barrage. But the German artillerymen had closely observed the advance of the first waves, noting the routes of march and registering their guns accordingly. When they opened the barrage, the killing accuracy was almost impossible for the British soldiers and their commanders to believe. The recollection of Lance Corporal J. J. Cousins of the 7th Bedfords combined shock and disbelief with the outrage of a man conscious of having been deceived: "Men were falling right and left of me, screaming above the noise of the shell fire and machineguns—guns we had been assured would have been silenced by our barrage. No man in his right mind would have done what we were doing."[17]

And yet these men continued to advance, even as their ranks were mercilessly winnowed, always at the ordered pace of just under two miles an hour, parading into the fire.

CHAPTER 6

An Aptitude for Folly

THE KING'S OWN YORKSHIRE LIGHT INFANTRY—THE KOYLIs—TRACED
their ancestry to the 53rd Regiment of Foot, which had been raised in
Leeds in 1755 and was subsequently renumbered the 51st. In 1881, after
amalgamating with other units, it became the King's Own Light Infantry
(South Yorkshire Regiment) and was again renamed, becoming the King's
Own Yorkshire Light Infantry. The ancestral units fought in the Seven
Years' War (1755–1764) and the Napoleonic Wars, including the Battle
of Waterloo in 1815. In World War I, the KOYLIs consisted of two battalions of regulars, three Territorial battalions, and eight battalions raised
as part of Kitchener's Army. Thus, most of the soldiers who fought at the
Somme were citizen volunteers, men of the "New Army."

Soldiers from this regiment were among those who were sent out
of the trenches in the predawn hours, in advance of the main attack,
and ordered to close within about forty yards of the enemy, lie down in
no-man's-land, and, at 7:30 on July 1, be the very first of the first wave.
Among those rising from prone positions in unhesitating response to a
platoon commander's whistle was Private Dick King. As he got to his
feet, he saw most of his platoon cut down within seconds of their attempt
to stand. Most had not even begun to move forward. King's brother,
Frank, was among those who fell. Or, rather, collapsed. He had not yet
stood up straight when he was shot through the arm and the lung.

Dick King saw this, but, under strict orders not to help the wounded,
he continued his advance toward the enemy. He was part of a two-man
team carrying a Lewis gun, a light (28-pound) machine gun that had

The ubiquitous, highly versatile Vickers machine gun was sometimes mounted on vehicles. Here it is rigged to the front of a motorcycle sidecar. NATIONAL LIBRARY OF SCOTLAND

been invented in 1911 by a US Army colonel with the imposing name of Isaac Newton Lewis. Finding little interest in his invention among the ultraconservative US Army command, he began manufacturing it chiefly in Britain. Like other light machine guns, the weapon was served by two men, a gunner and an ammunition feeder. It fired .303-caliber rounds at rates of between 500 and 800 per minute with a velocity of 2,400 feet per second and an effective range of 880 yards. It was an agile weapon that gave attackers some of the rapid-fire power of defenders.

King and his partner climbed a grassy slope in the middle of no-man's-land, a position that gave them just enough elevation to enable them to effectively rake a slice of the German trenches. Despite the anguish King must have felt over his stricken brother, he might have taken satisfaction in having lived to reach so promising a firing position. From here, he could expect to do some good in this battle. Then a salvo of German shells exploded on the slope. A few KOYLI men nearby survived. Dick King did not. He, his teammate, and the Lewis gun were blown to bits.[1]

Compressed within this sequence, somehow preserved from the prevailing anonymity of mass combat, is much of the essence of battle as it would unfold that day. Young volunteers attached to a storied regiment attack an objective they were assured had been rendered incapable of offering much resistance. The men are keyed up, having lain out in no-man's-land since well before dawn. At the sound of the whistle, they did not hesitate to rise. Some, like Frank King, were cut down before they even rose to advance. Others, like his brother Dick, were blown to pieces before they even began to fight. Such sequences would be repeated thousands of times on July 1, 1916, and many thousands more thereafter.

SACRIFICE

For the historian and the storyteller even a hundred years after the fact, the problem is how to write meaningfully about such futility. Of genius in the battle plan there was none. Of progress on the field there was very little and of what there was, none was sustainable. There was an obscene abundance of wounds and deaths. And there was sacrifice, astounding in volume and willingness.

Was it heroic? Some believe that sacrifice is by definition heroic. Others find futility incompatible with heroism. Among those who volunteered for service as an officer in the KOYLIs was Basil Henry Liddell Hart. The son of a Methodist minister, he had received the best education England had to offer, graduating from St. Paul's School to study at Corpus Christi, Cambridge. He fought in 1915 until he was sent home to recover from concussive injuries caused by a shell burst, but he recovered to fight at the Somme, survived to see most of his battalion wiped out on July 1, suffered three relatively minor wounds himself, and fought on until July 19, when he was so badly gassed that he was deemed unfit for further combat service. After the war, he emerged as one of Europe's foremost military historians and theorists, work that was profoundly influenced by day one of the Battle of the Somme and that included his most influential tactical conclusion: All frontal assaults in modern warfare are bound to fail. Having seen his regiment die, he had little confidence that military top command would act in accordance with his conclusion: "Another lesson of history is that the most dangerous folly of all is man's failure to recognize his own aptitude for folly. That failure is a common affliction of authority."[2]

Willingness to sacrifice, heroism, or an aptitude for folly, whatever it was that drove those sixty thousand British men and boys that July morning, it enabled them to walk at the steady pace of a stately parade and in some semblance of formation toward what they must have clearly seen would be the source of their destruction. They were not born and bred soldiers. They were not of the martial tribe that populated Tennyson's "Charge of the Light Brigade," professional troopers whose stock-in-trade was not to reason why but to do and die. Overwhelmingly, like the King brothers and like Liddell Hart, they were the volunteers who answered the call of Lord Kitchener. Civilians one day, they were soldiers the next, and casualties a short time after that.

Those casualties who were capable of walking—the "walking wounded"—generally kept walking, not back to the British lines, but ahead, on to the German trenches. Practically everyone capable of locomotion kept marching until they were shot down or blown up.

But why?

The great Irish poet William Butler Yeats thought he knew, when he wrote about the death, by friendly fire, of his friend Robert Gregory, a pilot flying for Britain in the Great War. Yeats wrote in the first person, from the perspective of Gregory:

> Those that I fight I do not hate
> Those that I guard I do not love . . .
> Nor law, nor duty bade me fight,
> Nor public man, nor cheering crowds . . .
> I balanced all, brought all to mind,
> The years to come seemed waste of breath,
> A waste of breath the years behind
> In balance with this life, this death.[3]

As Yeats imagined it, Gregory sacrificed his life to what had become a pervasive culture of nihilism. To live, to die, it was one and the same. And so the generation that had passed through the crucible of war became what the American expatriate writer Gertrude Stein would call the "lost generation." This was the conclusion of two poets, however. No soldier believed it. Soldiers also knew that their sacrifices were not for king or country. But much less were they from a sense of having nothing better to do. They were willing to die for the love of their brothers in arms. They sacrificed all from fear of letting down their mates, many of whom, in these Pals battalions, had been lifelong friends or neighbors.

POINTS OF CONTACT

After the fact of so much conscious, calm, and willful sacrifice, the next most astounding thing is that a much-reduced but still significant number of Tommies actually made it to the German front trenches and, even in their own mauled, small numbers, attempted to capture and occupy them.

Lance Corporal W. G. Sanders of the 10th Essex Regiment wrote of the German machine gun rounds "traversing at waist height against us . . . My men were falling all around, some shouting, 'I'm hit' or 'I've got it,' and some not a word." Still, Sanders and those remaining upright continued their advance—until "a bunch of Jerries loomed up from nowhere." Sanders's response was to "let a burst into them," which, to his surprise, prompted their immediate surrender.[4] Germans surrendered as well that first morning to Private A. Fretwell of the Sheffield City Battalion—or at least started to. When Fretwell approached the German trenches, some of the enemy compliantly emerged with their hands up. Then, however, "they saw how many of us had been hit [and] they changed their minds and ran back [to their trenches] again."[5]

The Germans might have been unimpressed by most of the greatly reduced units that lived to make contact with their front lines, but the British attackers were not deterred by the terrible toll machine guns and artillery were taking on their ranks. Lieutenant Philip Howe of the West Yorks had been ordered to penetrate the front line of German trenches and capture a rear line the British dubbed "Lonely Trench." The platoon he led had been significantly diminished by the journey through no-man's-land, but he pushed on. At the front trench, it was not a German phalanx that met him, but a single German officer—one German officer with a bag full of grenades, which he started throwing.

There is something to be said, after all, for the blind French and British insistence on an unconditional offensive posture. The Tommies could not have been blamed if, raked by machine guns and blasted by artillery (all supposedly neutralized by the biggest barrage of high explosives the world had ever seen), they had been reluctant to advance or had broken and run. But they were not reluctant, and they did not break. Even as their comrades fell in front, beside, and behind them, those still upright marched forward. Such was the case of Lieutenant Howe, who was determined that no Hun with hand grenades was going to keep him from following his orders and reaching his objective. Howe leveled at the German the only weapon a British officer carried into battle—other than his cane—a revolver. He fired repeatedly. The German did not fire back, but dodged left and right, continuing to reach for grenades and continuing to throw them. At last, it was a bullet from one of Howe's riflemen that put an end to the German officer and his grenades.

The real problem for the British in this first hour of the attack was not a few determined defenders. It was a great many determined defenders. The superbly constructed German trenches had preserved the lives of the vast majority of the German Second Army, which was holding this portion of the Western Front. Aside from some isolated early acts of surrender, most of General Otto von Below's troops emerged from their shelters after a week of relentless bombardment not demoralized but fighting mad. Most of the oncoming British were greeted not by an enemy with hands raised or even by a Teutonic Quixote brandishing a bag of grenades. Most were met with gunfire, and some, such as the members of the Glasgow Boys' Brigade, were met with defiance. As he approached the enemy trenches, Glasgow soldier L. Ramage saw "a wall of German soldiers standing shoulder to shoulder right along the parapet of their front-line trench, waving to us to come on."[6]

What had gone wrong?

The British troops on the ground were unaware of the basic miscalculation concerning the efficacy of an artillery barrage along so broad and deep a front. That was the main reason most of the enemy had lived to fight. The barrage was *never* going to do the amount of killing that was expected of it. But what the Tommies *could* see was a great deal of the enemy wire, which was supposed to have been blasted apart by the barrage, very much intact. Even more distressing was the large number of dud rounds littering no-man's-land and the frontline German trenches. "My first impression," first-wave Staffordshire private G. S. Young wrote, "was the sight of hundreds of unexploded mortar bombs." These were supposed to have torn up the German wire. To Young, they looked inert, like "footballs" (soccer balls), big and round—and bright orange-yellow. No, it wasn't footballs they resembled, Young corrected himself, but oranges.[7] And they were apparently just as harmless. In the days and weeks to come, a new "shell scandal" would break out in Britain. Before the ascension of David Lloyd George as minister of munitions and then as secretary for war, the *shortage* of British shells had been the source of public outrage. Now there was no shortage, but the quality of the ammunition, turned out by miscellaneous industrial concerns pressed into emergency service and ill equipped to meet the special demands of high-explosive munitions manufacture, was very spotty and the rounds unreliable.

The failure of the much-vaunted barrage, upon which all British hopes had depended, must have hit the Tommies very hard. Nobody had expected the effect of more than a million shells to come up so short. And the failure was doubly cruel. Not only had sixty thousand men marched into the unanticipated fire of nearly as many of the enemy, the preparatory barrage had also left a great deal of the enemy's wire completely intact. The British raiding parties sent out night after night before July 1 had largely failed to report the extent of the remaining entanglements. A private of the 2nd Seaforth Highlanders, J. S. Reid, wrote of how he "could see that our leading waves got caught by their kilts. They were killed hanging on the wire, riddled with bullets, like crows shot on a dyke."[8]

Such sights were both tragic and grotesque. Beyond terrifying, they were heartbreaking, especially among the closely knit Pals battalions. But for many of the survivors of the battle's opening hour, the tragedy was just beginning. It was one thing to go over the top with your comrades, in force, one of sixty thousand, and then quite another to find yourself alone, cut off, at or even behind the front trenches of the enemy. For these men, there were two choices: take cover and wait for the troops of subsequent waves to arrive, then join them; or take cover and wait for a German, very much alive, to capture or kill you.

"A Bone Yard without Graves"

The weeklong barrage had not just failed to improve the odds of a British victory; it made them longer. Exploding shells transformed an open no-man's-land into a cratered moonscape. This made any advance slower and far more difficult, especially because so much of the ground between the shell craters was sown thickly with intact wire. The more difficult the route of attack, the longer each attacker was exposed to enemy fire. Thus no-man's-land became a true killing field.

Even more formidable than the many relatively small shell craters were the nineteen enormous craters blasted out by the detonation of the mines the British had dug in the weeks leading up to the battle. Excavated under strongpoints and redoubts in the German lines, the mines were intended to wreak havoc on the enemy trenches and to do so almost simultaneously with the infantry onslaught. The mines did bring loss of life, but not nearly on the scale the British had planned. Far worse, they often became traps for advancing Tommies who sought shelter in them. The prospect of such shelter was a cruel illusion. Had the enemy fire come exclusively from the level of the trenches, the mine craters would have provided some protection. The German machine guns, however, were generally placed directly behind the first or second trenches, dug into the parados, the elevated berm intended to thwart attack from the rear. This position gave the machine guns just enough elevation to fire down into the bowls of the craters.

In *The Golden Virgin*, novelist Henry Williamson described the so-called Glory Hole, a conjoined grouping of mine and shell craters blasted between the German frontline trenches and the German-held fortified village of La Boisselle. Encompassing the opposing trenches—British as well as German—the "Glory Hole" created a five-hundred-yard void in the British line, a vast "bone yard without graves," as Williamson described it, littered with a mix of German and British corpses.[9]

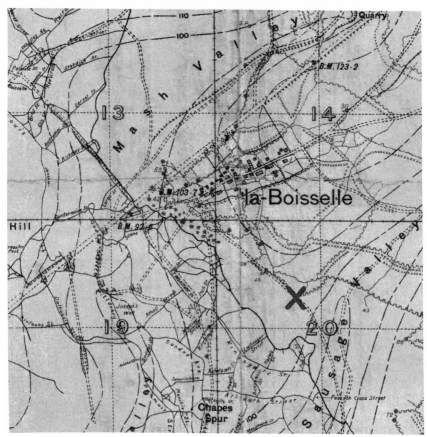

The trenches in the vicinity of La Boisselle. BRITISH ARMY HISTORICAL SECTION

The Tyneside Irish Brigade advances from the Tara-Usna Line opposite La Boisselle during the first day of the Battle of the Somme. Most of the men silhouetted here between trench and horizon would lie wounded or dead before the sun set.
IMPERIAL WAR MUSEUM PHOTOGRAPHIC ARCHIVE

THE SHAPE OF BATTLE

As self-destructive as it was destructive to the enemy, the battlefield bone-yard that was the "Glory Hole" embodied the chaos of the first day of battle. There was, however, a semblance of shape to the morning's events.

The attack was launched from the portion of the British front line facing German-held Foncquevillers at its northern end and German-held Maricourt at the southern end, where the British right flank touched the French left. The attack launched against Foncquevillers was the diversionary assault assigned to elements of General Edmund Allenby's Third Army. It was a full two miles north of the principal battlefield. As a diversion, this attack was intended to draw German resources away from the "real" fight; however, Haig could not resist upping the ante by ordering Allenby not merely to engage German forces in a diversionary action, but also to capture Gommecourt, a village from which his Third Army could pin down the enemy, preventing them from attacking the left (northern) flank of the Fourth Army or sending reinforcements southward. For a "diversion," it was an incredibly ambitious objective, and although it succeeded as a diversion, even this was something of a pyrrhic victory. The men of Allenby's 46th and 56th Divisions attacked without *any* artillery bombardment in advance. They went over the top and assaulted entirely unscathed German trenches.

Simultaneously with the infantry advance, Allenby did order a smoke barrage to mask the onslaught of his infantry. But the smoke did not so much hide the attack from the Germans as it signaled to them its very commencement. In response, they withdrew from their front line of trenches all but a skeleton force to their second and third lines. Tragically, the smoke prevented the Third Army attackers from seeing this withdrawal and thereby disguised the fact that the Tommies were advancing into a trap. It was a demonstration of the very essence of the German doctrine of defense in depth. In contrast to both the French and the British, who were under standing orders never to relinquish to the enemy a single yard of territory, German tactics made extensive use of the rear areas. The attackers were often drawn into the front trench and sometimes even the second-line trench, only to be counterattacked on the flanks, so that their advance was pinched off and the attackers cut off from their rear. The result of such enveloping counterattacks was a rapid multiplication of casualties. At Foncquevillers, the diversion cost the lives of 2,765 British soldiers, and nearly six thousand more were wounded. As for the Germans, losses were perhaps four hundred killed and twice that number wounded. While it is true that the British prevented the enemy in this sector from participating in the defense against the main attack to the south, Gommecourt was not captured—not on July 1 and not for the remainder of 1916. It remained within the system of German trenches. What also must be added to the price Allenby paid in killed and wounded was the temporary but extended unavailability of the 46th and 56th divisions. They were so badly mauled at Gommecourt that the survivors were transferred out of the Somme sector and sent to a so-called quiet sector to recover and to receive replacements.

South of this diversionary attack was the principal front, which was the responsibility of the Fourth Army. As envisioned by Haig and Rawlinson, the first day of the Battle of the Somme (which would also become known as the Battle of Albert, after the crossroads town behind which Fourth Army headquarters was located) was to be decisive. Fourth Army's objectives were all of a line of German-held villages that included, from north to south, Serre, Beaumont-Hamel, Thiepval, Pozières, Contalmaison, and Montauban. Of course, capturing these villages, which were themselves fortified strongpoints in the German line, also required destroying or capturing the German redoubts that defended them on the west. More than rudimentary gun emplacements, these were concrete-reinforced bunkers and fortlets.

It was a supremely ambitious set of objectives. Perhaps they would have been feasible if the weeklong artillery barrage had lived up to its billing. Taking these objectives was predicated on the artillery having achieved three things: the destruction of the wire entanglements in no-man's-land; the creation of ruin throughout the enemy trenches, dugouts, and redoubts; and the killing of a great many German soldiers *before* the British infantry began its advance. The failure of artillery to come even close to achieving these objectives—except at the far south end of the sector, near Montauban—doomed the main British attacks of July 1. North of Montauban, on either side of the road running north-

"Sausage Valley" and "Mash Valley" were open areas located roughly on either side of La Boisselle, Sausage Valley to the south, Mash to the north, with the vital Albert-Bapaume Road passing between them. Visible in the photograph is a Rolls-Royce truck and a multitude of field kitchens, which were stocked at this supply area before being deployed to feed their assigned units. IMPERIAL WAR MUSEUM PHOTOGRAPHIC ARCHIVE

east from Albert to Pozières and Bapaume, were two German-held areas destined to see much fighting. One, between Albert and Pozières, on the south side of the road, often had a huge tethered German observation sausage-shaped balloon above it and so was dubbed by the Tommies "Sausage Valley." Since mash always complemented an English sausage meal, the area on the north side of the road was designated "Mash Valley." As Fourth Army units advanced into these areas, they could not help noticing that they were thickly sown with unexploded British shells, one dud after another. Each was an evil omen of the darkest kind.

Sausage and Mash Valleys were about four miles north of Montau-ban, where the barrage had been most effective, and six miles south of Serre, the northernmost objective of the main Fourth Army attack. There, the barrage had been least effective, and when the Accrington Pals, an East Lancashire regiment, went over the top facing the enemy trenches at Serre, they marched directly into the fire of at least a hundred well-placed

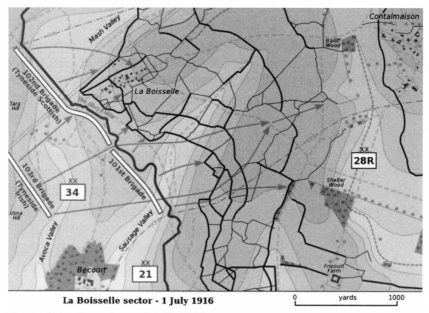

La Boisselle sector - 1 July 1916

The La Boisselle sector on July 1, 1916. WIKIMEDIA

machine guns, not a single one of which had been put out of action by a week of shelling. A signalman, whose job it was to remain behind in the East Lancashire trench to handle communications, watched as his "Pals" were "mown down like meadow grass" in no-man's-land. The sight sickened him, and he fell to weeping. He saw a flag signaling near Serre, but it soon fell out of sight, never to reappear. The signalman noted that many of the Accrington Pals were killed when they were forced to crowd together in order to squeeze through narrow gaps not in the German wire, but in their own. British engineers had not cleared enough of it on the night of June 30.

"MOST SATISFACTORY"

Uncut wire, whether British or German, was something that had been anticipated as a possibility, and it was agreed that infantry units encountering intact entanglements would fire a single white flare to warn those that followed. Unfortunately, *three* white flares were the signal for "objective gained," and in the confusion of battle, it was often impossible to distinguish one white flare from a succession of three. As a result, even when intact wire was reported, the intelligence rarely was received and understood. Pessimistic signalmen were likely to interpret *any* white flare as a sign that uncut wire was being encountered, whereas optimists would see the intention behind even a single white flare as an attempt to indicate that an objective had been taken.

General Haig was an optimist. Between the start of the battle at 7:30 and his receipt of the first reports shortly after eight o'clock, Haig, with relief, recorded in his diary that results were so far "most satisfactory," British troops having "everywhere . . . crossed the Enemy's front trenches."[10] The basis for these "most satisfactory" reports was, once again, problems with signal flares. When a unit made contact with the enemy's frontline trenches, it was supposed to send up a red flare. In fact, very few red flares were seen on July 1. For one thing, many of those carrying signal flares were killed in the advance across no-man's-land, well before the enemy trench was reached. For another, the flares themselves were notoriously unreliable. Many failed to ignite. Sighting few red flares, trench-based signalmen generally chose to assume the best, which was that the flares had been fired but not sighted and that, since British units were in contact with the German trenches, they *must* have begun successfully crossing them. Even more misleading, when the greatly depleted units did cross into German trenches and did manage to communicate this fact, they never specified what surviving fraction of the unit occupied the trench. Again, optimism in the rear lines prevailed, and the assumption was that the assigned segment of trench had been taken and was being held. In fact, in the overwhelming majority of cases, the trenches were occupied by numbers insufficient to hold them for long. Yes, British troops had crossed the enemy's frontline trenches in many places—only to be flanked, pinched off, cut off, and forced to fight and die or surrender and become POWs. Once any of these fates befell them, they were generally no longer in a position to communicate the bad news.

By nine in the morning, Haig was told that many units had reached the objectives they were slated to attain by ninety minutes into the attack. To all appearances, then, the attack was going swimmingly and as scheduled. But because the numbers of men out of each unit who had survived to attain their ninety-minute landmarks were so small, they were almost all cut off, killed, or captured by nine in the morning. Whatever fate befell them, they were unable to send up a warning flare, dispatch runners, or release carrier pigeons. As far as Haig knew—because this is what he was being told—his boys were advancing into the villages of Serre and Thiepval. The truth? Fourth Army men were in the front line of German trenches near these two villages, but they were taking fire from them and either dying or giving up.

Just to the south of Serre, the 2nd Battalion of the 10th Essex Regiment advanced to "Munich Trench," which was a strongly held position defending Beaumont-Hamel. The Essex troops swung around from the north. As the first wave made its way toward Munich Trench, the enemy unleashed an artillery barrage between the advancing British and the front trench they had just left. Thus the barrage fell between the first wave and the subsequent waves, which were either emerging from the trenches or still in them. Elements of the Essex first wave had already broken through the Germans' front trench, but, because of the barrage, they were now entirely cut off from support. While the isolated first British wave was besieged in the front trench the Germans had yielded to them, other enemy small units counterattacked the subsequent waves of Essex men, using shell craters as shelter. The German counterattack was costly to both sides and involved much hand-to-hand combat in the German frontline trenches as well as in no-man's-land. By sunset, however, the Germans retook their frontline trench. It was yet another example of an objective taken by the British only to be lost within hours. Some Tommies even managed to enter Serre itself, but their numbers were few, and they quickly withdrew.

BEAUMONT-HAMEL

Three miles south of Serre was Beaumont-Hamel. As elsewhere that morning, despite heavy losses suffered in no-man's-land, elements of two battalions of the Seaforth Highlanders in the first wave reached the German trenches, where, in an effort to break through the enemy line, 120 of the thousand-man battalion were killed and about three hundred more wounded. The attack here was an example of the best and worst of the

British effort on the Somme. In a war that often seemed anonymous in character, a faceless slaughter on a mass-produced industrial scale, a matter of unyielding material versus feckless men, instances of remarkable individual heroism stand out. Walter Ritchie was one of the humblest of the 2nd Battalion soldiers, a drummer. Seeing his fellow Highlanders falter, he ascended the parapet of one captured trench and, with machine gun fire singing past him, beat out the "charge" on his drum—over and over again. The Seaforth men responded by standing their ground and then advancing from one trench to the next.

Even as Ritchie rallied the soldiers of his battalion, two messages arrived at regimental headquarters. One ordered the regiment to hold their gains at all costs. The other ordered the regiment to withdraw immediately to its own front trenches. Both orders were quite clear—yet totally contradictory. Worse, neither bore a time stamp, so the sequence of their transmission was unknown. While regimental HQ dithered over a decision, the steady intensification of German machine gun fire made the commander's decision for him. The Seaforth Highlanders retired.

There was, however, a second wave slated to attack Beaumont-Hamel. While most of the battalions making up the force of sixty thousand that attacked on July 1 were from the North of England and the Midlands, with units from Ireland and London as well, one Dominion[11] regiment was also represented in combat that morning. The Royal Newfoundland Regiment traced its ancestry to 1795 and had fought in the disastrous Gallipoli Campaign in 1915, the only North American regiment present there. As bad as that had been, its ordeal on the first day of the Somme was even worse. As the battalion-size regiment waited to go over the top, its trenches began to overflow with the wounded and the dead from the first wave of the attack. The plan was for the advance of the Newfoundlanders to be covered on the right (southern) flank by the simultaneous advance of the Essex Regiment. Like the Newfoundlanders' trenches, those of the Essex men were becoming jammed with the bodies of the assault's first wave—some wounded, some dead. At 8:45 in the morning, the Newfoundlanders began to go over the top as scheduled. The Essex Regiment, however, was delayed by the dead, the dying, and the wounded. Thus the Dominion troops found themselves crossing a vast expanse of no-man's-land—750 yards—with their right flank completely exposed. The veteran troops of the 119th (Reserve) Infantry Regiment of the 26th (Württemberg) Reserve Division concentrated their interlocked fields of fire on the Newfoundlanders' naked right. Because the Newfoundlanders were the only British soldiers the Württemberg soldiers could see, they were targeted relentlessly.

Many Newfoundlanders were killed as they struggled to emerge from their trenches. Those who made it over the top were cut down within twenty minutes of setting foot on no-man's-land. A stark, stripped tree skeleton less than halfway across no-man's-land had become, by July 1, a familiar landmark. The Tommies called it the Danger Tree. That morning, few of the Newfoundlanders made it farther than the tree. Of twenty-two officers and 758 enlisted men committed to the attack, *every* officer was either killed or wounded, and 658 of the others also became casualties, killed, wounded, or missing. Some 110 survived without serious wound, but only sixty-eight answered roll call on July 2—the rest were physically and emotionally prostrate from having been attached to a unit in which casualties amounted to 90 percent.

"DEAD MEN CAN ADVANCE NO FURTHER"

The heroism of Newfoundlanders was conveyed in a letter to the dominion's prime minister from General Henry de Beauvoir de Lisle, the commanding officer of the 29th Division, to which the Royal Newfoundland Regiment was attached. He praised the "magnificent . . . valour" of an assault that "only failed of success because dead men can advance no further."[12]

Strangely, it was often harder to achieve and maintain heroic levels of valor in the trenches than it was in the thick of combat, fully exposed in no-man's-land. Second Lieutenant Edward Brittain, the brother of Vera Brittain, who would earn fame for her poignant wartime memoir, *Testament of Youth*, wrote to his sister of how the flood of wounded returning to the trenches from the first wave against Beaumont-Hamel created panic in his platoon, which was waiting to go over the top in the second wave. Second Lieutenant Brittain could not remember how he was able to get his men over the parapet, but, he wrote, "I only know that I had to go back twice to get them, and I wouldn't go through those minutes again if it meant the VC [Victoria Cross]."[13]

Between Beaumont-Hamel and Thiepval three miles to the south, the Ancre River flows in a northeasterly arc. Positioned on the heights on either side of the Ancre were some fifteen thousand Irish troops, including the Royal Dublin Fusiliers and the thirteen battalions of the 36th (Ulster) Division, among them the Royal Inniskilling Fusiliers, the Royal Irish Rifles, and the Royal Irish Fusiliers. The Inniskilling Fusiliers, fighting on the left bank of the Ancre, managed to get its 1st Battalion to the German trenches, but then they were pinned down and could not break through. The battalion's call for reinforcement went unanswered, and two-thirds were wiped out before the surviving third managed to withdraw. Among other Inniskilling battalions, casualties exceeded 50 percent.

The Royal Dublin Fusiliers left their trenches at nine in the morning and advanced against Beaucourt Station, a mile and a half southeast of Beaumont-Hamel. The regiment's 1st Battalion became entangled in its own wire and was badly mauled by German machine guns. The 2nd Battalion was able to avoid the wire, but suffered similar casualties nevertheless. Many members of all the Ulster units became casualties along the river. Many men were killed or wounded before they even advanced beyond their own wire. The Royal Irish Rifles were almost wiped out as they attempted to traverse the six hundred yards of no-man's-land that separated them from the Germans. When the few survivors reached within fifty yards of the enemy wire, they halted. Watching from a British artillery post, a junior officer demanded to know why they stopped short. "Why don't they move?" he demanded of his major. The older man's reply was stark: "They will never move more."[14]

The regiments attached to the 36th (Ulster) Division were each attempting to break through to positions from which elements of the division could attack and take the Schwaben Redoubt, a heavily fortified, concrete-reinforced bunker that extended to a depth of more than twenty feet below ground level. As formidable as this objective was, as noon approached, the Ulstermen were swarming all over the redoubt and took five hundred prisoners of war. They seized and held the German line just behind the eastern edge of the redoubt, but, by nightfall, still unreinforced because no reinforcements could reach them, the Ulstermen withdrew to the captured front line of German trenches. The attack was renewed from that position the next morning, and a handful of the Irish even occupied what they called Stuff Redoubt, part of the German second line. This represented a total advance of one mile from the Ulster trenches. Along a front in which movement was measured in yards, it was an extraordinary achievement. If more men could be rushed through this point, a breakthrough in the northern portion of the main attack area was possible. Instead, the Ulstermen soon found themselves on the receiving end of a massive artillery barrage—not a German barrage, but a British one. The British artillerymen could not imagine that the Irish had gotten this far. Worse for the Ulster lads, they had no way to communicate with the British artillery.

Sergeant Felix Kircher, German 26th Field Artillery, watched the British barrage eat up the Ulstermen. He was amazed at the progress made by what he almost affectionately called "the Tommies." He later pointed out that his men, rear-line artillery observers, had no weapons to speak of. "We would have had to surrender but, then, the English artillery began to fire at our trench; but a great deal of the shells were too short."[15] To Kircher's astonishment, the attackers retreated. Those they left behind in the German trenches were just a few of the fifty-five hundred Ulstermen who died near the River Ancre. Their bodies were within yards of breaking through the second line of German trenches.

CHAPTER 7

South of the Ancre

MANY OF THE SURVIVORS OF THAT FIRST MORNING OF BATTLE TO THE
north of the Ancre River were those who had lived to make significant
progress toward or even into the German trenches. They saw their comrades fall and fall in great numbers, but they lived and attained some
objective. The point of view of these individuals was often surprisingly
optimistic, even triumphant. A second lieutenant, Eric Miall-Smith,
wrote home to describe what he called a "glorious victory" and proudly
claimed that he had "done my bit" by killing four Germans. As his unit
approached the enemy trenches, the Germans "threw down their arms
and rushed forward to shake our men by the hands."[1]

The "big picture," especially on the south bank of the Ancre, was very
different, as Cecil Lewis, a Royal Flying Corps airman on observation
duty, reported. Troops on the ground could either place large canvas
groundsheets to indicate their unit's progress or fire flares when an observation aircraft was spotted. Lewis saw no groundsheets at all and just
two flares on a front encompassing the operations area of an entire corps.
"From our point of view an entire failure," he duly noted, in his logbook
that morning, of the attacks in the Mash Valley and Sausage Valley area.
He returned for another look in the afternoon and once again reported "a
complete failure," admitting later to being "bitterly disappointed."[2]

In most places along the Somme front, Allied and enemy trenches
were separated by hundreds of yards, usually from five hundred to nine
hundred. In most places, the Germans had positioned machine guns to

create overlapping, interlocking fields of fire. Sometimes they opened up on the British attackers as they came out of their trenches. Sometimes they began the slaughter as the Tommies worked their way through narrow gaps in the British wire. Elsewhere, artillery and machine guns took their toll in the middle of no-man's-land or at the German wire. The expanse dividing the trenches was, for a magnificently well-entrenched enemy, an almost limitless opportunity for killing. And so the British rarely reached their objectives in anything like sufficient numbers to hold them for long.

The men of the 36th (Ulster) Division, for example, took the Schwaben Redoubt but soon relinquished it for lack of reinforcements. That was the usual pattern on July 1, 1916. Reduced by terrible losses suffered while going over the top and then advancing through no-man's-land, men from the early waves would claw their way to the frontline German trenches. Some of the enemy would surrender, but most made a tactical withdrawal to the second line of trenches. From here, they fought the invaders of their first line, and the British would struggle to hold out until the arrival of reinforcements. The problem was that, by the time the first or second wave had attacked, German artillery and machine guns had thoroughly "registered" on the routes of advance across no-man's-land—the places where shell holes and uncut wire yielded to reasonably clear ground. Common sense suggests that the first and second wave of an attack would take the brunt of everything the defenders had to throw against them and that, therefore, subsequent waves would have an easier time. In this war, however, common sense counted for remarkably little. Heavy as their losses were, the first and second waves typically survived longer than those who came behind them. By the third and fourth waves, the enemy knew precisely where to concentrate its fire. This not only doomed the later waves, it also meant that the attackers in the early waves who had taken an enemy trench were now left there without the possibility of reinforcement. Depending on their situation at a particular time and place, they might be cut off and killed or captured, or they might, like the Ulstermen at the Schwaben Redoubt, be forced to withdraw from their prize.

Thiepval

While the tragic struggle over the Schwaben Redoubt raged, Scottish units a mile south attacked the Leipzig Redoubt, which dominated a German salient that projected southwest from Thiepval Wood and the village of Thiepval toward Authuille and Authuille Wood. Here, the Germans neither surrendered nor made a tactical withdrawal, but instead defended their strongpoint fiercely. The attack raged against them just as fiercely. It was a battle of endurance. Sergeant James Turnbull of the Highland Light Infantry's 17th Battalion (the Glasgow Commercials, a Pals battalion) threw Mills bombs at the defenders for some sixteen hours straight. In civilian life, he had earned some renown as a cricketer who could bowl with the best of them. Cricket, too, is a game of endurance, and while the men of his platoon struggled to catch their breath, he kept throwing—until a sniper finally got a bead on him.

In the meantime, the Newcastle Commercials, a Pals battalion of the Northumberland Fusiliers, attacked the village of Thiepval itself. These were the men whose brigade commander had told them they would need no rifles, just a walking stick, when they went over the top—and then would find Thiepval a dead zone, "not even a rat will have survived."[3] Few of the Commercials survived to reach the German wire, which made it impossible for the British to advance southeastward beyond Thiepval. A battalion that tried, the South Yorkshire coal miners of the 9th (Service) Battalion of the York and Lancaster Regiment, was shredded by machine gun fire. Four hundred twenty-three were killed, and a mere handful survived to reach the German trenches. The 70th Brigade, to which the Commercials belonged, lost a pair of lieutenant colonels—two of its four commanding officers.

Ovillers and La Boisselle

Two miles south of Thiepval lay Ovillers, and a mile south of that village was the town of La Boisselle. Just behind the German front lines, these two places—mostly ruins now—were the targets of the 8th Division. To reach Ovillers, the Tommies would have to cross eight hundred yards of no-man's-land through Mash Valley, which exposed them to fields

British soldiers of A Company, 11th Battalion, Cheshire Regiment, occupy a German trench near the Albert-Bapaume Road at Ovillers-la-Boisselle in July. IMPERIAL WAR MUSEUM PHOTOGRAPHIC ARCHIVE

of enemy machine gun fire; however, the enemy waited until the men were within two hundred yards before opening fire with machine guns and artillery. Miraculously, perhaps seventy men reached a small section of German trench. They managed to take and hold approximately three hundred yards of it, but, never reinforced, soon retreated into no-man's-land, which, in places, they found to be knee-deep in corpses.

La Boisselle was the objective assigned to the 102nd Brigade (Tyneside Scottish) of the 8th Division. It occupied high ground between Mash Valley on the north and Sausage Valley to the south. A Lieutenant Bernard White of the 20th Battalion, Northumberland Fusiliers, was in the first wave. He and his platoon were supposed to serve as pilots for the rest of the attack, but observers quickly lost sight of them. Someone did catch a glimpse of White on a parapet of the German trenches, hurling Mills bombs, but he did not live for long on that eminence. Still, it was long enough for those who followed to identify their point of attack. In Sausage Valley, the German trenches were overrun at several points near the spot where Lieutenant White had been seen, but a 40 percent casualty rate made it impossible to hold any occupied trench for long. And when a British detachment headed directly for the Sausage Valley Redoubt, the Germans opened up on them with flamethrowers. Two more 8th Division lieutenant colonels were killed in this attempt to neutralize the redoubt.

The detonation of the great Lochnagar mine beside La Boisselle was intended to facilitate the attack. Although it did kill almost an entire company of the German 5th Reserves, it had nothing like the universally lethal effect the British had imagined it would. When twelve British battalions of the British 34th Division entered the German frontline trenches adjacent to the blast site, they were stunned by the sudden emergence of machine-gunners from dugouts so deep and so strong that they survived the Lochnagar mine detonation. Now they were in position to deliver a deadly flanking attack, dealing out what one German lieutenant described as "a hurricane of defensive fire from the machine guns" in addition to patiently aimed rifle fire.[4]

As at Ovillers, the Germans waited until the British were within about two hundred yards of their trenches before unleashing their "hurricane." According to a German lieutenant colonel who later described the attack, at first the British were bold, taking advantage of the elevation of the frontline parapet to throw Mills bombs. As the machine guns methodically swept the British ranks, however, the number of attackers rapidly diminished. The lieutenant colonel noted that, quite suddenly, not only did the attack cease, but an eerie silence fell over the battlefield. Next, just as suddenly, Tommies rose up from the ground—this time taking to their heels in the other direction, back to the friendly trenches near Albert. The Germans were not letting them go quietly. They directed machine gun fire against their retreat, and when some retreating soldiers took cover, groups of German troops took off after them, flushed them out, killed most, and captured the rest. The Germans kept up their fire for more than two hours, determined to make the British withdrawal as costly as possible.

CONTALMAISON

The village of Contalmaison is south of Pozières and southeast of Ovillers. This put it well behind the German front lines. With sublime optimism, General Henry Rawlinson had assigned this village to units of the 34th Division as their objective for day one. Attacks on places much nearer the British trenches—Thiepval, La Boisselle, and Ovillers—failed. Nevertheless, members of units that had been badly whittled away by artillery and machine guns came close to taking Contalmaison, penetrating a thousand yards behind the German front trenches in one of the deepest thrusts along the front. Yet they could hold nothing that they initially gained, and since they were much farther advanced into enemy territory than the others in this portion of the front, it took longer for overtaxed British stretcher bearers—the men who were dispatched in the final wave of the July 1 attacks—to find them, retrieve them, and bring them back to the dressing stations.

In this war, each side sought not to kill but to wound as many as possible. A wounded casualty exacted a greater cost on the enemy than a dead casualty. A killed man was lost, and that was the end of it. Each wounded man, however, required two to four stretcher bearers to attend to him and retrieve him. This was an extraordinary expense in manpower. Moreover, the bearers did not carry rifles. They were unarmed men who lumbered across no-man's-land. They were killed and wounded in great number. Private Davie Starrett, 9th Battalion, Royal Irish Rifles, recalled how, under relentless shell fire, "stretcher bearers fell every minute." Most of those who managed to reach the nearest dressing station "were wounded carrying wounded."[5]

Collecting all the wounded from the killing fields of Sausage and Mash Valleys consumed forty-eight hours—with those who had participated in the Contalmaison attacks suffering the longest, writhing in no-man's-land over two days and one or even two nights. Despite the agonizingly slow rate of evacuation, more than five thousand wounded Tommies jammed dressing stations within the first twenty-four hours of the attacks through Sausage and Mash Valleys. "It was a terrible sight to see the wounded coming down in hundreds," Gunner William Grant of D Battery, 154th Brigade, 36th (Ulster) Division recalled.[6]

At advanced dressing stations, the wounded were transferred to whatever vehicles were available. Handcarts, horse-drawn wagons, gun limbers, caissons, personnel and supply trucks, and ambulances were pressed into service. Men who were in any degree ambulatory were compelled to make their own way, with neither stretcher nor other conveyance. "Those who could possibly crawl at all, had to get from the trenches to the dressing station," Grant wrote. The distance was about three miles. Each time Grant and his fellow artillerymen came back from the guns with empty ammunition wagons, they picked up as many of the crawling wounded as they could and packed them onto their wagons, dropping them off at the dressing station on their way to the ammo dump. "But," Grant observed, "a lot of them were too badly wounded to stand the jolting of the wagon, and preferred to go on their own."[7]

Near Contalmaison, the stretcher bearers worked as far forward as the *third* German trench. From here to the nearest dressing station was a two-and-a-half-hour trudge across the two abandoned German trenches and no-man's-land. Blessedly, after the morning attack diminished, so did fire against the stretcher bearers. They made their way across the shell-pocked terrain by arduous footwork but in relative safety. Still, they never knew when a sniper would take a random shot or when machine guns and artillery would once again open up. That long, punishing journey terminated at a forward aid or dressing station capable of giving the injured precious little succor. Bandages were applied and labels were attached specifying the nature of the wound and the medical attention needed. Then the men were sheltered as best as they could be, there to await wagons or trucks or ambulances to carry them to the casualty clearing station (CCS) behind British lines. Each CCS was a minor hospital facility manned by military physicians and nurses of the Royal Army Medical Corps. They were often assisted by troops of the Royal Engineers and Army Service Corps. At the CCS, a physician would determine whether a man could be treated right then and there sufficiently to return him to the front or whether he needed to be transported to a base hospital. No casualty remained at the CCS for long. It was either back to the front or off to a base hospital, where a further decision would be made. Could the man be treated at the base hospital and returned to the front or perhaps assigned to "light duty" in the rear echelons? Or were his wounds serious enough to warrant being invalided back to England? Wounds of this severity ranged from the truly catastrophic and life-altering down to those just sufficiently disabling to disqualify a man from further combat service. No one wanted to lose a limb, be paralyzed, or blinded, but there was a desirable wound—one that conferred honor on the victim, yet, without ruining his life, rendered him unfit for further military service and ensured that he would be sent home. This much-prized injury was called a "Blighty wound," because it was a one-way ticket out of hell and back to "Old Blighty"—England.

CCS facilities were more triage and transfer station than hospital. They were located near railroad tracks to make it easier to get men onto trains bound for base hospitals. In contrast to the dressing stations, the CCSes were large and gave at least as much of an impression of permanence as did field barracks. Nevertheless, they often had to be abandoned and moved when the course of battle took a threatening turn.

MAMETZ

South of Contalmaison and a mile and a half south of La Boisselle is Fricourt, another village held by the Germans on July 1, 1916. In contrast to Contalmaison, Fricourt was just behind the enemy's front lines and therefore seemed particularly vulnerable. Its capture was assigned to 10th Battalion, West Yorkshire Regiment, which stepped off at 7:30 that morning in four rapidly successive waves. With admirable dispatch, the battalion overran the frontline trench and began its advance toward the second line, only to be raked by machine gun fire from the well-fortified rubble of the village of Fricourt itself. One of the bitterest ironies of the intense and prolonged British artillery barrage preceding the infantry assault was that, in destroying a village, it did not so much deprive the German occupiers of that village as it transformed intact buildings into rubble that not only impeded infantry assault, but multiplied available positions of concealment and cover for machine-gunners and snipers. For this reason, the Yorkshiremen had no idea of what they were advancing into. Within ninety minutes of leaving their trenches and having tasted sweet triumph by capturing the German first-line trench, half of the

In this panoramic view of a portion of the July 1 attack, British troops advance against German trenches near Mametz. The chalky earth excavated in this area makes the German trench lines vividly clear. MINISTRY OF INFORMATION OFFICIAL COLLECTION, ROYAL ENGINEERS NO. 1 PRINTING COMPANY

battalion fell to the machine guns of Fricourt. It was a classic German defensive trap. The first-line trench was separated from the second by a gradual slope. This afforded the enemy machine-gunners a perfect view of the attackers as they stood exposed between the two lines of trench.

In front of Fricourt, the German line bulged toward the west and then turned sharply east for about a mile, toward Mametz. Here, near a place called Casino Point, two British mines were detonated, one charged with five hundred pounds of high explosives, the other with five *thousand* pounds. Together, these created sufficient havoc to aid the men of the Devonshire Regiment in pushing the Germans out of Mametz and, as we will see, out of nearby Montauban as well. The victory at Mametz was a significant achievement, and yet it, too, came at a cruel cost. At the edge of the small village was a large crucifix. The Germans deemed it the perfect hiding place for a machine gun, the emplacement for which was cut into the base of the crucifix. The Devonshire men knew of the existence of the machine gun at this location even before they began their advance toward Mametz. Their hope, however, was that the weeklong preparatory barrage had neutralized both the gun and its crew. As the attackers approached, however, it was clear that the crucifix had come through essentially unscathed. The Devonshire soldiers had no choice but to resign themselves to the probability that the gun was active.

It was. Within seconds, 159 men of the Devonshire Regiment fell, cut down by a machine gun nestled in the cross of Jesus. All four of one company's officers, the captain and three lieutenants, were killed, and no officer who was left alive in the entire regiment escaped wounds serious enough to take them out of the battle. Astoundingly, the men of the regiment carried on the successful attack against Mametz without their officers.

Richard Henry Tawney, a sergeant in the 22nd Manchesters, took part in the attack on Mametz. In August 1916, while the Battle of the Somme still raged, he published an account of the assault in the London-based *Westminster Gazette*.[8] He wrote of how the chaplain blessed the men as they began their march from their village billets to the assault trenches. He wrote of how, as they set off from the edge of a wood, the evening felt poignantly perfect, "the immense overwhelming tranquillity of sky and down, uniting us and millions of enemies and allies in its solemn, unavoidable embrace." This, it seemed to Tawney, "dwarfed into insignificance the wrath of man and his feverish energy of destruction."

The sergeant described the two-mile walk from the billets to the front trenches, a tiresome ordeal for men burdened with "rifle and other traps" and having to come to a stop "every ten or twenty yards." Once the platoon reached the front trench, there was the need to jostle for space with another platoon, the company having been assigned to attack in two lines, launched from the same trench but timed to separate themselves by a hundred yards.

Once the men had sorted themselves out, many risked being trampled by curling up to doze at the bottom of the trench or in whatever concavity could be found in the trench wall. Tawney himself managed to claim a cubbyhole, but no sooner did he start to catch precious sleep there than an officer stuck his head in, said he was sleepy, and asked if there was room.

"But I thought, 'Not so, my son. This is a holiday, and out of school we're all equal. Go find a hole for yourself.' So I pretended to be fast asleep, and he went away." That officer, Tawney observed, "was killed in the course of the day."

The sergeant did not long slumber. For one thing, he was troubled by conscience, "afraid the lads might think I was shirking," and, for another, there had arisen a "symphony" of eruption. It was the detonation of the mines near Casino Point. This did not come across as a distinct explosion but was a visceral sensation as if "the air were full of a vast and agonized passion, bursting now into groans and sighs, now into shrill screams and pitiful whimpers, shuddering beneath terrible blows, torn by unearthly whips, vibrating with the solemn pulse of enormous wings. And the supernatural tumult did not pass in this direction or that. It did not begin, intensify, decline, and end. It was poised in the air, a stationary panorama of sound, a condition of the atmosphere, not the creation of man." Tawney felt as if "the trench would be sucked away into a whirlpool revolving with cruel and incredible velocity over infinite depths."

Such feelings were interrupted by the warning that came down the rank of men: "five minutes to go." The company captain now ambled by and asked to borrow Tawney's watch. He was "brave man and a good officer. . . . It was the last time I saw him."

At 7:30 precisely, they went up the ladders, double-timed it through the gaps in their own wire, and then "lay down, waiting for the line to form up on each side of us. When it was ready we went forward, not doubling, but at a walk." They had a full nine hundred yards to the enemy trench, their first objective, and then fifteen hundred more to a "further trench where we were to wait for orders. There was a bright light in the air, and the tufts of coarse grass were gray with dew."

I hadn't gone ten yards before I felt a load fall from me. There's a sentence at the end of The Pilgrim's Progress *which has always struck me as one of the most awful things imagined by man: "Then I saw that there was a way to Hell, even from the Gates of Heaven, as well as from the City of Destruction." To have gone so far and be rejected at last! Yet undoubtedly man walks between precipices, and no one knows the rottenness in him till he cracks, and then it's too late. I had been worried by the thought: "Suppose one should lose one's head and get other men cut up! Suppose one's legs should take fright and refuse to move!" Now I knew it was all right. I shouldn't be frightened and I shouldn't lose my head. Imagine the joy of that discovery! I felt quite happy and self-possessed. It wasn't courage. That, I imagine, is the quality of facing danger which one knows to be danger, of making one's spirit triumph over the bestial desire to live in this body. But I knew that I was in no danger. I knew I shouldn't be hurt; knew it positively, much more positively than I know most things I'm paid for knowing. I understood in a small way what Saint-Just meant when he told the soldiers who protested at his rashness that no bullet could touch the emissary of the Republic. And all the time, in spite of one's inner happiness, one was shouting the sort of thing that N.C.O.'s do shout and no one attends to: "Keep your extension"; "Don't bunch"; "Keep up on the left." I remember being cursed by an orderly for yelling the same things days after in the field-hospital.*

Sergeant Tawney and his company "crossed three lines that had once been trenches, and tumbled into the fourth, our first objective. 'If it's all like this, it's a cake-walk,' said a little man beside me, the kindest and bravest of friends, whom no weariness could discourage or danger daunt, a brick-layer by trade, but one who could turn his hand to anything, the man whom of all others I would choose to have beside me in a pinch; but he's dead."

That "cakewalk" came to a sudden end as rifle and machine gun fire began to pour down on the fourth trench. Men began to die. "'I am in terrible pain,'" one called out to Tawney. "'You must do something for me; you must do something for me; you must do something for me.' I hate touching wounded men—moral cowardice, I suppose. One hurts them so much and there's so little to be done." Despite being under strict orders not to attend to the wounded, Tawney tried to ease the stricken man's equipment off of him and to pull him down off the parapet, where he lay writhing, and into the trench. But it was just too crowded, and so the sergeant took a spade from a fellow soldier and began furiously building up the parapet to provide more cover for the man.

Far away, a thousand yards or so half-left, we could see tiny kilted figures running and leaping in front of a dazzlingly white Stonehenge, manikins moving jerkily on a bright green cloth. "The Jocks bombing them out of Mametz," said someone, whether rightly or not, I don't know. Then there was a sudden silence, and when I looked round I saw the men staring stupidly, like calves smelling blood, at two figures. One was doubled up over his stomach, hugging himself and frowning. The other was holding his hand out and looking at it with a puzzled expression. It was covered with blood—the fingers, I fancy, were blown off—and he seemed to be saying: "Well, this is a funny kind of thing to have for a hand." Both belonged to my platoon; but our orders not to be held up attending to the wounded were strict. So, I'm thankful to say, there was no question what to do for them. It was time to make for our next objective, and we scrambled out of the trench.

Tawney realized that he and his men were three minutes late in beginning the advance to the next objective. "The artillery were to lift from the next trench at the hour fixed for us to go forward. Our delay meant that the Germans had a chance of reoccupying it, supposing them to have gone to earth under the bombardment. Anyway, when we'd topped a little fold in the ground, we walked straight into a zone of machine-gun fire. The whole line dropped like one man, some dead and wounded, the rest taking instinctively to such cover as the ground offered. On my immediate right three men lay in a shell-hole. With their heads and feet just showing, they looked like fish in a basket."

Only later did Tawney realize that he had been quite unaware of the number of men who were falling and dying around him.

For the moment the sight of the Germans drove everything else out of my head. Most men, I suppose, have a Paleolithic savage somewhere in them, a beast that occasionally shouts to be given a change of showing his joyful cunning in destruction. I have, anyway, and from the age of catapults to that of shot-guns always enjoyed aiming at anything that moved, though since manhood the pleasure has been sneaking and shamefaced. Now it was a duty to shoot, and there was an easy target. For the Germans were brave men, as brave as lions. Some of them actually knelt—one for a moment even stood—on the top of their parapet, to shoot, within not much more than a hundred yards of us. It was insane. It seemed one couldn't miss them. Every man I fired at dropped, except one. Him, the boldest of the lost, I missed more than once. I was puzzled and angry. Three hundred years ago I should have tried a silver bullet. Not that I wanted to hurt him or anyone else. It was missing I hated. That's the beastliest thing in war, the damnable frivolity. One's like a merry, mischievous ape tearing up the image of God.

After the Germans who had emerged from cover to fire on his platoon returned to their trenches, Tawney looked around him. Most of the platoon lay dead or dying. "My platoon officer lay on his back. His face and hands were as white as marble. His lungs were laboring like a bellows worked by machinery. But his soul was gone. He was really dead already; in a minute or two he was what the doctors called 'dead.' 'Is there any chance for us, sergeant?' a man whispered. I said it would be all right; [more men] would be coming through [to] us in an hour, and we would go forward with them. All the same, it looked as if they wouldn't find much except corpses."

Suddenly, determining losses seemed of paramount importance. The "worst of it was the confusion; one didn't know how many of us were living or where they were. I crawled along the line to see. A good many men were lying as they'd dropped, where they couldn't have hit anything but each other. Those able to move crawled up at once when spoken to, all except one, who buried his head in the ground and didn't move. I think he was crying. I told him I'd shoot him, and he came up like a lamb. Poor boy, he could have run from there to our billets before I'd have hurt him."

Against the protests of the nearest officer ("a boy . . . at the end of his tether"), Tawney proposed to venture out in search of A Company, thinking it was better to consolidate all available strength than to try to go it alone with a much-diminished force. "Of course it was idiotic. If our company had lost half or more of its strength, why should 'A' Company have fared any better?"

Anyway, as I crawled back, first straight back, and then off to my right, everything seemed peaceful enough. One couldn't believe that the air a foot or two above one's head was deadly. The weather was so fine and bright that the thought of death, if it had occurred to me, which it didn't would have seemed absurd. Then I saw a knot of men lying down away to the right. I didn't realize that they were dead or wounded, and waved to them, "Reinforce." When they didn't move, I knelt up and waved again.

That is when he was hit.

What I felt was that I had been hit by a tremendous iron hammer, swung by a giant of inconceivable strength, and then twisted with a sickening sort of wrench so that my head and back banged on the ground, and my feet struggled as though they didn't belong to me. For a second or two my breath wouldn't come. I thought—if that's the right word—"This is death," and hoped it wouldn't take long. By-and-by, as nothing happened, it seemed I couldn't be dying. When I felt the ground beside me, my fingers closed on the nose-cap of a shell. It was still hot, and I thought absurdly, in a muddled way, "this is what has got me." I tried to turn on my side, but the pain, when I moved, was like a knife, and stopped me dead. There was nothing to do but lie on my back. After a few minutes two men in my platoon crawled back past me at a few yards' distance. They saw me and seemed to be laughing, though of course they weren't, but they didn't stop. Probably they were wounded. I could have cried at their being so cruel. It's being cut off from human beings that's as bad as anything when one's copped it badly, and, when a lad wriggled up to me and asked, "what's up, sergeant?" I loved him. I said, "Not dying, I think, but pretty bad," and he wriggled on. What else could he do?

Tawney raised his knees to ease the pain in his stomach. In response, bullets came over, and he quickly put his knees back down. "By a merciful arrangement, when one's half-dead the extra plunge doesn't seem very terrible. One's lost part of one's interest in life. The roots are loosened, and seem ready to come away without any very agonizing wrench."

Through the morning, afternoon, and evening he lay, wounded, in a space between the German trenches. From time to time, he would call out for stretcher bearers. They never came—until, suddenly, in the failing light of day's end, he became aware of a man standing beside him. "I caught him by the ankle, in terror lest he should vanish. In answer to his shouts—he was an R.A.M.C. [Royal Army Medical Corps] corporal—a doctor came and looked at me. Then, promising to return in a minute, they went off to attend to someone else. That was the worst moment I had. I thought they were deceiving me—that they were leaving me for good." But he came back.

He listened like an angel while I told him a confused, nonsensical yarn about being hit in the back by a nose-cap. Then he said I had been shot with a rifle-bullet through the chest and abdomen, put a stiff bandage round me, and gave me morphia. Later, though not then, remembering the change in his voice when he told me what was amiss, I realized that he thought I was done for. Anyway, there was nothing more he could do. No stretcher-bearers were to hand, so it was out of the question to get me in that night. But, after I had felt that divine compassion flow over me, I didn't care. I was like a dog kicked and bullied by everyone that's at last found a kind master, and in a groveling kind of way I worshipped him.

R. H. Tawney would survive the war to earn academic acclaim as an economic historian and even wider renown for his social criticism and Socialist activism. He ended his account of the assault on Mametz by noting that his company had been "about 820 strong. . . . A friend, an officer in 'C' Company . . . told me in hospital that we lost 450 men that day, and that, after being put in again a day or two later, we had 54 left. But Mametz had been taken. I suppose it's worth it."

MONTAUBAN

Two miles east and slightly north of Mametz is Montauban. Among the British forces tasked with taking this objective was the 55th Brigade, whose members were huddled in the attack trenches when, at 7:27 that morning, fifty-five hundred pounds of high explosives detonated the pair of British mines at the eastern end of the front against which the 55th was to advance. The men began going over the top as the blast debris continued to rain down. The lingering cloud of dust and debris was a reassuring sight, suggesting the certainty that a great many of the enemy who had been intent on killing them had now been blown to bits or buried.

What the men of the 55th did not know, as they clambered up the trench ladders, was that among the defenses the Germans had established here were "flame projectors." Military historians generally consider this to be the original—and now obsolete—term for *flamethrower*, but it is probably more useful to distinguish between flame projectors and flamethrowers. As flame weapons developed during World War I, man-portable and tank-mounted flamethrowers increasingly replaced the more static and cumbersome flame projectors, which consisted of long flexible hoses connected to tanks of fuel and propellant. The tanks were sheltered in the second trench, and the hoses were run out through portions of no-man's-land directly in front of the first trench. At the end of the hose was a pipe of about eight feet in length, with a nozzle at the end. A crew of two operated this business end of the weapon, one initiating and directing the stream of flame, the other, just behind him, helping to guide the unwieldy device. As luck would have it, the Germans had laid out several flame projectors before the two mines had been detonated. The hoses, intact, were at the periphery of the blast craters. Thus the weapons not only survived, but were positioned precisely at the point through which and around which many men of the 55th Brigade would attack.

The flame projectors burst into action in time to burn many of the attackers alive—or to send them scattering directly into the field of fire from German machine guns. While the mine detonations had killed enemy in the front lines, their effect on the British themselves was even more deadly. They not only signaled the beginning of the attack, they indicated exactly the routes through which it would come.

Terrible as the flame projectors and machine guns were, they were not enough to check the attack. This time, the ongoing British artillery support was both effective and well coordinated with the infantry advance. The two main strongpoints defending Montauban, the Pommiers Redoubt and the Glatz Redoubt, pounded by the creeping barrage, were very quickly overrun. *This* was the way artillery was supposed to work with infantry. Despite heavy counterattacks, enough men were alive and unwounded to rush into the redoubts, occupy them, *and* hold them. As planned, subsequent attack waves were able to reach their objectives, reinforce the first wave, and thereby consolidate their gains. By 10:05, some two and a half hours after the attack had begun, Manchester and Scots units stormed into Montauban itself. To their surprise, the village, ruined by the weeklong British barrage, was undefended—save for a lone fox seen slinking across a ruined lane.

By eleven o'clock, the British troops had walked through the streets of the village proper and entered what they called Montauban Alley, just beyond the most northerly houses. About a hundred German soldiers were positioned there. They gave up without firing a shot.

All that remained in the outskirts of Montauban was a brickworks known as La Briqueterie. It had been the little town's only industry and was now mostly a ruin, reduced to rubble by the British pre-attack bombardment. Some lofty smokestacks survived more or less intact, however, and these the enemy was using to observe the battle. The British attackers cautiously probed near La Briqueterie. Eliciting no opposition, they decided to rush the objective. At 12:34, a single German machine gun opened fire, claiming some casualties before the gunners were killed. The abrupt silencing of the machine gun brought numbers of German officers and men out of their dugouts, hands raised high. The prize POW was the commanding colonel of the German 62nd Regiment, along with his adjutant and headquarters troops. The officers and men of No. 2 Group, 21st Field Artillery, also surrendered.

British losses were heavy: seventy-six officers killed along with 1,664 of all other ranks. These men, alive and lively when the day began, were silent now. But so was Montauban, in British hands. Yes, the losses were heavy, but *this* is the way all the British attacks were supposed to go. Haig and Rawlinson envisioned *this* as the result to be obtained everywhere along the front, from Beaumont-Hamel and Thiepval in the north to the point at which the British and French armies made contact at Maricourt in the south. Everywhere one German-held village after another was supposed to have fallen to the irresistible force of British men and arms. In most places, this did not come to pass. Here, at Montauban, it did.

There was a feeble German counterattack by night, at 9:30 p.m., from a quarry in a place called Caterpillar Valley, but as Sir James Edward Edmonds, Britain's official war historian, proudly wrote years later, the attack "was driven off by fire, and night fell with XIII Corps in solid occupation of its conquests."[9]

CHAPTER 8

South of Bray:
France's Fight on the Somme

In 1916, some twelve hundred people lived in Bray-sur-Somme, perhaps a hundred fewer than the number who call it home today. A small place, it has been nevertheless continuously occupied since the era of Gaul and Rome. During most of its history, from its earliest days, it was both a crossroads settlement and the location of four Somme River fords. This strategic position marked it as a frequent target in times of war, especially during the Middle Ages, when it was regarded as important enough to merit the protection of walls and moats at its western and northern margins and an earthen palisade to the east. The walls, which guarded Bray's most vulnerable frontage, had four gates, each complete with portcullis.

Late in August 1914, when the Great War was still a war of maneuver, the German army invaded and occupied Bray. In late September, during the First Battle of Albert, French forces shelled Bray heavily, forcing the German occupiers to withdraw on October 4, but leaving much of the town in ruins. Nevertheless, its position remained strategic. Located on the north bank of the Somme, behind the front line that had congealed during the fall of 1914, and with a major road connecting to Albert and smaller roads feeding to the south and east, Bray served as supply dump and the location of facilities for the rest and recuperation of French soldiers. The small, battered town also marked the point through which the line ran separating the British front from the French. The British covered everything north of Bray, the French everything south.

As originally conceived, of course, the offensive in the Somme sector was supposed to be a much grander Anglo-French affair—until the crisis in Verdun gutted the French contribution, draining manpower from the Somme. The young American poet Alan Seeger, son of New York, briefly resident in Mexico, Harvard classmate of future Nobel laureate T. S. Eliot and *New Republic* founding editor Walter Lippmann, uncle to the future folk singers Pete, Mike, and Peggy Seeger, had joined the French Foreign Legion on August 24, 1914, to fight in the "European War." In June 1916, Seeger, then twenty-eight, found himself fretting in the Somme sector. Like many French soldiers, Seeger had been "adopted" by a *marraine de guerre*—literally, a "war godmother," a young woman, who, like many in France during the Great War, took it upon herself to correspond with young troops. On June 4, he wrote to her, "I hardly think we shall not be here much longer. . . . The last rumor is that we are soon to go to Verdun to relieve the 2nd Moroccan division. That would be magnificent, wouldn't it?—the long journey drawing nearer and nearer and nearer to that furnace, the distant cannonade, the approach through the congested rear of the battle-line full of dramatic scenes, the salutations of troops that have already fought, 'Bon courage, les gars!' and then our own début in some dashing affair. *Verdun nous manqué*. I should really like to go there, for after the war I imagine Frenchmen will be divided into those who were at Verdun and those who were not. . . ."[1]

Yes, the big show was at Verdun. That was the scene of what young men like Seeger pictured as the highest drama, with France itself at stake. Still, by June 15, he was managing to work up some enthusiasm for whatever might happen at the Somme. The talk was of something big. "I am not going to write you any more at length before these big events come off," he wrote not to his war godmother now, but to his actual mother back in the States.

Words are perfectly futile at such a time and serve no earthly purpose.
I have already said all I have to say,—how I am glad to be here,

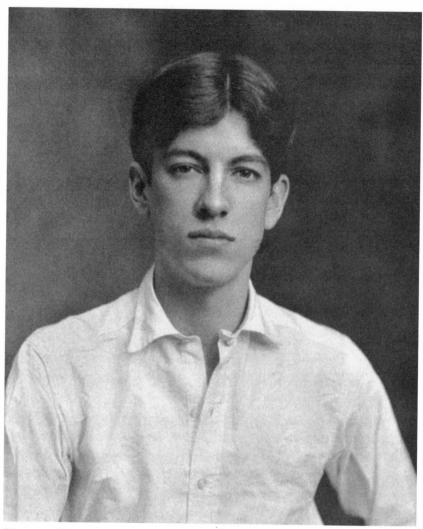

The young Harvard-educated American poet Alan Seeger joined the French Foreign Legion so that he could fight in the "European War." His best-known poem begins, "I have a rendezvous with death. . . ." It was a rendezvous Seeger kept at the Battle of the Somme. WIKIMEDIA

have no regrets, and would wish to be nowhere else in the world than where I am. We both have to be brave, and you, even, one thing more,—patient. When we go into action, you will know it, for the French communiqué will be brilliant that day for the first time since we helped make it so last Fall in Champagne. . . . If we do as well as the Russians are doing in Galicia, we ought to have some wonderful moments. If wounded, will telegraph immediately. . . .[2]

On June 28, he wrote to a friend, "We go up to the attack tomorrow. This will probably be the biggest thing yet. We are to have the honor of marching in the first wave. . . . I will write you soon if I get through all right. If not, my only earthly care is for my poems. . . . I am glad to be going in [the] first wave. If you are in this thing at all it is best to be in to the limit. And this is the supreme experience."[3]

THE FRENCH TRIUMPHS OF JULY 1

As it turned out, the Anglo-French offensive on the Somme front would not step off until July 1, and Alan Seeger and his Foreign Legion unit would not get into the action until July 4. By midday of July 1, however, the French Sixth Army managed to overrun and capture all of the German first-line trenches, except for the area around the tiny village of Frise (population between one and two hundred in 1916). Located on the Somme Canal, Frise was surrounded by watery marshland that not only made entrenchment difficult, but impeded any attack on the hamlet itself. Even without Frise as a prize, however, the first day of French conquest was a remarkable achievement, especially when contrasted with the British struggle that had unfolded through July 1. By the end of the day, French casualties were comparatively light, the greatest loss being some four thousand men taken prisoner.

Were the French better or more determined soldiers than the English? Were they more effectively led? The answer to the first question is *no* and to the second, *probably not*. Close to Bray, where the British and French flanks made contact, the British also had their only unalloyed successes on July 1, the capture of Mametz and Montauban. The truth is that German artillery was not as numerous at the southern end of the

The Church of Frise did not survive the Battle of the Somme. WIKIMEDIA

Somme front and had not been used nearly as well as it had along the northern, British front.

Still, the French acted with great vigor. No sooner was the German front line in their control than French Territorial troops rushed in to clear the battlefield of debris, unexploded ordnance, and the dead. This accomplished, artillerists rolled up batteries to support the infantry's advance from the captured first-line German trenches to the second line. The British, in contrast, were never so methodical. In the northern portion of their sector, German resistance prevented a systematic attack, but even on the southern end, the British relied mainly on infantry to push forward, without the advantage of close artillery support.

I Colonial Corps, to which Alan Seeger's Foreign Legion unit was attached, had left billets at Bayonvillers during the night of June 30–July 1 to march closer to the firing line. Seeger must have been disappointed to learn that the Legion was being sent to the town of Proyart, south of the Somme River and just under four miles south of Bray. They were to be held here as reserves, and when, at eight o'clock on the morning of July 1, orders were read out at roll call, the Legionnaires were told that the general offensive would step off at nine—without them. Seeger would not be in the first wave after all. Instead, he was put on "shell fatigue" with his comrades, assigned to the hard labor of unloading eight-inch artillery shells from the *camions* (trucks) that had delivered them to the Legionnaires' reserve position.

In the meantime, the colonial regiments of I Colonial Corps *were* sent to the front, where they participated in taking the German first line that day. Seeger and the others could only watch as thousands of German POWs were marched back from the front. Along with the prisoners came the ambulances, carrying both French and German wounded. Like famished men, the Legionnaires begged news from any French soldier who passed. What was happening at the front?

What was happening, it seemed clear, was victory. As Rif Baer, an Egyptian who was one of Seeger's closest friends among the Legionnaires, reported, everything they "could learn seemed to augur well," and when, at about four in the afternoon, they finally left Proyart for

A French aerial observer or pilot-observer took this photograph, from an altitude of about five hundred feet, of French troops attacking on the Somme Front. The smoke is from a smoke shell, used to generate a smokescreen to mask movement from the enemy. NATIONAL ARCHIVES AND RECORDS ADMINISTRATION/US WAR DEPT.

Fontaine-lès-Cappy near the French first line, "Alan was beaming with joy and full of impatience for the order to join the action." In fact, "Everywhere delirious joy reigned at having driven the enemy back without loss for us." The Legionnaires were convinced "that no further resistance would be met and that our shock attack would finish the Germans."[4]

They spent the night of July 1–2 at Fontaine-lès-Cappy, and then, in the morning, marched toward what had been the German first lines.

"My dream is coming true," Alan Seeger told his Egyptian comrade-in-arms, "and perhaps tomorrow we shall attack. I am more than satisfied, but it's too bad about our July 4th leave. . . ."[5]

THE COLONIALS

The European nations fighting in World War I transported some 650,000 troops from their colonial empires to fight on the European continent. Of these, roughly a half-million fought for France alongside eight million Frenchmen. France's colonial army on the continent included 175,000 Algerians, 40,000 Moroccans, 80,000 Tunisians, and 180,000 sub-Saharan Africans, referred to collectively as "Senegalese infantrymen." French colonials were especially well represented at both Verdun and the Somme.

At 4:30 p.m. on July 1, elements of the I Colonial Corps, supported by the artillery that had been brought up to the captured German first positions by midday, succeeded taking Frise, which had withstood the French assaults that morning. From here, the colonials attacked the German second line, breaking through it near the village of Herbécourt (a little less than four miles from Fontaine-lès-Cappy), which they then surrounded. From the outskirts of Herbécourt, the French attack turned due south, where it was repulsed at Assevillers, the Germans finally using their artillery to significant effect. This setback notwithstanding, the I Colonial Corps took Assevillers at nine o'clock on July 2. French aerial reconnaissance reported on that day that the Germans had evacuated. This was very good news, of course, but it was also standard tactical practice for the Germans, who, fighting exclusively on French territory, often withdrew from first, second, and even third lines, drawing the enemy deeper into the territory it controlled and setting it up for a flanking attack. But in this instance, the French had momentum on their side. The fall of Assevillers led to the capture of Flaucourt and Feuillères farther east. During July 1–2, the I Colonial Corps took more than five thousand prisoners—the endless lines Seeger and his friend observed marching to the rear. From Flaucourt, with its abandoned German artillery park, French cavalry troops were sent to probe closer to the River Somme, which here meandered well behind enemy lines. Their probe extended the French advance to 4.3 miles, giving it the distinction of being the deepest Allied penetration on the Western Front since trench warfare had set in during the early fall of 1914.

The 2nd Colonial Division of the I Colonial Corps advanced beyond the tiny village of Feuillères and pushed the enemy out of the *boucle*, or loop, which is created by the Somme's sudden turn to the south at Péronne, one of the ancient towns along the river. This advance put the French face-to-face with the southern segment of the Germans' third position. Long occupied by the enemy, Péronne, looming on the east bank of the river, was one of the true prizes of the Somme sector.

During the evening of July 1, elements of the French XXXV Corps took Estrées-Deniécourt, south of Assevillers and southwest of Belloy-en-Santerre. Early the next day, the Germans launched a counterattack and clawed back half of Estrées. Nevertheless, in the space of forty-eight hours during July 1–2, French forces had broken through on a broad five-mile front. Most significantly, the I Colonial Corps had achieved something the British were nowhere able to do at the Somme. They created a salient that pushed just to the east of Maricourt about three miles north of Frise. This looked like real progress. Unfortunately, it was as much a liability as an asset. The salient was continually bombarded by German heavy artillery, which was firing from the relative safety of the east bank of the Somme. The Germans made ample use of tethered observation balloons and observer aircraft to assist the artillery in precisely registering on French strongpoints in the salient. What is more, German attacks repeatedly enfiladed the salient, and French movement through the Flaucourt Plateau, located two miles southeast of Frise, between the French and German lines, was made impossible— at least by daylight.

JULY 4, 1916

On July 4, the Foreign Legion was tasked with capturing the villages of Barleux and Biaches, which were on the southern edge of the Flaucourt Plateau. Their capture would relieve pressure on the Maricourt salient. The two objectives quickly fell to the Legionnaires, but the Germans counterattacked fiercely from the northeast in the afternoon. These counterattacks spread to La Maisonette and Belloy-en-Santerre.

About four o'clock in the afternoon, two battalions, including Alan Seeger's, were ordered to counter the counterattack at Belloy. Seeger's company formed the reserve of the battalion. As the companies of the first wave formed up on a plain thick with tall wheat, Seeger and his Egyptian friend Rif Baer saw the fixed bayonets of the Legionnaires glinting just above the wheat. Seeger's company waited as the companies of the first wave bounded forward, and then they, too, advanced into the wheat. An order was shouted, and they lay down, awaiting their turn to advance. The company was divided into two sections. The first, which was the right and vanguard of the company, included Seeger. Rif Baer was in the second section, which formed the left wing of the wave. On signal, Seeger's section rose to their feet and advanced toward the far right margin of Belloy. Rif Baer "caught sight of Seeger and called to him, making a sign with my hand." The young man answered with a smile. "How pale he was! His tall silhouette stood out on the green of the cornfield [wheat field]. He was the tallest man in his section. His head erect, and pride in his eye, I saw him running forward, with bayonet fixed. Soon he disappeared and that was the last time I saw my friend. . . ."[6]

Another Legionnaire published an account of the assault on Belloy-en-Santerre in *La Liberté*, the Paris newspaper.

It is six o'clock of an ideal summer evening. Assigned to take the southern part of Belloy, the 3rd Battalion presses "straight forward, beneath the crash of bursting shells, across a chaos of detonations. . . . The men hurry on, clutching tightly their arms; some set their teeth, others shout."[7]

The first two companies of the battalion have three hundred yards to traverse before they reach the southern edge of Belloy. "*En avant!* But suddenly, hands relax their grasp, arms open, bodies stagger and fall, as the clatter of German mitrailleuses spreads death over the plain where, but a moment before, men were passing." (The *mitrailleuse* was a multi-barrel volley gun similar to a Gatling gun and capable of firing multiple rounds simultaneously or firing bursts in rapid succession.) Hiding beside the road from Estrées to Belloy, the gunners take the men "in flank, cutting to pieces the 11th company" amid "Cries of anguish . . . from the tall grass." Those who remain unwounded or, if wounded, are still capable of fighting call out "for their chiefs. But all, officers and subalterns, have fallen. 'My captain . . . My lieutenant . . . Sergeant. . . .' No answer." And then a voice calls out: "No more chiefs left. Come on, all the same, *nom de Dieu!* Come on! Lie flat, boys, he that lifts his head is done for. *En avant!*"[8]

With that, the Legionnaires crawl forward to continue the attack at a crawl. "The wounded see the second wave pass, then the third. . . . They cheer on their comrades: 'Courage, fellows, death to the Boches! On with you!'"[9]

And the high grasses shudder, their roots trodden by the men, their tops fanned by the hail of projectiles.

From the sunken road the German mitrailleuses work unceasingly. . . .

Now, in all the plain, not a movement; the living have passed out of sight. The dead, outstretched, are as if asleep, the wounded are silent; they listen, they listen to the battle with all their ears, this battle so near to them, but in which they have no part. They wait to hear the shout of their comrades in the supreme hour of the great assault."[10]

From the distance of the outskirts of Belloy, fragments of the order drift to the ears of the wounded. "*En avant! Vive la Légion. Ah. . . . Ah. . . . Ah. . . .*"[11]

The "notes of a bugle pierce the air; it is the brave Renard who sounds the charge." With that, the Legion "in a final bound, reaches the village. . . . The grenades burst, the mitrailleuses rattle . . . ." To the wounded lying in the field, the span seems "beyond measure, interminable, a time of anguish, during which one pictures man killing man, face to face, in hand to hand conflict." And then the cry "arises, swells, grows louder, louder: 'They are there, it is over, Belloy is taken!'"[12]

The fall or winter before the Battle of Belloy, a small battle in a big war, Alan Seeger wrote the only poem for which he is remembered today. At that, it is a poem many remember only because it became a favorite of President John F. Kennedy:

> I have a rendezvous with Death
> At some disputed barricade,
> When Spring comes back with rustling shade
> And apple-blossoms fill the air—
> I have a rendezvous with Death
> When Spring brings back blue days and fair.
>
> It may be he shall take my hand
> And lead me into his dark land
> And close my eyes and quench my breath—
> It may be I shall pass him still.
> I have a rendezvous with Death
> On some scarred slope of battered hill,
> When Spring comes round again this year
> And the first meadow-flowers appear.
>
> God knows 'twere better to be deep
> Pillowed in silk and scented down,
> Where love throbs out in blissful sleep,
> Pulse nigh to pulse, and breath to breath,
> Where hushed awakenings are dear. . .
> But I've a rendezvous with Death
> At midnight in some flaming town,
> When Spring trips north again this year,
> And I to my pledged word am true,
> I shall not fail that rendezvous.

Alan Seeger was one of the first to fall in that little battle. "Mortally wounded, it was his fate to see his comrades pass him in their splendid charge and to forgo the supreme moment of victory to which he had looked forward through so many months of bitterest hardship and trial." It was said that, like the "other generous wounded of the *Legion fallen*, he cheered on the fresh files as they came. . . ."[13]

Like their British allies, French troops were under strict orders never to pause in aid of the wounded. "In that zone of deadly cross-fire there could be but one thought,—to get beyond it alive, if possible. So it was not until the next day that his body was found and buried, with scores of his comrades, on the battle-field of Belloy-en-Santerre."[14]

Foch Decides

The German counterattacks at Belloy, La Maisonette, and Biaches resumed throughout the night of July 4 and continued into the morning of July 5. Colonial troops retook most of Estrées-Deniécourt on July 5. The progress in the French sector of the Somme encouraged General Ferdinand Foch, commander of the Army Group North. Magnificently mustachioed in the manner of Kitchener, erect as a ramrod, and with deep-set, piercing eyes, he was the very embodiment of the French army's embrace of the doctrine of attaque à outrance, "attack to uttermost," attack at all cost.

Foch had been born not in the heart of France, but on its southern periphery, at Tarbes, in Hautes-Pyrénées. Educated by Jesuits, he did not choose the priesthood—his brother's path—but instead enlisted in the French 4th Marine Infantry Regiment in 1870, during the Franco-Prussian War. This taste of army life persuaded him to remain in the military, and, at the end of the war, in 1871, he enrolled in the École Polytechnique. Although this was not Saint Cyr, *the* military academy, it was a fertile field for training French officers, and he received his lieutenant's commission in 1873—a year early, thanks to a postwar officer shortage. Despite his Catholic background, usually a handicap in the staunchly secular army of the new republic that followed the abdication of Napoleon III, Foch was promoted in due course to captain and in 1885 entered the Staff College, to be trained for service in the upper echelons of the French military. He was called back to the college in 1895 to serve as an instructor and earned a reputation as an innovative military thinker. His doctrinal and theoretical focus was always propelled by his visceral advocacy of offense. Yet this never overshadowed his analytical side. While others did their best to put the humiliation of the Franco-Prussian War behind them, Foch examined it relentlessly, meticulously, determined to learn from the mistakes so as not to repeat them in what everyone assumed would, sooner or later, be another war with Imperial Germany.

As an instructor at the Staff College, Foch was instrumental in shaping the character of the French army in the years leading up to World War I. No mere rabble rouser, he wrapped his ideas on extreme offensive in the theories of Carl von Clausewitz, who, as a Prussian, had never been popular in French military circles. For all his emphasis on the political and strategic dimensions of war, Clausewitz may have been most radical in his idea that victory begins and ends with a *will* to conquer. Foch embodied this in lectures and books—which, in some ways, proved *too* effective. For while Foch took pains to marry the conquering will to qualities of military competence and prudence, many of his disciples embraced only the idea of conquest, and the army that entered the war in 1914 was dominated by a cult of the offensive, with Ferdinand Foch as its less than thoroughly willing leader. His lectures and writings drove the creation of Plan XVII, the simplistic battle blueprint with which France sought to defeat Germany by head-on offensives propelled less by strategic ingenuity, tactical agility, and logistical preparation than by élan vital and a will to win. The hollow core of Plan XVII doomed France to disaster in 1914, and Foch's reputation initially suffered in consequence. Nevertheless, given command of XX Corps at the start of the war, he was part of a fleeting invasion of Germany and thus one of the few top commanders to actually put a forward-moving offensive into action. Moreover, although he was soon forced to retreat under intense counterattack, he commanded an effective stand at Nancy, where he temporarily halted the German juggernaut of August 1914.

Fortunately for France—and fortunately for Foch—Joseph Joffre recalled him from Nancy to defend Paris, which was in imminent danger of falling early in September 1914. His calm and inspiring leadership in the crisis was crucial to achieving the "Miracle on the Marne," the French victory in the First Battle of the Marne (September 5–12, 1914). The outcome not only saved the capital but ended Germany's chances for a quick victory by transforming the Western Front into a war of attrition between static lines of entrenchment.

As a result of the Marne, Joffre promoted Foch to command of the French Ninth Army and then of Army Group North. During September 25–November 4, 1915, he collaborated with the British in the Loos-Artois Offensive, which is also known as the Third Battle of Artois. Fought north of what would become the scene of the 1916 Somme offensive, the campaign in Artois had a strategic purpose similar to the later battle. As the 1916 operation was originally intended to be the Western Front portion of a coordinated Anglo-French, Italian, and Russian mega-offensive striking Germany simultaneously from the west, south, and east, the 1915 operation was to be roughly coordinated with Italian attacks across the Isonzo River in the south and a British attack at Loos-en-Gohelle. Both Field Marshal Sir John French and General Sir Douglas Haig objected to attacking in this area because they considered the ground unfavorable, no heavy artillery was available, ammunition supplies were still critically low, and the BEF had insufficient manpower reserves to draw on. Lord Kitchener, in his capacity as minister of war, overruled these objections. He was determined that the British give affirmative aid to their ally.

Predictably, the offensive failed. Less predictable was the scope of the losses. While the Germans suffered an estimated fifty-one thousand casualties, the French lost 48,230 killed, wounded, missing, or made prisoner, and the BEF an even more devastating 61,713. Yet Foch survived, continued in command of Army Group North, and remained aggressive. Seizing on the French successes in the southern portion of the Somme front during July 1–5, 1916, he issued orders on July 6 to continue the attack on *both* banks of the Somme. He added the resources of the French Tenth Army to those of the Sixth to ensure that his forces would have the capacity to exploit any further breakthroughs.

XX Corps

Foch's order came after the attacks of the I Colonial Corps and action by the officers and men of his former command, the XX Corps. As was not the case with the colonials, who operated south of the Somme River, XX Corps, on the north bank, had to coordinate closely with the British. Supplies to both the French and the British were delayed because of a transportation bottleneck in the beleaguered Maricourt salient. A planned XX Corps attack on Hardecourt, northeast of Maricourt village, had to be delayed until the British could begin operations on the extreme southern end of their front at Bernafay and Trônes woods. XX Corps artillery bombarded Hardecourt beginning on July 3 and continuing for the next forty-eight hours. Finally, just before seven o'clock on the morning of July 5, XX Corps infantry advanced via saps (covered trenches) toward Hardecourt and the surrounding area, and then followed a creeping barrage into the battered village itself. Hardecourt, Hem, and the Bois Fromage were all taken by 6:30 on the evening of July 5, only to be counterattacked vigorously during July 6–7. Territory changed hands repeatedly during this time, but the French advance generally held.

By July 8, it became apparent to Foch that the British failures to achieve significant progress, combined with the poorly developed road net on the French side of the Somme front, made it impossible to deliver sufficient reinforcement on the German-controlled side of the Somme to capture Maurepas, an enemy stronghold one mile east of Hardecourt. During July 7–8, the British took the German second position from Longueval to Bazentin-le-Petit and were now positioned for an attack on Guillemont, southwest of Ginchy and northeast of Montauban. They launched the attack, which promptly failed. Thus, from late in the day on July 7 through July 8, objectives throughout the area east of Bray repeatedly changed hands as a result of one German counterattack after another, in the villages and in the woods.

XXXV CORPS

While possession of woods and adjacent villages—all ruins—changed almost hourly during July 7 and 8, farther south, the French XXXV Corps attacked Barleux, about three miles southwest of Péronne. The Germans held Barleux stubbornly, and the attack failed. In the meantime, the attempt to rush ammunition and artillery forward to support this and other eastward attacks jammed the country roads, forcing the suspension of the operation against Barleux as ammunition supplies dwindled. Late on July 9, Barleux, along with Biaches, was finally captured, and elements of the XXXV Corps used these ruined villages as jumping off points for assault operations designed to gain control of the Amiens–Vermand

Road near Estrées-Deniécourt. The French carried off these attacks on July 10, but heavy German resistance repulsed every attempt. Next came a counterattack on Barleux, which briefly put that ruin back into German hands, whereupon a force of colonials joined elements of XXV Corps in an attempt to retake both Barleux and the nearby Bois Blaise. Although the Germans were flushed out of the woods, which were then occupied by the French, the attempt to retake Barleux was beaten off by German machine-gunners well hidden in the surrounding wheat fields.

A VERSION OF VICTORY

To look at a historical map of the Battle of the Somme, it would appear that by July 14, Bastille Day, after two weeks of battle, the French succeeded in pushing back the German front line nearly to Barleux (which, however, was again in German hands as of July 14) and, to the south, beyond Flacourt. The July 14 French advance ended just east of Hardecourt. This certainly looks like significant progress—and more than enough to put the British to shame. Although the Tommies had achieved their July 1 objectives on the south end of their front, everywhere else, as we will see in the next chapter, they had failed.

It is, however, one thing to look at a map one hundred years after the battle it documents and quite another to try to imagine how life and death actually were, on the ground, on that first day and first two weeks of July 1916. Without question, the French achieved a better result than the British. But what, really, did they achieve?

The line that looks permanent on the map actually marked the division between territory that was *firmly* held by the Germans to the east and, to the west, territory that was *tenuously* controlled by the French. Much of the time this territory writhed under attack. Possession of this or that objective—a pile of rubble that had been a village, once charming or homely, a stand of ruined trees that had been a lush forest—would change hands, often more than once in any twenty-four-hour period. What the French had "won" was a landscape roiling with artillery and hand grenade detonations, torn by machine gun blasts, and punctuated by sniper fire. Looking toward the north and the British with a mixture of discouragement and superiority, the French called this scene south of Bray "victory."

CHAPTER 9

The British Follow Up

POLITICIANS, THE PUBLIC, THE PRESS, AND THE SOLDIERS THEMSELVES disputed Sir Douglas Haig's qualities as a commanding general in 1916 even as historians continue to do so today. While his military leadership is legitimately subject to question, it is difficult to deny that he was ever less than a good soldier. When Joseph Joffre announced that, because of the Verdun crisis, the French army would contribute to the Somme offensive a mere fraction of what he had promised, Haig expressed grave doubts about the BEF's ability to shoulder the main burden even of an offensive narrowed in scope. But when Joffre framed the situation in terms of duty owed to an ally, Haig responded like a good soldier, said *Oui, mon general,* and set about organizing his front.

Having reduced their level of participation and responsibility, the French acquitted themselves well fighting along a limited front south of Bray. In obedience to the will of the French chief, whom he acknowledged as his senior, Haig assigned to the BEF a mission with unrealistic objectives. Predictably—indeed, inevitably—his armies fared tragically over all of their designated front, except for the extreme southern portion of it, where German defensive preparation was weakest. Thus, in an effort to satisfy Joffre, Haig disappointed him by failing to accomplish more than two-thirds of the mission he had accepted. It had not been for lack of trying. The mounting death toll among the Tommies was ample proof of that.

PRO PATRIA MORI

The performance of the British soldier was never in question on the Somme. Everywhere in the initial attacks that stepped off at 7:30 in the morning of July 1, they marched in parade order against guns they were told the Royal Artillery had silenced. Everywhere, the citizen soldiers of Kitchener's Army demonstrated their willingness to die for king and country. Like the Light Brigade in the Crimean War or the Confederate troops of Pickett's Charge at the Battle of Gettysburg in the American Civil War, the British soldiers of July 1, 1916, marched into their own assigned Valley of Death or up the slope of their own designated Cemetery Hill. Overwhelmingly, those few who reached the German trenches did so in hopelessly reduced numbers and cut off from all possibility of reinforcement. Those who were not killed, wounded, or captured in no-man's-land were, by and large, killed, captured, or wounded at the German wire or in the German trenches.

America's iconic general of World War II, George S. Patton Jr., would have understood what went wrong in the British sector during that tragic morning in July. In his *War and Peace in the Space Age*, Lieutenant General James M. Gavin recalled "George Patton's last words to us before we left Africa [for the invasion of Sicily] . . . 'No dumb bastard ever won a war by going out and dying for his country. He won it by making some other dumb bastard die for his country.'"[1] The British troops of 1916, whose commanders had a blind faith in artillery coupled with almost no actual intelligence regarding the remarkable extent of German defensive preparations, went into combat ready to die. The Germans, who had prepared a defense in depth, which included a system of entrenchments built for survival rather than glory, went into combat ready to fulfill what was, for all practical purposes, the British death wish. Operating from cover, they tactically deployed their machine guns and artillery, the instruments by which so many would die.

On the British side, the morning's tragedy was executed with parade-ground precision. At precisely 7:30, officers' whistles shrilled, and men advanced everywhere. Ordered to walk calmly and maintain the integrity of their wave, wave after wave, the attacking troops were killed with a commensurate orderliness. The machine guns cut them down not with wild savagery, but with the discipline of a skilled reaper harvesting grain. Men of the second wave waiting to follow the first watched from the trenches as their comrades died, not in an ecstasy of chaos, but cut down in a line, weapons dropped from suddenly strengthless hands, arms reflexively raised to the smoke-choked heavens, knees buckling, one man down after another, sometimes left to right, sometimes right to left, rank upon rank.

When the German artillery opened up on the men of the second and third waves, it was with an uncanny accuracy. Soldiers thought of death by artillery burst as one of war's most random events. But when artillery was handled with skill, death became more a matter of cool-headed trigonometry and time. By observing the initial waves in the attack, seasoned artillerists patiently "registered" the guns under their command, elevated them to concentrate the rain of shells precisely where the attackers *would* be. It was not an instance of shells hitting their intended targets, but of those targets approaching, just as predicted, to meet the incoming rounds. The German artillerists did not so much inflict death on their enemies as they brought their enemies and death together, at a calculated time and place, in a choreography of devastation. And once the artillerists registered on one wave, it was a matter of quick calculation to adjust elevation to advance the line of falling shells in tempo with the enemy's advance. Time the barrage correctly, and the falling shells would always be there to greet the advancing soldiers.

Once the attacks of morning had been launched, the thrill of battle shattered. Mistaking precision for planning, the British commanders had laid out a timetable for July 1, 1916, with the confident specificity of train masters. It was assumed without question or doubt that a week of intensive artillery fire would kill most of the enemy. From this the assumption simply followed that the initial waves would succeed in taking their objectives. It was assumed that the successive waves would have nothing to do but mop up, penetrate the broken German lines, and occupy what had been the rear German positions. It was assumed that all the attacks in the initial phase of the Somme offensive, the phase in which the German front lines were to be broken, would unfold perfectly by mid-morning.

By nine o'clock, however, it was apparent up and down the British front that the clockwork timetable would not be met. The orderly advances of 7:30 were now ragged, entirely without coordination. What had begun as a grand advance, timed to the second, was now a piecemeal follow-up based on little solid intelligence. Because the men of the first waves had either become casualties, were struggling with inadequate numbers to hold on to first-line German trenches, or, enveloped by the enemy in those trenches, were cut off and fighting desperately to find a means of retreat, information was coming back neither to British commanders in the field nor to high command far to the rear. By the time reasonably accurate news did reach the decision makers, it was already irrelevant to present circumstances.

The absence of timely information had a paradoxical effect on the course of the battle through the rest of the morning and into the afternoon. Postponement or cancellation of follow-up attacks was unthinkable for the good soldier Haig, especially in view of the progress the French had made in their much smaller sector. This do-or-die/do-and-die mindset, coupled with the absence of real-time data—namely, a realistic tally of setbacks and outright disasters created by the grim reality of the failed artillery barrage—meant that everyone fell back on the timetables drawn up before the attack had begun. Religious faith perpetually confronts a great cloud of unknowing. Similarly, without information flowing back from a vast front, commanders turned to the only thing in which they could believe. Enveloped in the cloud of unknowing that is the fog of war, they put their faith in the timetable as they would the stone tablets of the Commandments. Accordingly, they continued to send their thousands into the teeth of a resistance that—in their plan—could not possibly exist.

On the eve of battle, some envied those who had been chosen for the first waves. To men like Foreign Legionnaire Alan Seeger, being the first to clash with the enemy was what combat, as a life experience, was all about. Even for those whose attitude toward war was less romantic, there was a thrill in being the first. In most soldiers, however, the natural instinct for self-preservation favored the follow-up positions on the assumption that they would be meeting an enemy mauled and weakened and therefore less likely to possess the means of taking their lives. Quite sensibly, therefore, most soldiers did not envy the first waves at all.

Yet in this battle, the troops who led the opening of an assault enjoyed—however briefly—an enviable advantage over those who followed. Having seen and heard, albeit at a distance, a weeklong artillery barrage, having been assured by commanders at every level that few if any of the enemy could survive such a barrage, having been trained and rehearsed for the opening assault in what surely would be an operation to "mop up" what little the high-explosive shells had left, the first waves brimmed with confidence. Fear is natural, but so is hope—and hope fueled by the assurances of older, wiser men in officer's uniforms, veterans of the colonial wars England had always won, was especially strong.

The men in the waves that straggled into formation during the mid-morning to noontide hours no longer had hope, let alone confidence. Although their commanders received nearly no intelligence from the leading edge of the attack, the troops waiting in the trenches were hearing plenty. If you were hit in no-man's-land and could still walk or crawl, you did not wait for stretcher bearers who might arrive in hours or not at all. Bleeding, agonizing, passing in and out of consciousness, you clawed your way back to your trenches. Men like these had stories to tell, stories of machine gun fire and artillery fire from an enemy who, far from having been blasted into oblivion, was, it seemed, hardly touched by a week of shelling. There were tales told by wounded men who had remained where they had fallen in no-man's-land and watched their comrades as they were swallowed up in the German line. There were stories, many stories, of men who could not find a way through or around the German wire that the artillery barrage had failed to destroy, though its destruction had been promised and therefore assumed. Survivors spoke of seeing men cut down like wheat in a field, cut down in their serried ranks, upright one second, prostrate the next, a harvested crop. But even more terrifying were the word pictures painted of men bumbling into barbed wire, hung up upon it in grotesque postures, shredded by machine gun bursts, and left in their shreds of gore and rags like an army of scarecrows that had been stripped and torn by some cyclonic wind.

In the face of all this, what compulsion was it that continued to propel thousands of men through the mid-morning and mid-day of July 1? Some were compelled by a sense of duty. Others, until recently ordinary citizens, had become soldiers thoroughly conditioned to follow orders. Many advanced out of fear of letting down their comrades or yielding to a cowardice that would make a mockery of others' sacrifice. Others, doubtless, were resigned to their fate, to keeping their assigned "rendezvous with death." And for those who were not moved by any of these sentiments, there were at least two additional aids to at least the appearance and function of courage.

One was rum. Private G. Brownbridge, 13th Northumberland Fusiliers, was scared, but not as scared as the young second lieutenant standing next to him, "shaking like a jelly. . . . He was just a youngster, about my own age. . . . I shouted at him to get over the top but he just looked at me forlornly and couldn't seem able to speak. I whipped out my bottle of rum, I had been saving it for several days, and offered it to him but he must have been a teetotaler as he only took a sip. I told him to take a good drink, which he did. You never saw a man find his courage so quickly." Brownbridge concluded: "If we hadn't our rum, we would have lost the war."[2]

The other means of counterfeiting heroism was the "battle police" or Military Police, known as Red Caps—though, in the trenches, the characteristic soft "flat-hat" caps with red tops above visor and band were replaced by the standard washbasin helmet and a red MP armband. The French army was already notorious for its willingness to shoot its own men as instructional examples to encourage absolute obedience. Generally speaking, the relationship between officers and men throughout the French army was defined by mutual contempt. The British liked to think of their military as above all that, and it is certainly true that the junior officers of Kitchener's Army tended to have great empathy with enlisted men whose qualifications as soldiers were probably on a par with their own, if not at a higher level. Nevertheless, Red Cap contingents were part of every unit deployed to the front, and they had orders to stop anyone who left the attack trenches without permission. When officers' whistles blew to send men over the top, the Red Caps were tasked with walking through the trenches to ensure that no fit man lingered behind. The mode of enforcing their charge was left up to MP commanders, non-coms, and individual soldiers. Wounded almost immediately after beginning his advance, Pete Kirkham, of the 5th Manchester Pals, turned back to the trenches. There he encountered "two very young soldiers" who "had been too scared to follow their mates over the top." He did not stop to speak to them, but continued to make his way to the dressing station when he was stopped by a pair of battle police, revolvers at their hips. They asked him where he was going. By way of response, Kirkham showed them his wound, and they let him pass. "I had only gone a few yards when I heard two pistol shots from close by. I feel *sure* that these two unfortunate boys had been 'executed for cowardice.'"[3]

Nobody had any way of knowing at the time, but the Battle of the Somme would not be decided in a morning, a day, a week, or even a month. By the time Subaltern Max Plowman was writing about his experience at the Somme, it was August, and frontline summary executions were sufficiently common for him to note that he had "just come from a meeting of officers before the C.O., at which he told us we are going back to make an attack. . . . He was needlessly emphatic about the word 'Retire' and its deletion from our vocabulary. We haven't come out here to retire. Even so, if an officer did use the word, I doubt if we should obey that strict injunction to shoot him. We shan't win this war shooting one another. And all those details about battle police being appointed and instructed to shoot loiterers: are they necessary? . . . Alas for the old romantic pictures of the colonel leading his men into the fray! His last words to them now are these scarce-veiled threats."[4]

DISORDER AND DETERMINATION

Subaltern Plowman complained that anyone overhearing his colonel delivering battle instructions "would think we were criminal conscripts. . . . If only the romantic British public knew! Yet, in the words of our battle-hymn, 'They'd never believe it.'"[5] Throughout the day of July 1, those who went over the top did so amid a swelling stream of wounded returning to friendly trenches. A few individual soldiers might have frozen when ordered over the top, but there is no record of any unit so much as hesitating to follow an attack order.

Typical of a unit assigned to follow up the initial assault with a "secondary infantry attack" was the 11th Sherwood Foresters, a Pals battalion. It was assigned to follow three other battalions already in the field, overtake them, and advance to Mouquet Farm (the Tommies called it "Mucky Farm"), some sixteen hundred yards east of the center of Thiepval. They were to take up positions in trenches hastily dug in advance of the main British first trench. The day before the battle, some of the Foresters had helped dig dugouts in the assembly trenches for the 9th Yorks and Lancs to use in an attack that was to proceed that of the Foresters. The dugouts were excavated to the customary British specification, which boiled down to "not too deep." British command avoided doing anything that might encourage men to remain under cover a second longer than deemed necessary. As the Foresters walked by these dugouts, which had no more than two feet of head cover, they saw that a German bombardment had killed or wounded many of the men who had labored beside them. "That place was full of dead men," Private F. W. A. Turner recalled, "torn-off limbs and badly wounded who begged for help, but we dared not stop." The communication trench connecting the advance trench with the dugouts "almost ran with blood that morning."[6]

Things were not much better for the 11th Sherwood Foresters once they assumed their positions in the advance trench, awaiting the signal whistle. Even before it sounded, a machine gun began "spraying the top of the trench, flicking up dirt from the parapet. When the whistle blew, the first man up my ladder was an American, Private Martin. As soon as he reached the top he was shot through the wrist. He came straight back. 'I've got mine,' he said. 'I'm off.'"[7] With luck, the wound would leave him his hand and the use of it. With even more luck, it would be judged a "Blighty wound," sufficiently severe to merit a trip back to England. However it might turn out, it at least saved Private Martin from death in this particular action in this particular battle.

The 11th Sherwood Foresters never did succeed in taking "Mucky Farm." The following month, it would become the site of a significant Somme battle spanning August 10 to September 26. I Anzac Corps—

Australians and New Zealanders—would begin that fight, but it would be the Canadian Corps that succeeded in capturing the position on September 16, after five weeks of fighting. By taking the farm, British commanders intended to hold the high ground just east of German-held Thiepval, thereby threatening from behind the town and the entire German salient that bulged west from it. The Germans did not want that to happen and, in a fierce counterattack, almost immediately recaptured the farm. Ten days later, on September 26, elements of the 6th East Yorkshire (Pioneers) Regiment retook it.

Even having failed in their assignment, the Foresters fared better than most of their comrades during the July 1 follow-up attacks. Most of these efforts were squashed almost as soon as they were launched. Men would go over the top. For many, a machine gun bullet to the head

Fred Leist, an official Australian war artist, painted *Mouquet Farm, Pozières* (watercolor over pencil on cardboard) in 1917. It depicts the wrecked buildings at this farm, which became a much fought-over objective in the Somme battle. AUSTRALIAN WAR MEMORIAL

or chest sent them toppling backward into the trench. A few rungs up the ladder, and their battle—often their life—had ended. For most of those who survived the effort simply to crest the parapet of their own trench, a machine gun round or an artillery shell more often than not ended the advance somewhere in no-man's-land. "I hadn't gone far," wrote Lieutenant A. Sainsbury of the 2nd Royal Dublin Fusiliers, "I couldn't now and couldn't then be sure whether I had actually got to our own wire, so disfigured was the landscape by the shelling, when I felt a thud in the upper leg."[8] Private E. Houston of the Fusiliers' Public Schools Battalion, asked those who had not been in battle to "Imagine stumbling over a ploughed field in a thunderstorm, the incessant roar of the guns and flashes as the shells exploded. Multiply all this and you have some idea of the Hell into which we were heading." The Public Schools Battalions were Pals battalions originally made up of former public school (what Americans would call *private* school) students. As the war continued and the ranks of these battalions thinned, non–public school troops were "drafted to" (assigned to) the battalions. Such was the case with Private Houston, and it gave him a particularly poignant perspective on his youthful comrades-at-arms. "They were a nice lot of lads and I hated to think of them going up against trained men of the German Imperial Army."[9]

Except in the southern sector, the British primary attacks had failed. The few troops who managed to reach the German trenches were cut off. The secondary attacks, later that morning, failed even more completely in that even fewer men made it as far as the German trenches. Most who were not killed or wounded while emerging from their own trenches or at their own wire or somewhere in the middle of no-man's-land were pinned down at the German wire. Here they sheltered as best they could in shell holes. To move forward was impossible, and the prospect of retreating back across exposed no-man's-land was, if anything, even worse. Show yourself, and you were a target.

In fact, the Tommies who had found cover in shell holes were not helpless. Their Lee-Enfield 0.303-inch rifles were perhaps the best shoulder weapons available in 1916. Designed by an American, James Lee, they were the most modern combat rifles on the front, having begun manufacture in 1907. Although the German Mauser was also an excellent weapon, it was older, its magazine was smaller—five cartridges versus ten for the Lee-Enfield—and the design of its bolt action could not match the rapid fire capability of the British weapon. From their positions in no-man's-land, the Tommies could snipe at any German who showed himself above a trench parapet. Spread out and disorganized as they were, however, the British troops of the secondary advance found it generally impossible to continue their attacks beyond the German wire. As Private H. C. Bloor of the Accrington Pals put it, "I just couldn't see how any of us would get out of it alive and, so far, I hadn't done anything to the Germans. I made up my mind to get one of them, at least, before I was killed." After settling himself into "a comfortable position," Bloor aimed and fired. "One of the Jerries threw up his arms and fell backwards and the others ducked down."[10]

Sniping from shell holes was a sign of supreme frustration among stranded troops. If anything, however, their officers felt even more desperately stymied. Casualty rates among officers of all ranks were high, but they were stunningly high among officers of field grade—majors and above. Appalled by the lack of progress and heavy casualties, unable to communicate with men isolated in shell holes, these officers often ventured out into no-man's-land, where German riflemen easily picked them off. One brigadier general, C. B. Prowse, impatient waiting in the rear while his brigade failed to inch forward, decided to sort things out himself. One report said that he was hit by machine gun fire while he was in the process of personally attacking a machine gun emplacement with the only weapon a general officer carries into battle—his walking stick. Although this made for an attractive story, Prowse was actually wounded by an exploding shell. He died at the dressing station.

The British troops lying out in no-man's-land, crouched down in the muddy water of a shell hole, a hole often shared with the dying and the dead, believed they would be wiped out at any moment. It was true that if a soldier suffered a lapse of attention and allowed his head to poke above the rim of the hole, some attentive German would almost certainly take a shot. But the Germans were so thoroughly indoctrinated in the maintenance of a strictly defensive posture that they almost never counterattacked in force.

Instead, they remained in their trenches, sniping toward no-man's-land and defending vigorously any attempt the British made to penetrate the wire and attack the trench. Defense in depth was deep indeed.

MORNING ENDS

By noon, the Battle of the Somme was four and a half hours old. The first two hours had seen some sixty thousand infantrymen attack sixteen miles of front. Many were killed or wounded as they struggled over the top. Many more were felled in no-man's-land. Others found shelter in shell holes. Some made it as far as the German wire. Fewer still, here and there, managed to occupy the first line of German trenches, where they were soon killed, wounded, or captured. Only on the far right front of Rawlinson's Fourth Army line did British arms achieve success, especially with the capture of Montauban.

In the secondary actions that unfolded before noon, another forty thousand men were committed to battle, making a total just shy of one hundred thousand fielded by noon—fully 129 battalions. According to plan, these secondary attackers were supposed to exploit all the gains of the early morning. Ideally, they would open gaps in the German lines sufficiently wide to allow the cavalry of Sir Hubert Gough to ride, penetrating far into the enemy-held territory of Northern France.

It did not happen.

Instead, Generals Haig and Rawlinson were faced with a sixteen-mile front, two-thirds of which had been attacked not merely without success, but with disastrous results. To the far north, where Edmund Allenby's Third Army had made a diversionary attack against Gommecourt and Beaumont-Hamel, there was some success, but at a staggering pyrrhic cost. The Schwaben Redoubt outside of Thiepval, south of Gommecourt, had been neutralized by the doughty Ulster Division, but the village of Thiepval itself remained in German hands and harbored men, artillery, and, worst of all, machine gun nests. Disaster had been averted in and around both Gommecourt and Thiepval, but the threat was far from ended. All the solid successes were confined to the southern third of the British front. The butcher's bill at noon was estimated to be fifty thousand killed or wounded. Most of these casualties came in the first hour of combat.

The soldiers had not failed. Their commanders, having created a plan founded exclusively on best-case assumptions, had failed the soldiers. At the top, Douglas Haig, fearful of failing the promises he and his government had made to Joseph Joffre, failed his own soldiers as well. He committed them to an attack in which he never really believed.

Those were the big failures behind the morning of July 1, 1916. Other failures flowed from them. An army consists of a tooth and a tail. The tooth makes direct contact with the enemy. The tail supports everything the tooth needs to stay alive and do its job. The failure of the tail that morning was serious, but was not the fault of the men whose job it was to support the fighters. The tail functioned well where the battle went according to plan. In other words, over approximately a third of the front, supplies got to where they were needed and were supposed to be. Where the battle broke down, however, which was across two-thirds of the front, logistics became difficult or impossible. Communications and supply were a shambles.

A similar failure afflicted the heavy machine gun teams, the field artillery, and the trench mortar squads, all of which were supposed to coordinate closely with the infantry. Again, where the attacks went well, these supporting players were able to position themselves for maximum effort. But where the battle dissolved into chaos, the artillery and machine guns could not move in close enough to coordinate with the infantry. The front was insufficiently stabilized to risk the big machine guns and the heavy field artillery.

If an observer of battle that long morning could harden his heart sufficiently to see the entire operation as a giant, diabolical machine, he would have concluded that it was being torn apart by the friction of clashing gears that had seized up for want of lubrication. Hastily dug trenches, too shallow to afford real protection, disintegrated under enemy artillery fire, turning the British front lines into a rugged landscape almost impossible to negotiate. Take a topography transformed by high explosives into a moonscape and combine it with a volume of wounded nobody had anticipated, and the war machine began destroying itself. Many of the wounded went for hours, even days, unattended and uncollected in no-man's-land. The return of those fortunate enough to find transportation from the front quickly clogged the trenches, making it nearly impossible for soldiers to move within them or even to position themselves for attack. To give General Rawlinson his due, he had actually devoted a great deal of thought to evacuating and caring for a high volume of wounded. Accordingly, he requested eighteen ambulance trains to handle evacuation of the wounded quickly. Yet, two hours into the battle, only one train showed up.

THE GERMAN PERSPECTIVE

It was not good to be a German soldier confronting the British right wing that morning. The German artillery positions facing the southern end of the British line were uncharacteristically weak, and more than a few German infantrymen gave up with little or no fight. The British attack came so quickly and with such ferocity that a wave of demoralization ran like a shudder through this end of the front.

Elsewhere, however, north of Montauban and environs, the German defense in depth operated with rigorous discipline. Within an hour or two after the initial attack, when a German soldier looked west, he saw not the approach of wave after wave of Tommies, but a shell-pocked no-man's-land sown thickly with the khaki of the dead and wounded. Karl Blenk, *Musketier* of the 169th Regiment, one of a machine gun crew, wrote of the "wailing and lamentation from No Man's Land and much shouting for stretcher bearers from the stricken English. They lay in piles but those who survived fired at us from behind their bodies."[11]

Blenk was amazed at how the first wave of attackers had approached at a walk. "Later on," however, "when the English tried again, they weren't walking this time, they were running as fast as they could but when they reached the piles of bodies they got no farther." Blenk watched as British officers "gesticulated wildly, trying to call the reserves forward, but very few came."[12]

The German had no way of knowing how many men his machine gun had cut down. But he did note that it was prescribed practice to change the weapon's barrel after five thousand rounds had been fired. "We changed it five times that morning."[13]

NOON ORDERS

If distance from the action means anything, British headquarters probably knew less about the actual course of battle than anybody else. The higher up the headquarters, the farther back it was and, accordingly, the less it knew. Nevertheless, by noon of July 1, the reports from the front reaching headquarters were getting more accurate—and more tragic. The remote commanders responded to the generally very bad news by ordering yet more units into battle. Some were fresh. Others were already badly battered and depleted. It made no difference to headquarters. But when his divisional CO telephoned Brigadier General H. Gordon to renew the attack in the afternoon, Gordon was heard to speak into the instrument, "You seem to forget, sir that there is now no 70th Brigade."[14]

CHAPTER 10

Flyover

AIRCREWS OF THE SIX SQUADRONS OF THE ROYAL FLYING CORPS (RFC) supporting General Henry Rawlinson's Fourth Army took to the skies at four o'clock on the morning of July 1. In the slice of time between first light and the start of the attack at 7:30, the crews did their best to report on the effect of the week's artillery bombardment. Either the observers did not have much of a view—the early morning was very misty—or much time, because they were unable to convey the extent to which the barrage had failed. Mostly, the observers reported the strange absence of large numbers of Germans in the front-line trenches. Commanders on the ground concluded from this that the bombardment had killed large numbers of Germans. This interpretation discounted the fact that the aerial observers had not only commented on the absence of upright Germans, but also horizontal ones. Where were the living soldiers? Where were the dead?

For whatever reason, the initial aerial reconnaissance yielded little insight. Once the attack began, some of the fliers turned their attention to reporting from altitudes of five hundred to one thousand feet on the progress of each unit. Others, flying obsolescent, spindly, 72-mile-per-hour, vintage 1912 BE 2c aircraft, cruised the entire breadth of the British front searching out the locations of the German artillery batteries that were pounding the advancing British infantry. Using crude "Morse buzzers," the aerial observers transmitted data in real time via "wireless" (radio) to the British artillery in a frantic effort to direct effective counterbattery fire. The Morse code messages were received by well-trained

The Nieuport 17 was introduced to the Western Front in January 1916 and proved itself one of the best fighter aircraft in World War I. Produced in France, it was used by all the Allied nations. WIKIMEDIA

RFC wireless operators seconded to the principal artillery batteries. It was an assignment few members of the flying corps relished, since they operated so dangerously close to the front lines. The airmen tapped out hundreds of requests for fire and then flew round and round at a dangerously low altitude the better to direct that fire. But so many British guns were involved that it soon became impossible to accurately direct the fire of any particular battery, let alone individual gun.

INVENTING AIRPOWER

The RFC deployed three flying "brigades" to the Somme in addition to a four-squadron wing. The operating strength on the Somme front was a total of twenty-seven squadrons flying 410 airplanes with an additional 216 under repair and servicing at aircraft depots. By the end of the Somme offensive in November 1916, the Somme deployment had lost 782 aircraft—a staggering 200 percent casualty rate. Still, the pilots and their planes managed to drop 292 tons of bombs, achieve air superiority in the skies over the front, and take more than nineteen thousand aerial reconnaissance photographs.[1]

Wallowing in mud and misery, trapped in catastrophic machine gun crossfire, relentlessly shelled, British as well as German infantrymen looked anxiously, longingly, and enviously to the sky whenever they heard the drone of engines overhead. There, above, was a battlefield of purity and clarity, they believed, a realm in which warriors faced each other man to man and machine to machine. There, above, was a natural element that still allowed movement and maneuver in battle. Yes, you might be killed. Yes, it promised to be a terrible death—by some combination of fire and a fall from a great altitude. Yet it seemed to many on the ground infinitely better than hugging the muddy earth, waiting for the next sweep of a machine gun and the next shell to fall—waiting, without the possibility of meaningful advance, without, really any reliable means of fighting for your own life. In the air, up there, your life depended on your skill and daring. You had a chance. You were not helpless. You were a man, not the cohabitant of trench rats. You were a knight, not cannon fodder.

Airpower seemed the future of war to infantrymen stuck so perilously and painfully in the present. At the level of high command, however, the future of the air arm was doubtful, and Major General Hugh Montague Trenchard was determined to create that future before it could be taken away. The general surely remembered a time when everyone said *he* had no future. Born at Windsor Lodge on Haines Hill in Taunton, England, in 1873, he was the son of an infantry captain who was married to the daughter of a captain in the Royal Navy. Although neither parent was particularly distinguished, Hugh Trenchard was proud of having descended from Sir Raoul de Trenchant, who had fought by the side of William the Conqueror at Hastings in 1066. His deep heritage was not, however, sufficient to carry him through the preparatory school to which he'd been sent. In everything but math, he did poorly and lagged woefully behind his classmates. Fortunately, the British military would take just about anyone, provided the prospect's aspirations were not too lofty.

Hugh's mother, however, had lofty aspirations. She wanted her son to hold a command in the Royal Navy. Accordingly, he was sent to a "cramming school" specifically set up to prepare candidates for admission to HMS *Britannia* (ex-*Prince of Wales*), a retired warship that served as residential barracks for Royal Navy cadets. When Hugh failed his entrance exam, he was sent slinking off to another "crammer," this one designed to prepare candidates for commissions in the army.

Hugh Trenchard started cramming for his army exams at the age of thirteen. By sixteen, he had failed twice to gain entrance into the military academy at Woolwich—and could not even return home because his father had become bankrupt and lost the family house, so that the boy had to rely on relatives for room and board. Desperate for an alternative, he took examinations for a commission in the Militia, which had the lowest requirements of any of the services. He failed in 1891 and again, 1892. While serving as a "probationary subaltern" in a militia artillery unit, he eked out a barely passing grade in 1893, was duly commissioned a second lieutenant in the 2nd Battalion, Royal Scots Fusiliers, and packed off to serve in India.

With his career prospects having escalated from bleak to grim, he served in India until the Second Boer War erupted, upon which he eagerly volunteered for service in South Africa. Shortly after he arrived, he was severely wounded in the chest. He underwent surgery for the removal of a lung. Left partially paralyzed and with a severe limp, he was invalided back to England, where a physician advised recuperating in the clean, dry, cold air of Switzerland. Soon bored by his Alpine surroundings, Trenchard took up bobsledding and promptly had a high-speed crash—from which he emerged bloodied, but also cured of his partial paralysis. Now able to walk unaided, he returned to South Africa and active service, seeing the Boer War through to its conclusion and then serving in Nigeria.

Trenchard discovered flying in 1912, became a certified pilot, and was soon appointed second-in-command of the army's Central Flying School. He worked his way rapidly up the ranks of the diminutive Royal Flying Corps, becoming commander of the RFC in France in 1915. After the war, Trenchard would go on to create the Royal Air Force (RAF), but, in July 1916, he focused on the Somme as the campaign in which he would prove the worth of aircraft in war. In the Somme campaign, he presided over the creation of two things entirely new in the military art. The first was the creation of a *planned* air campaign. The second was integrating that campaign closely with the ground attack, to give ground forces what became known as close air support.

The first task at the Somme was achieving air superiority in the skies over the sector *before* the British Fourth Army attack began. Flying more planes than the Germans had available, Trenchard soon owned the skies above the British front. He was now ready to carry out six distinct missions. The three most important were observational: aerial reconnaissance, aerial photography, and observation and direction of artillery. The next three were combat roles: tactical bombing in support of the ground offensive, contact patrols to harass the enemy on the ground and thereby support the infantry, and, finally, aerial combat to ensure the ongoing suppression of the German air service in the sector. It was a program that, in itself, was nearly as ambitious as Haig and Rawlinson's plan for the ground forces. The difference? Trenchard would succeed—albeit at a heavy cost that can fairly be described as pyrrhic.

AERIAL VICTORY

On July 1, however, the air campaign began with what was an unquestionable triumph—one that British as well as German ground troops anxiously observed. Early in the morning, before the infantry attacks stepped off, two DH.2 fighters from Number 32 Squadron intercepted *ten* German bombers crossing the lines at Festubert, a farming village twenty-one miles southwest of German-held Lille. In the lead DH.2 was the squadron commander, Major Lionel Rees. His wingman in the other DH.2 was Lieutenant John Simpson, a Canadian. Unfortunately, Rees and Simpson became separated as they approached the German bombers; nevertheless, Simpson—though outnumbered ten to one—attacked the German formation. Almost instantly, he was hit eight times in the head by machine gun fire from one of the German aircraft. Although he was dead, his aircraft circled down to the ground almost gently.

Separated from Simpson, Rees had not seen the attack, but he did see the German formation invading British airspace. Like Simpson, Rees bucked the ten-to-one odds and attacked. With nerves of steel, he held his fire until he had closed to within one hundred yards. Then he opened

The Airco DH.2 was a mainstay fighter of the Royal Flying Corps, even though it was becoming obsolete by the time of the Battle of the Somme. The DH.2 was a "pusher," its propeller mounted in the rear instead of at the front in aircraft with more conventional "tractor" propellers. The rear-mounted prop allowed the pilot to fire his forward-facing machine gun without worrying about hitting the propeller. WIKIMEDIA

up, damaging two German aircraft. This was sufficient to send the other eight German craft scurrying back into German-controlled airspace. (It was later revealed that one of Rees's bullets had ended the life of the formation's commander and, finding themselves leaderless, the Germans aborted their mission.)

Rees did not simply let them go. He pursued—so vehemently that one panic-stricken German pilot dropped his bombs—on *German* infantry positions. Rees pressed his pursuit across the German lines. As Rees closed in on the slow bombers, gunners in the German aircraft fired back at him, and Rees took a round in the leg. Undaunted, he continued his attack:

> *I closed, just as I was about to open fire, a shot struck me in the leg putting the leg temporarily out of action. I fired another drum,*

but not having complete control of the rudder, I swept the machine
backwards and forwards. I finished firing about 10 yards away, and
saw the observer sitting back firing straight up in the air. . . . I then
recovered the use of my leg and saw the leader going towards the lines.
I got within long range of him. He was firing an immense amount
of ammunition. Just before he reached the lines I gave him one more
drum. Having finished my ammunitions I came home.[2]

Mass-produced weapons of incredible destructive power had made
the Great War an anonymous affair, an enterprise with few individual
heroes in that the public had few names to conjure with. On the morning
of July 1, 1916, within view of thousands of soldiers, Lionel Rees, operating one of the most advanced products of the industrial age that had
armed World War I, single-handedly turned back ten German bombers
from the British lines, stopping them from dropping their ordnance on
the Tommies.[3]

Lionel Rees earned the Victoria Cross for his action an hour and a
half before the infantry attack began at the Somme. That he was the only
RFC pilot to receive this most coveted of British decorations during the
entire campaign does not betoken any failure of airpower. It was just that
medals were not issued for missions that, although very costly, became
routine as airpower became fully integrated into the battle.

GRIM WITNESS

The dearth of VCs among airmen during the Somme campaign also
reflects the top priority given to reconnaissance and observation—haz-
ardous duties for which decorations are rarely awarded. The RFC airmen
were in the best position to observe and evaluate the battle. As they
reported on the progress of the ground attack, they must have understood
before anyone else—before the soldiers on the ground and well before
the commanders in the rear—that the attack was failing. They could
report with satisfaction that troops were going over the top all across the
front at 7:30 a.m. and that they were advancing into no-man's-land in
remarkably good order. But the pilots also had a bird's-eye view of the
German trenches, whose eerie emptiness they had reported on just before

The French Salmson 2 was widely used for battlefield reconnaissance, including furnishing real-time artillery reports to aid the Royal Artillerymen in registering their guns. WIKIMEDIA

the infantry attack was launched. Now, with the attack under way, they saw the enemy infantry emerging from dugouts, the trenches suddenly filling with troops, and machine gun nests just as suddenly blazing to life with the murderous fire that cut down rank upon advancing British rank. From the air, the men must have looked like so many marionettes whose strings were slashed, one after the other.

The pilots must also have been among the first British officers to feel the heartbreak of frustration in this offensive. *They* could see where and why the attacks were failing—how those few elements of the attacking forces that managed to reach the German first-line trenches had been greatly reduced by casualties and were almost immediately cut off by enveloping attacks as they seized the frontline trenches. *They* called in the need for reinforcements, urgently, and with pinpoint accuracy. As the pilots loitered over the trouble spots, *they* could also clearly see that the reinforcements were not forthcoming. What is more, they could also see the reason why. Whereas portions of the first and second waves of the attack, though raked by machine gun fire, reached their objectives, albeit in diminished numbers, the third and fourth waves were simply decimated by German artillery fire. In addition, German heavy artillery quickly knocked out British field-telephone communication, seriously disrupting command and control.

Despite their horror at what they were seeing, the observers calmly continued to carry out their assignments. Detecting enemy units forming up for counterattacks up and down the entire Fourth Army front, the contact patrols used their Morse wireless equipment to report the German movements and counterattacks in real time. To ensure that the messages came through, some pilots wrote notes on kneeboards, swooped low over field headquarters, and dropped their dispatches. Without question, the air units were providing the most accurate and timely information available from any source on the progress of the attack. The breakdown came not in the reporting, but in the evaluation and interpretation of the reports on the ground. Because the aerial observation often contradicted reports from ground commanders, headquarters became confused, not knowing which sources to trust.[4] Common sense should have suggested that the pilots and air observers, both on account of their aerial perspective and their observational objectivity, would be in a position to supply the most accurate information. Reports from the ground, in contrast, were subject to the fog of war, and it was known that field unit commanders were always either too optimistic or too pessimistic in what they reported. But the use of aircraft was sufficiently novel and unfamiliar to senior commanders that they could not bring themselves to rely more heavily on this most valuable information. Consistently, by the time Rawlinson's HQ had collated the reports from all sources, the commanders were doomed to act on what had become "expired" information.

This was true both of the main Fourth Army attack as well as the diversionary attack, to the left of Rawlinson's Fourth Army, by the Third Army, under Edmund Allenby. Pilots of RFC Squadron 15 and Squadron 4 watched as the Third Army's VIII Corps and X Corps, respectively, attacked along a front stretching from Thiepval north to Serre. Here, the difference in observational intelligence supplied by forward ground observers and aerial observers was dramatic. Whereas the ground observers could supply nothing better than generalized progress reports with a necessarily narrow perspective, the flying observers were capable of identifying the most significant British penetration on this front, the 36th (Ulster) Division's remarkable assault on the Schwaben Redoubt. Number 4 Squadron reported several German artillery batteries scrambling in response to defend against what they clearly feared would be a full-scale British breakthrough.

Squadron 4 observers noted that the enemy was not massing troops around the Schwaben Redoubt, but the need for reinforcements to hold the Ulstermen's gains was urgent.[5] Headquarters responded by directing Captain C. A. A. Hiatt of Squadron 4 to fly over the fighting that had erupted at Thiepval, the German-held and German-fortified village located on the northern periphery of the Schwaben Redoubt. When, based on the airmen's reports, it became clear that vigorous German counterattacks made reinforcement impossible, X Corps headquarters ordered the timely withdrawal of attacks on Thiepval and (to the north) Beaumont-Hamel as well.[6] This was an instance doubly rare in the entire Somme campaign—a lifesaving tactical withdrawal, and one that was ordered on the basis of aerial observation.

The level of detail the airmen were able to record was often astounding. Flying above Pozières, located on the vital Bapaume road a little more than a mile southeast of Thiepval, Lieutenant T. W. Stallibrass, Squadron 3, recorded in his logbook the action of a "Hun 4.5-battery behind a hedge." It was still firing, despite an intense British ground attack. "This battery was a good one and the commander a sportsman, as he was being heavily strafed by several of our heavies and lighter guns and shells were falling on and round his battery, but he refused to stop firing. Eventually only one gun was left which he kept in action and was still firing when we returned to our 'drome' [aerodrome, or airbase]."[7]

Good News

Although the reality most fliers were compelled to report was grim, they were also uniquely positioned to transmit intelligence on precious British breakthroughs. During the July 1 advances, a Squadron 9 aircrew flying over XIII Corps on the British right—the flank on which the only truly significant British progress took place—reported the breakthrough of 30th Division against an enemy front line that offered remarkably light opposition. It was also this squadron that conveyed the news of 18th (Eastern) Division's occupation of Pommiers Trench and its capture of Pommiers Redoubt, which defended the fortified German-occupied village of Montauban. When the two-man crew of a Squadron 9 BE 2c aircraft, Captain J. T. P. Whittaker and Second Lieutenant T. E. G. Scaife, saw the reflection of the tin markers affixed to the packs of British troops advancing on Montauban, they scanned the ground for any German positions that might particularly menace them. Seeing an enemy battery just beginning to come into action at Bernafay Wood, Whittaker swooped down to seven hundred feet, fired his machine guns, and sent the men of the battery scurrying. This accomplished, Whittaker and Scaife continued their contact patrol with a strafing attack on German trenches east of Bernafay.

Whittaker and Scaife's action was a case study in how close ground support was supposed to work. It saved British lives and also furnished progress information to General Haig, which he found so significant that he decided to begin concentrating the rest of the day's efforts between La Boisselle and the British point of contact with the French left at Bray. As late afternoon turned into early dusk on July 1, Haig telephoned Rawlinson to tell him that the bulk of Fourth Army would no longer take responsibility for the sector from La Boisselle north to Serre. Rawlinson was ordered to detach his two northernmost corps and put them under the command of General Hubert Gough, who would now cover the northern portion of the front. The rest of Fourth Army would focus on the British right—the southern portion of the front, which was showing real progress.[8]

DAY'S END AND AFTER

Nightfall grounded the RFC. During the first day of battle, each individual aircrew had flown between six to twelve hours, proving the endurance of both men and machines.[9] The onset of darkness marked the end of the darkest day in the history of the British army. July 1, according to preliminary reports, had cost the BEF close to sixty thousand casualties, killed, wounded, and missing.[10] Days later, the official butcher's bill was reported as 57,470 casualties (including 19,240 killed or died of wounds).[11] The attack had been made along an sixteen-mile front, but had achieved an advance of no more than a mile on only three miles of that front.

In this bloodbath of July 1, one pilot (Lieutenant Simpson) had been killed, four aircrew wounded, and nine reported missing out of a total of 110 airmen collectively flying some 108 hours above an intensely active battlefield.[12] General Trenchard enclosed a note with the casualty figures he sent on July 2 to Major William Sefton Brancker, the War Office's assistant director general of military aeronautics: "Considering [casualties are] practically a bare 2% of the whole lot engaged and its [sic] not as if they only went over the lines once as most of them did two or three trips, I think it is a very small percentage for pilots. The [losses of] machines are a little bit heavier."[13]

In the course of a campaign that stretched to November 17, 1916, air losses would become far, far heavier as the RFC contended with an increasing German air presence and engaged in more combat missions, including extended bombing runs in which slow, obsolescent BE 2c aircraft flew without escort deep into German-held territory. Ground-based anti-aircraft artillery and machine guns—even rifle fire—took a heavy toll on these lumbering machines. A resolutely determined Trenchard responded by adding fast, modern fighter escorts to the missions. He reported to Brancker at the end of the first week of the Somme battle:

> *I have lost a good many machines lately and a certain number of pilots, but really they had done splendidly. We have done 1,200 hours' flying a day which makes you think a bit, and a lot of pilots have done five to six hours' flying a day, and this is going on day after day. I have lost, as you know, eight machines at low bombing, I am afraid that some of the pilots are getting a bit rattled, and it's not popular. I have put in for two V.C.s. Contact patrols working with the infantry have been a great success this time, and the artillery work has been extraordinary. The fighting is going well, and the pilots are doing splendidly. We have crashed a good number of Fokkers and brought down a good many more than they admit. . . It's a bit of a strain with so many hostile machines and anti-aircraft guns about. . . The depots*

are getting overworked mending machines that are shot to pieces and crash, issuing stores and repairing transport.[14]

Throughout the rest of the campaign, Trenchard continued to push his aircraft and crews. On July 1, 410 RFC aircraft were reported as "serviceable." By November 17, 782 had been destroyed in combat or in accidents. On this same date, 550 aircraft were reported as "serviceable." This meant that during the Somme campaign, Trenchard had brought in 922 aircraft, either new or rebuilt. On average, ten aircraft were replaced each month.

Overall, the casualty rate among machines was nearly 200 percent. Among pilots the final casualty rate, as of November 17, averaged just about 100 percent. On July 1, 426 pilots were available. As of November 17, that number was 585, reflecting a continual influx of additional and replacement airmen. During five and a half months of battle, 308 pilots had been killed, wounded, or went missing in combat and another 268 were listed as "non-battle casualties." Among observer crew, 191 were killed, wounded, or missing.[15]

Hugh Trenchard, whose early military career mostly consisted of a narrow escape from death, was unyielding in his adherence to an offensive doctrine and strategy throughout the Battle of the Somme. His aircrews paid a terrible price for his relentless determination. In contrast to the ground forces at the Somme, who also suffered catastrophic losses and gained nothing, Trenchard did achieve a strategic victory, albeit one of pyrrhic dimensions. By the end of the Somme offensive, the British had gained little or no ground, and the war would grind on for another two years. Trenchard's RFC, however, ended the campaign having gained control of the skies above the Somme. Difficult as it may be to imagine, this must have saved many British lives.

Yet even this costly victory had unintended consequences. In April 1917, General Trenchard would take his Royal Flying Corps into combat in the Battle of Arras (April 9–May 16, 1917), applying the same relentlessly offensive doctrine that had given him air superiority at the Somme.

But 1917 was not 1916. In the space of a year, the German air force—the *Deutsche Luftstreitkräfte*—had developed very significantly, both technologically, with new and advanced aircraft, and in the quality of its pilots. Ground defenses had also improved, with better anti-aircraft artillery and more effective techniques. Most consequential of all was the arrival of Manfred von Richthofen, the celebrated "Red Baron," Germany's "ace of aces," who led an elite squadron of fliers dubbed the Flying Circus. So prolific a menace was Richthofen and his command that April 1917 over Arras earned the epithet "Bloody April." On average, an RFC pilot lasted just eighteen hours flying over Arras before he was shot down.[16] In just four days, between April 4 and April 8, the RFC lost seventy-five aircraft and 105 aircrew.[17] Critically short of pilots, Trenchard had to bring in callow replacements fresh out of flight school. Their inexperience only multiplied RFC losses. In this way, British airpower went from a costly triumph at the Somme to a humiliating and tragic defeat at Arras. It would recover, but only as German air resources, both human and technological, dwindled.

CHAPTER 11

Remains of the Day

At 7:30 on that July 1 morning, the British attacks began, and men began, very rapidly, to die in great number. The killing commenced and continued without interruption until an eerie interlude settled across the opposing trenches and no-man's-land shortly after noon. It was as if both sides had agreed, wordlessly, to take a breath, to feel the mounting heat of what, somewhere on this planet, must surely have been a lazy summer afternoon.

But as nature abhors a vacuum, so battle, once begun and in search of resolution, cannot abide a lull in the slaughter. Lieutenant General Henry Sinclair Horne, commanding XV Corps in General Henry Rawlinson's Fourth Army, decided to salvage in the afternoon some of what had failed so terribly in the morning. Horne was an artillery officer, a graduate of the Royal Military Academy at Woolwich and, after service in the Second ("Great") Boer War and other appointments, was named Inspector of Artillery in 1912. On the face of it, Horne was perfectly suited to the Great War, which was, above all and despite the resistance of both French and British commanders, an artillery war. Horne's most significant tactical contribution to the Battle of the Somme was his perfection of the "creeping barrage," in which the attacker's artillery laid down its barrage in carefully timed "lifts" that moved just ahead of the advancing artillery. More than any other tactic, this adapted heavy artillery—in World War I an essentially defensive weapon technology—to the needs of the attacker.

Fricourt, a village of perhaps four hundred people, was less than a mile from Mametz. It had been exempted from direct attacks that morning on the assumption that capturing objectives close to it, including Mametz, would cause it to fall as well. This had not happened, and although there was nothing intrinsically special about Fricourt, it was held by Germans. For that reason, General Horne decided that it should be taken before July 1 ended.

LIEUTENANT HOWE'S WAR

Two divisions of XV Corps were deployed along the front line, the 21st on the right and the 7th on the left. Held in reserve was another XV Corps division, the 17th (Northern). It was from this unit that Horne detached a single brigade, the 50th, and assigned it to the 21st Division just for the day. Pursuant to the order, the 50th was marched to the first-line trenches directly opposite Fricourt.

For most of the men of this brigade, this would be their baptism of fire. Only one battalion, the 10th West Yorks, had seen action in the morning, but they had suffered heavy casualties, so just a handful of men and a single officer, a Lieutenant Philip Howe, were alive and sufficiently whole to enter the line that afternoon.

By 2:00 p.m., no one had yet told those assembled in the frontline trench what their objective was and when they were going to attack it. Lieutenant Howe was therefore surprised when companies C and D of the 7th East Yorks suddenly lumbered into the trench he and the few survivors of the 10th West Yorks occupied. He was downright shocked when the commanding officer of the battalion, a lieutenant colonel, asked him if he would care to join in the attack on Fricourt.

When, sir? Howe asked.

In a half hour, the C.O. answered.

It is doubtful that Howe was delighted by this invitation. It had not been presented as an order, but he understood that practically every man assembled or assembling in the trench was not only New Army but *new* to the New Army. As someone who had actually experienced combat, Howe was deemed a seasoned veteran, even though the only combat he had seen was a miserably failed attack earlier in the morning. He could not shirk his duty. The neophytes needed all the stiffening they could get. He accepted the invitation.

It was not just having been given no more than a half-hour's notice that dismayed Lieutenant Howe. It was that none of that half hour had been filled by a preparatory artillery barrage. General Horne, although he was one of the BEF's most prestigious artillery specialists, had not ordered a preparatory barrage. What he had ordered was an immediate frontal attack on German-occupied Fricourt, at the height of daylight, using a Kitchener's Army infantry brigade that had yet to see combat.

Howe had already participated in one bloody failure this morning. He must have been convinced that he was about to be part of another, launched with even fewer resources, no preparation, and in the middle of the day following a two- or three-hour lull in combat along the front. The lieutenant was veteran enough to appreciate the hopelessness of what he was about to do.

But he did it nevertheless. He followed the East Yorks commanding officer to the foot of the parapet ladder. When whistles blew along the line at 2:33 sharp, that lieutenant colonel was the first man up the ladder and over the top. Howe was right behind him. Looking to his right and to his left, he saw the rest of the East Yorks scramble over the top. He was in the middle of this first wave.

Of course, the Germans defending Fricourt were more than ready. They had seen everything. How could they not have? And they put their carefully positioned machine guns into action as soon as the first men appeared over the parapet. The fire met the attackers no more than sixty feet from the British trenches. For three minutes, the gunners directed a spray of bullets across the advancing British line much as a method-ical gardener might play a hose along a neat, gently curving flowerbed. Lieutenant Howe felt the searing lash of a round graze his cheek before slicing through the sling of his rifle and wounding his hand. At 2:36 p.m., officers and non-coms shouted the command to withdraw back to the trench. The initial sally was hopeless. In the space of 180 seconds, 123 men had been wounded or killed.

Even as those who could still move under their own steam tumbled back into the trench, more East Yorks were arriving to fill it. Lieutenant

Howe gathered his survivors, and the tiny contingent of "veterans," having added three minutes to their combat records, began the march back from the front trench to brigade headquarters.

Marching to the rear, Howe and his much-reduced unit encountered another commanding officer, this one the lieutenant colonel of the 7th Green Howards, which, like his own 10th West Yorks, had had a catastrophic morning. This was caused when one of the battalion's companies attacked in error, without orders and without support. Reasoning that the mistake had been made because the company commander had misread preparatory orders as action orders, the battalion CO decided to withhold the particulars of a planned afternoon attack until just before the attack was to step off. Like the East and West Yorks, the Howards went over the top at 2:30. The only grumbling heard concerned the failure to be offered a pre-battle rum issue—for lack of adequate notice.

There was at the time considerable debate in the British army over the wisdom of issuing rum just before action. Some insisted that the ersatz courage generated by alcohol was indispensable to an attack. Others argued that the men drank too much and, as a result, made mistakes as well as lost their fighting edge. What the 7th Green Howards' experience at 2:30 on July 1 proved was that going up against well-defended enemy trenches protected by interlocking fields of machine gun fire was lethal, especially on a sunny afternoon, whether you were drunk or sober. As Private W. W. Askew, of the 7th Green Howards, reported, "We mounted the parapet; some of us got out, some of us didn't but we were under a murderous attack of machine-gun fire. We were falling like ninepins."[1]

And now, incredibly, the lieutenant colonel of the Howards was asking Philip Howe if he and his men cared to join in another attack this afternoon.

The pull of duty no longer seemed quite so strong. Howe excused himself on account of his gashed face and wounded hand, and he pointed out that the few men he still had under his command were spent. He learned later in the day that, between them, the East Yorks and the 7th Green Howards managed to lose four hundred men, killed and wounded, without having gained so much as an inch of ground.

DIVERSIONARY

The actions in which Philip Howe partook were toward the right, or southern, end of the British Somme front. Real gains had been made here in the morning, and, under Haig's orders, the principal thrust of the British attack was therefore shifted from the northern parts of the front to here. Yet, at the extreme northern end of the British sector, the front facing Gommecourt, the diversionary attacks by units of Edmund Allenby's Third Army were still under way—with some success but at great cost.

The VII Corps, under Lieutenant General Sir Thomas D'Oyly Snow KCB numbered among its components the 46th (North Midland) Division, which Snow ordered to attack the salient around Gommecourt at 12:15 sharp. The objective was to make contact with and tie into the 56th (London) Division, which was under heavy counterattack by Germans on the southern end of the salient. If they could link up, the two divisions might be able to penetrate the salient, forcing the Germans to fall back on Gommecourt.

On paper, the operation made some sense. In three-dimensional reality, however, it was thoroughly hopeless. To begin with, Gommecourt was heavily defended by a numerically superior body of very good German troops, whereas both the London Division and the North Midlanders were not even New Army. They were Territorials—essentially the reserve of a reserve, with many men overage. They had already been through disastrous engagements at Ypres and the Battle of Loos. At the latter in September 1915, thirty-seven hundred of the North Midlanders had fallen in the span of ten minutes while attempting to take the Hohenzollern Redoubt. Their commanding officer, Major General E. J. Montagu-Stuart-Wortley, who had served with distinction since 1877 in such far-flung theaters as Afghanistan, South Africa, Egypt, Turkey, Malta, and Sudan, now found himself leading Territorials in a mere diversion that nevertheless had all the dangers of a major battle for a key objective without any prospect of making any worthwhile gains. Indeed, in a morning attack against Foncquevillers all six battalions of the 46th (North Midland) Division had been repulsed at high cost and within half an hour of the battle's commencement. All but one battalion commander had been killed or wounded.

Montagu-Stuart-Wortley appreciated that the London Division had made significant headway against the Germans at the Gommecourt salient, but that a German rally had built up substantially superior numbers, cutting off the Londoners and pinning them down. By 12:15, the hour originally appointed for the North Midlanders to attack, the Londoners were beset at the salient on three sides, thanks to failure of another part of the morning's diversionary action, an attack on Serre. He could hardly have been eager to join the fray, but he surely felt a sense of obligation to rescue the Londoners. Yet he could meet neither Snow's demands nor his schedule. Snow demanded a full effort, even as Montagu-Stuart-Wortley's brigade commanders pointed to the depleted condition in which the morning attacks had left them. Anything approaching a full effort, they said, was impossible. Unwilling to simply disobey Snow, Montagu-Stuart-Wortley determined to make a creditable token attack with two companies, one from the Sherwood Forest brigade and the other from the Staffordshire Brigade. Snow also demanded that the attack step off at 12:15—but the trenches were a quagmire of mud and were now jammed with casualties from the failures of morning. It proved nearly impossible to get even two companies in position to go over the top. After postponing the attack to 1:30, Montagu-Stuart-Wortley was forced to put it off until 3:30—the Londoners getting pounded all the while.

At last, at 3:30, Montagu-Stuart-Wortley ordered his token attackers over the top: two companies. A fully manned British army company at the time consisted of 250 men. On this occasion, with the heavy casualties already suffered, the two companies together mustered perhaps two hundred men, total. The commanding officer of the Sherwood Forester brigade had been waiting and watching. He had been promised a preparatory artillery barrage and, in the bright daylight, a smokescreen as well. A few artillery pieces fired desultory volleys, but nothing that amounted to a substantial barrage. Even worse, most of the mortars capable of firing the smoke bombs to generate the smokescreen had been knocked out of action. For all practical purposes, there was no smokescreen as H-hour approached. Accordingly, the brigade commander told the company commander to call off the attack. In the absence of both a decent barrage and a smokescreen, it was suicide—especially in such small numbers. It was not worth dying for a token.

Runners were immediately dispatched to each of the company's four platoons, but only three were able to deliver their messages before it was too late. On the front covered by one of the platoons, the whistles shrilled. All twenty men of this understrength platoon clambered over the top. Captain V. O. Robinson reported that "every man except one, the platoon sergeant, was hit."[2] Other reports listed just two men who escaped death or wounding.

Among the company from the Staffordshire Brigade, almost everyone had been killed or wounded by artillery bombardment while they were huddled in an overcrowded trench waiting for the attack. When a runner announced at about three o'clock that the attack would commence at 3:30, the few survivors wandered their trench in search of other able-bodied men. All the officers had been killed, and Private G. S. Young recalled that "we made jokes as to who would blow the whistle for the attack, if we could find one on a dead officer. Fortunately the attack was cancelled."[3]

It was fortunate for those left alive in two already depleted companies, but it was most unfortunate for the beleaguered 56th (London) Division. After enduring thirteen hours of nonstop fighting as they occupied the German front trenches outside of Gommecourt, the isolated division finally withdrew, without having ever made contact with the 46th Division. As for Gommecourt, it remained a German possession.

Snow's plan was clearly hopeless from the beginning. But the fact that the 46th (North Midland) Division had failed to aid a successful division in dire need, that it had not attacked as ordered, and that it subsequently emerged from the combat of July 1 with the lowest casualties of the thirteen British divisions engaged that day brought down the wrath of VII Corps commander Thomas D'Oyly Snow. He entered his condemnation into the official record, complaining that "the 46th Division . . . showed a lack of offensive spirit," which he could "only attribute . . . to the fact that its commander, Major-General the Hon. E. J. Montagu-Stuart-Wortley, is not of an age, neither has he the constitution, to allow him to be as much among his men in the front lines as is necessary to

Before the Battle of the Somme, this was a grand château in Gommecourt. The rest of the village emerged from the battle in similar condition. NATIONAL LIBRARY OF SCOTLAND

imbue all ranks with confidence and spirit."[4] Snow convened an official Court of Inquiry on July 4, 1916, but General Sir Douglas Haig personally intervened before the court delivered its findings. He sent Montagu-Stuart-Wortley back to England in disgrace. Although there was no court-martial, his assignment to the 65th (2nd Lowland) Division in Ireland was a badge of dishonor. This was a backwater division that never saw action on the Continent. Montagu-Stuart-Wortley retired from the British army shortly after the end of the war, on July 31, 1919. Until the day of his death in 1934, at the age of seventy-six, he appealed through military and civilian channels for redress of the injustice he had suffered. His appeals went unheard.

Thiepval

By mid-afternoon, the German stronghold of Thiepval had been neutralized by the Ulster Division, but it was still very much in German hands (see chapter 9). The division's men were tired and, even worse, their ammunition was dwindling. Murderous machine gun fire had once again begun to emanate from the town. "The peaceful road which now runs . . . towards Thiepval was a place of carnage that day," reads a modern guide to the Somme battlefields. "The Official History says that it was 'subsequently known as Bloody Road, owing to the mass of dead heaped up on it at the end of the day.'"[5]

By three in the afternoon, the Ulstermen, who had made such progress against both the Schwaben Redoubt and Thiepval itself, were beginning to crack under increasingly well-coordinated German counterattacks. The Ulster units, whose success during the first half of the day stood in vivid contrast to the disasters elsewhere on the British front, were wearing out and becoming demoralized. When a particularly vigorous counterattack came out of Grandcourt, many troops from the 8th and 9th Royal Irish Rifles (also known as the East and West Belfasts, respectively) simply broke and ran. A Lieutenant Colonel F. O. Bowen, in command of a Pals battalion called the Belfast Young Citizens, led a contingent that turned those men back—"at revolver point." Bowen admitted that it had become "a desperate show, the air stiff with shrapnel, and terror-stricken men rushing blindly." Clearly a perceptive officer, Bowen noted, "These men did magnificently earlier in the day, but they had reached the limit of their endurance."[6]

Bowen's own Belfast Young Citizens had not yet reached *their* limit. About an hour after he and his men persuaded the East and West Belfasts to return to combat, Lieutenant Colonel Bowen received a message from the captain commanding the D Company of his own battalion: "hanging on but hard pressed," the message read. The captain who wrote it "was never heard of again."[7]

The 49th (West Riding) Reserve Division—Territorials all—was sent to aid the Ulstermen at nine in the morning. Despite the nature of their mission, they advanced with little sense of urgency until, reaching Thiepval Wood, they received a stern message instructing them to be at Thiepval village by four. It did not seem possible. Moving through the marshy Thiepval Wood was slow going, but once the 49th emerged from the shelter of those woods, things became far worse. The unit found itself raked by machine gun fire emanating from the village. "We went forward in single file, through a gap in what had once been a hedge," Private J. Wilson of the 1/6 West Yorks wrote. He noted that "only one man could get through [the gap] at a time. The Germans had a machine-gun trained on the gap and when it came to my turn I paused." By a stroke of luck, the machine gun fire paused, too. Wilson assumed the weapon had jammed or had run out of ammunition. Seizing the opportunity, he dashed through the gap, "but what I saw when I got to the other side shook me to pieces. There was a trench running parallel with the hedge which was full to the top with the men who had gone before me. They were either dead or dying."[8]

Just as the 46th (North Midland) Division could not reach the imperiled 56th (London) Division near Gommecourt, so the West Yorks of the 49th (West Riding) Division were ordered to cut short their attempt to relieve the Ulstermen—at least while it was still daylight.

As for the Londoners, they never would be rescued that day. After capturing the German frontline trenches, these Territorials continued to punch above their weight, but, receiving no reinforcement, they were hopelessly cut off. Seven battalions of the London Division had attacked Gommecourt on July 1. By the end of daylight, more than seventeen hundred men lay dead, twenty-three hundred wounded, and about two hundred taken prisoner. Of the wounded, most still languished in no-man's-land as night fell. Ten, twelve, fourteen hours they had lain in the dust under the July sun. Some battalions were virtually wiped out, the London Scottish, for instance, losing 616 of its 871 men, and the Queen's Westminster Rifles all twenty-eight of its officers.

THE LEIPZIG SALIENT: 97TH BRIGADE ATTACK

Before night fell on that first day, the British had some successes—at Mametz and Montauban (chapter 7) and in General Allenby's northern diversion, though at heartbreaking cost (chapter 6). The French, who had a front of only three miles, did even better, taking their major objectives within the first three hours of the battle (chapter 8).

All of these successes—"victories" is too strong a word to describe any of them—occurred on the right wing, the southern portion of the

A German photographer took this picture of the body of a British soldier some-where on the Somme front. He has suffered a head wound, but, never tended to by stretcher bearers of either side, he appears to have died from exposure and thirst. IMPERIAL WAR MUSEUM PHOTOGRAPHIC ARCHIVE

Somme front. Elsewhere, by the late afternoon, the small numbers of British soldiers who had somehow attained their objectives in the German trenches had either managed to return to their own lines or had met their end, some in the enemy trenches they occupied, others in their bid to retreat across no-man's-land.

But in two locations, the Quadrilateral Redoubt, a few hundred yards east of Ginchy and about two miles northeast of Montauban, and the Leipzig Salient, near Authuille on the road to Thiepval, the Tommies were cut off from any avenue of retreat. They must have felt not merely abandoned but completely forgotten. Throughout most of the afternoon, the Quadrilateral was quiet, "very quiet," Private E. C. Stanley of the 1/8th Royal Warwicks recalled, "so I had a sleep and then I wandered around, talking to some of the men."[9]

A Royal Flying Corps observer took this photograph of a British gas bombardment by the 18th (Eastern) Division against German trenches in front of Montauban during the week before the British infantry attack stepped off at 7:30 on the morning of July 1. Visible at the top of the photograph is Bernafay Wood. The village of Montauban is near the top-left. The road running diagonally across the photo from Montauban to the bottom-right connects to the village of Carnoy, which was located behind the British front line. IMPERIAL WAR MUSEUM PHOTOGRAPHIC ARCHIVE

What men? By this time, all that was left out of the entire battalion were eleven.

At the Leipzig Salient, it was anything but quiet. Fighting raged around the isolated British position all day. That morning, the 17th and 16th Highland Light Infantry (HLI), with the 2nd King's Own Yorkshire Light Infantry (2nd KOYLI) supporting them, had been the right-wing components of Brigadier General J. B. Jardine's 97th Brigade, which was deployed along an eight-hundred-yard front. At 7:23 in the morning, minutes before the main attack, the first-wave companies of the 17th HLI crept into no-man's-land, positioning themselves thirty to forty yards from the enemy's front trench. As soon as the weeklong preparatory barrage lifted just before the general attack, they rushed the trench.

The 17th HLI achieved total surprise and were able to take a portion of the trench. This encouraged a general assumption among British commanders that the Leipzig Redoubt, within the Leipzig Salient, would simply fall in due course. When this happened, another battalion, the 11th Border, was to attack German positions in and near Authuille Wood. Once these threats had been neutralized, the remainder of the entire 97th Brigade would advance toward Mouquet Farm and take the major strongpoints near it, ultimately attaining Bazentin Ridge. With this high ground in British hands, the advance could continue eastward to the next German defensive line between Mouquet Farm and Grandcourt. The schedule called for this objective to be reached by 10:10 in the morning.

As it turned out, the two Highlander units, catching the Germans by surprise, actually did seize the Leipzig Redoubt along with its garrison. From here, the 17th HLI advanced 150 yards to the Hindenburg Trench deeper within the salient itself. Machine gun fire from a German strongpoint dubbed the Wonderwork suddenly mowed down many of the briefly triumphant, boldly kilted Highlanders. It was at this point that Brigadier General Jardine proved he was not the run-of-the-mill British career officer. Acting on reports from the 161st Brigade Royal Field Artillery (RFA) that the 17th HLI had been pinned down and the infantry advance thus halted, Jardine defied standing orders that forbade any deviation from the corps commander's battle plan. He moved two batteries of the 161st Artillery Brigade so as to redirect their fire from the planned bombardment to bombardment of the German defenses directly behind the redoubt. This allowed the 17th HLI, cut off from behind, to retreat to the redoubt.

The Germans throughout the salient were suffering a high degree of British infiltration, but they nevertheless managed a well-organized counterattack beginning at 1:45. By 4:10 p.m., they had recaptured much of what the British had taken—except for the Leipzig Redoubt, which, by this time, was occupied not only by the Highlanders, but also by a portion of the 2nd KOYLI.

In the meantime, the 11th Border Battalion, having cleared German resistance in Authuille Wood, advanced, per the battle plan, toward Mouquet Farm. It was about an hour into the attack, 8:30 in the morning, and the battlefield ahead of them was a blur of smoke and dust. The Borderers took this as a sign that everything was going according to plan. In fact, they walked into a machine gun trap, the fire emanating from Nordwerk. Casualties were high, and only a few members of the shredded battalion were able to tie into the 17th HLI. Other 11th Border survivors withdrew back into Authuille Wood, where they holed up until well into the afternoon.

On the left flank of the 97th Brigade's attack, the 16th HLI and the left flank companies of the 2nd KOYLI found it impossible to advance against the Wonderwork strongpoint because they were unable to occupy the German front trench opposite it. The reason for this was one of the frequently encountered unintended consequences of heavy preparatory bombardment. The cover the attackers had counted on the captured German trench providing had been obliterated by the British shelling. There were no longer any trenches to capture.

Not to be thwarted, the men of the 16th HLI rose up to charge the Wonderwork without benefit of any covered intermediate position. Predictably, they were cut down by machine gun fire. As intense as the British preparatory barrage had been, it had missed the well-covered machine gun nests, which had been positioned for fire against the gaps in the German wire. Few of the 2nd KOYLI, essential to the support of the Highlanders, were ever able to reach the Leipzig Redoubt.

Looking toward Mouquet Farm from a British communication trench dubbed Centre Way, we see the faint smoke of three shells bursting within the German trenches. Two Australian soldiers (with helmets) crouch in a trench at the far right. The foreground is piled with sandbags. The photograph was taken between July 23 and early September 1916, during which time the Australian 1st, 2nd, and 4th Divisions launched (between them) nineteen attacks on German positions in and around Pozières—or what was left of it. AUSTRALIAN WAR MEMORIAL

THE LEIPZIG SALIENT: 96TH BRIGADE ATTACK

The attack on the salient by elements of the 96th Brigade began far less promisingly than the 97th Brigade attacks. Leading the 96th Brigade effort were the 16th Northumberland Fusiliers and the 15th Lancashire Fusiliers. No sooner did they leave their trenches than machine guns opened up from heavily defended Thiepval and cut them down before they could advance more than a few yards.

Dutifully, the 16th Lancashire advanced into the trenches the two fusilier units had left, while the 2nd Royal Inniskilling Fusiliers were held in reserve behind the front trenches. The 16th Northumberland began an advance directly against Thiepval, but, like the fusiliers, were mowed down by perfectly laid fields of continuous machine gun fire.

Some one hundred men from the devastated 15th Lancashire managed to penetrate the German front line and rushed the village of Thiepval. They linked up with Tommies from the 36th Division, who had broken through German defenses north of the village. The only intelligence of this link-up within the German-occupied village came from Royal Flying Corps (RFC) observers, since all land communication had been cut off. At 10:30 a.m., the 32nd Division commander, Major General W. H. Rycroft, ordered both the 97th and 96th Brigades to hold their positions while new attacks from the north were urgently organized.

But each attempt to advance from the north failed. The massed machine gun fire was too intense. An increasingly desperate Rycroft called his corps commander, General T. L. N. Morland, at 11:40 and proposed that a fresh assault be made—this time not directly from the north down upon Thiepval, but from behind the village. His idea was to skirt Thiepval from the north, slip toward the south, and then make a flanking attack from the east, the German rear. Morland agreed, and Rycroft planned to reinforce the southward advance of the 2nd Inniskilling, called out of reserve, with elements of the 49th Division. Together, these men would attack Thiepval from the east. Simultaneously, the 14th Brigade would reinforce the imperiled British units hanging onto the Leipzig Redoubt. Once they had secured the redoubt, they would launch from it an attack against the German-occupied Hindenburg and Lemberg trenches.

This complex flanking operation was preceded by a barrage from 12:05 to 1:30, directed against positions around Thiepval: the Thiepval Spur, the Wonderwork, the Nab Valley trenches, and the Nordwerk. Unfortunately, the shelling was spread far too thin to be effective, and when the 2nd Inniskilling and other elements of 96th Brigade moved out of the cover of Thiepval Wood, they were met with heavy machine gun fire and forced to return to the Wood.

Another 14th Brigade unit, a portion of the 2nd Manchester Battalion, ventured out from Authuille Wood, using communication trenches for cover before moving forward on the left. This area was not swept by

German machine guns, and by 1:45 two companies made it into the Leipzig Redoubt. Their attempt to attack the Hindenburg and Lemberg trenches, however, was foiled by German "bombers"—hand grenade throwers. Unable to advance from the Leipzig Redoubt they occupied, the reinforced British now found their own numbers too great for the extent of German trench they had managed to capture. Tightly packed into the trenches, they could not maneuver. By nightfall, they continued to hold the Leipzig Redoubt but were at an offensive stalemate, in effect having become the prisoners of their own conquest.

QUIET AGONY

Most histories of the Battle of the Somme, which spanned July 1 to November 18, 1916, concentrate on that first day of battle; some even do so exclusively. This is understandable since the first day contained the main British offensive effort and was the blackest day the British army ever endured. A total of 57,470 men became casualties, including 19,240 killed in action. French and German accounting for July 1 was far less accurate. The French reported approximately seven thousand casualties, the Germans some eight thousand killed and wounded in addition to forty-two hundred taken prisoner.

Just as July 1 stands out from the months of Somme combat that followed it, so the morning of July 1 overshadows the rest of the day. Across most of the British front, with vivid locally concentrated exceptions, the Somme sector was eerily quiet. Many men hunkered miserably in their trenches. They were the lucky ones. Those who had gone over the top and had not reached their objectives or had fallen back on their own lines were stuck in no-man's-land as darkness settled on Picardy. The luckier of these managed to find shell holes that offered shelter and, often, the companionship of other soldiers. The less fortunate were more exposed, and the least fortunate were wounded, lying on the field, waiting for stretcher bearers who might or might not arrive before they succumbed to their injuries, were shot by snipers, or blown to pieces by an artillery round.

CHAPTER 12

Armies of the Night

THE DAYLIGHT HOURS OF JULY 1, 1916, ALONG THE SOMME FRONT WERE filled with slaughter. The night of July 1–2 was quieter but no less terrible. It was consumed with the aftermath of the day's slaughter, a blasted countryside populated by thousands of men, stranded in no-man's-land during the daylight hours, now creeping back to their own lines. This mostly horizontal exodus was shivered by spasms of murder and attempted murder. Four members of the 1st London Rifle Brigade, who had been lying out in no-man's-land, pinned down near Gommecourt throughout the day, decided to use the cover of darkness to make a run for their own trenches. But "the Germans were soon all around us and stick grenades started coming at us. We decided it was hopeless," recalled Lance Corporal T. R. Short, "and stood up to surrender." In response, some twenty of the enemy charged the now-unarmed Tommies, bayonets fixed. "A split second before connecting my stomach with a bayonet, at which I nearly passed out in terror, a terrific shout of 'Halt!' came from somewhere and, showing how disciplined the German soldier is, the one coming at me slid flat on his back, his rifle went straight up in the air and his legs shot between mine."[1]

DULCE ET DECORUM EST
Bill Soar, bugler of the 1/7 Sherwood Foresters (Robin Hood Rifles), had been hit in the arm but, cloaked in night, he staggered back to the British trenches. When he reached the barbed wire, a trigger-happy sentry manning a machine gun fired a burst—and only afterward demanded

the figure stumbling toward him identify himself: friend or foe. Soar shouted out his name and battalion and was told to approach. He stepped forward, bumbling into the thick of the wire entanglement several yards beyond the parapet. He had no helmet, no rifle, no pack. All had been lost or left in no-man's-land. Now he was compelled to unfasten his trousers and leave them on the wire. In a bloody tunic and his drawers, he returned from battle.

The famous line from Horace comes to mind, the Latin words that the most celebrated of the British war poets, Wilfred Owen, used in his best-known and bitterest poem, *"Dulce et Decorum Est"*: "The old Lie; *Dulce et decorum est pro patria mori"*—It is sweet and dignified to die for your country.[2]

Soar kept his life but left something of his dignity on the barbed wire. Many other Tommies who became entangled on the barbed wire, either their own or the enemy's, lost both life and dignity. Some died instantly, others, severely wounded, succumbed only after hours of agony that, for those who heard and saw their suffering, brought to mind the Crucifixion. Whether a man was caught in his own side's wire or that of the enemy, no one dared venture out to make a rescue. If the moans became either sufficiently unnerving, enervating, or irritating, or if they evoked sufficient sympathy, a rifleman might end the man's misery with a bullet.

Sometimes, more extreme measures were taken. Shrapnel severely wounded the foot of J. W. Stansby, second lieutenant in the 1/6th North Staffs, a territorial unit. As he lay helpless, unable to walk, a rifle round passed through his hand. He went down within fifteen minutes of having gone over the top in the attack of 7:30 a.m. He had made it as far as the German wire. Following that first quarter-hour, the sum of his experience of the Battle of the Somme was lying near the enemy's wire all day long, in agony and in anticipation of being shot, bayonetted, or blown up at any moment. It being the height of summer, darkness fell late, and when it did, the Germans in the trenches opposite him "threw volleys of hand grenades into the wire," intent on finishing off anyone there. When they "came out to pick up the pieces," Stansby wrote, "I was carried into the German front-line trench and taken down into a dugout where I was searched and my wound dressed."[3] Having failed to blow Second Lieutenant Stansby to pieces, the enemy treated him with whatever compassion belligerents conventionally show their prisoners in "civilized" warfare.

Private Albert McMillan, of the 16th Middlesex (Public Schools) Battalion, heard his sergeant order that night the few survivors of his company to surrender. They were hopelessly cut off, and a number of German rifles and machine guns were trained on them. Their hands went up, and the Germans beckoned to them from their trench. McMillan and his sergeant tenderly handed down to waiting hands in the trench one of their own. The man had been severely wounded in the groin. Seeing this, one German soldier responded without pity but with simple truth: "*Nicht mehr Kinder machen*," he laughed. "No more children for you."[4]

Most historians believe this photograph depicts the Public Schools Battalion (a Pals battalion officially designated the 16th Battalion, The Middlesex Regiment) at "White City," a British strongpoint opposite Beaumont-Hamel. Some, however, believe it is actually the 1st Battalion, The East Lancashire Regiment. In either case, the photograph shows the built-up area behind the second-line British trenches. Large dugouts are reinforced with a multitude of sandbags. IMPERIAL WAR MUSEUM PHOTOGRAPHIC ARCHIVE

As British soldiers capable of walking, limping, or crawling made their way west through no-man's-land that night, others, the stretcher bearers, fanned out toward the ominous east in search of those wounded who could not move on their own. The stretcher bearers were part of the very last wave of any attack, but no soldier who had any experience of combat ever said they had it easy. Unarmed, the bearers made tempting targets for an enemy who was frustrated and angry over having been bombarded and shot at all day. As Captain Charles Hudson of the 11th Sherwood Foresters wrote, "Stretcher-bearers were wonderful people. Ours had been the bandsmen of earlier training days. They were always called to the most dangerous places, where casualties had already taken place, yet there were always men ready to volunteer for the job, at any rate in the early days of the war. The men were not bloodthirsty. Stretcher-bearers were unarmed and though they were not required to do manual labour or sentry-go, this I am sure was not the over-riding reason for their readiness to volunteer."[5]

First-person and eyewitness accounts of stretcher bearers in action are scarce. No assignment in war was more psychologically draining or physically arduous, especially since no-man's-land was scarred by shell craters, sown with barbed wire, and littered with unexploded ordnance. Mud was often a knee-deep quagmire that made moving nearly impossible. "It is amazing the amount of reserve endurance that is stored in the human frame," a New Zealand stretcher bearer, Private Linus Ryan, recalled in a manuscript titled "My three years in khaki." He wrote about the Battle of Passchendaele (July 31–November 10, 1917), but the experience of bearers at the Somme must have been similar:

> *Our rate of progress [to the battlefield] was a veritable crawl. We were verging on the condition of collapse. Our feet were just two concentrated lumps of pain—trench feet. The gas we had experienced . . . had affected our throats . . . our voices were a mere whisper. We did not have sufficient energy to hold up our heads and as we staggered back not a word was spoken, but possibly they all felt—as I felt—that if there was another patient waiting . . . I would just break down and cry. And there was another patient—three or four in fact! Ben Thorn,*

our leader . . . said 'Come on boys, hoist him up', and once again we staggered and fought with the clinging slime.

That trip was a nightmare. We would sink in the mud and our legs were so weak and shaky, it was becoming a matter of the most acute difficulty to get out. We had one consolation. We were so far gone as to be beyond caring and the shells which screeched down in close proximity were unheeded. We reached the Somme [a dressing station]—we had to reach there. Somehow or other we got back too and when we got back and found another man awaiting us, somehow or other we hoisted him to our shoulders and . . . staggered away again with our burden.[6]

On many Western Front battlefields, the Somme included, the stretcher bearers were forbidden to venture far out into no-man's-land during the day. So they waited until dark to search for the wounded in the field. At this time of year, they had no more than six hours of true darkness in which to work, yet reaching a single wounded soldier lying midway out in no-man's-land might take an hour or more. Returning with him might consume as much as two hours, depending on the weather, the depth and extent of the mud, and the presence of other obstacles. It took four nights to pick up most of the British wounded from the first day's fighting. In at least one case, however, a man endured eleven days and nights in no-man's-land before he was discovered.

Sleeping with the Enemy

In those few places along the British front where an attack succeeded in taking a section of German trench, nightfall brought either the terrifying sense of being cut off from the bulk of one's comrades and liable at any time to be swallowed up by the enemy or, where British numbers were sufficiently large, the heady sensation of not only having survived combat but having won the battle. In both cases that night, an extra rum ration was distributed. Where the British had established a reasonably firm foothold, reinforcements were sent up during the night to stiffen the captured position. A company of the 1st Royal Irish Fusiliers advanced through the dark to reinforce the Quadrilateral Redoubt. After arriving, the company's sergeants volunteered to look for wounded men beyond the redoubt. As they stealthily searched, the quiet was broken by the sound of voices—German voices. One of the sergeants responded by hurling a Mills bomb in the direction of the voices, scattering (perhaps killing) the Germans, who, the sergeant discovered, had been setting up not one but two machine gun nests intended to rake the redoubt in the morning. The sergeant pushed one of the weapons into a seemingly bottomless shell hole. He summoned another sergeant to help him haul the other machine gun back into the redoubt.

The occupants of the captured Quadrilateral Redoubt were surely grateful to the vigilant sergeant of the company of newcomers. At the same time, they must also have been well aware that, but for the sergeant's presence and sharp ear, they could all have awakened to a stream of machine gun bullets. Amid the pride in victory and the relief that came with survival, those who occupied the trenches in the redoubt had been made keenly aware that they were sleeping with the enemy and doing so in his territory. If the Germans should decide to mount a concerted attack against them, they were done for.

For those few units receiving reinforcements or the even fewer that had taken their objectives without having lost most of their number in the process, the greatest satisfaction was taken in "the fact that so many of us were still alive," according to Private R. G. Robertson of the 4th Liverpool Pals. He and his mates passed the night singing the likes of "It's a Long Way to Tipperary" and "Keep the Home Fires Burning" by way of celebration.[7]

HOME TRENCHES

As precarious as the captured trenches were, the home trenches, from which the attacks had been launched that morning, cannot have felt all that much better. Although there was little gunfire and no shelling, the night was far from peaceful. Generals Haig and Rawlinson had planned the battle with only one outcome in mind: success. But what they had actually achieved was an all but total failure. The volume of wounded this—the costliest single day in the history of the British army—produced was overwhelming and so unexpected that injured and dying men clogged the trenches, not figuratively, but literally.

It was a scene out of Dante. Those who were unwounded or could at least walk struggled to move from place to place in the trench. Frequently, a groan, a scream, or a curse was all that alerted the ambulatory that they had trod upon someone who could not move on his own. Even worse were those occasions when a soldier just trying to get somewhere in the trench felt the soft give of uniformed flesh yield under his boot—but without the attendant verbal protest. That meant just one thing. He was walking on the dead. And as the wounded piled up unattended, the volume of the dead increased.

The darkness, the crowding, the chaos greatly delayed evacuation of the wounded. Men who had suffered fourteen hours of torment in no-man's-land had been rescued by stretcher bearers only to be dumped among other wounded, the dying, and the dead. It was a monumental task even to begin to triage them all and evacuate those in greatest need.

The prevailing chaos that night brought not only suffering, it created grave and imminent danger. Surely, the Germans on the other side of no-man's-land had some inkling of the confusion reigning in the British lines. If there was ever a time for them to launch an attack, it was now. Few men were focused on the enemy. The war, that night, was not in no-man's-land, but right here—in the trench, underfoot or elbow to elbow with the injured, the dying, and the dead. If the enemy had chosen to attack on that grim night, the British lines would have crumbled in many places. The Battle of the Somme might well have ended in a day or a week, most likely in a defeat as total as any the Allies had suffered during the disastrous opening month of the war.

That the Germans did not attack certainly signaled their weariness. Even more, however, it betokened their commanders' resolute determination to remain in an aggressive defensive posture. Even with the foe so temptingly vulnerable, they did not dare to venture out of their ample trenches and deep dugouts. The plan and the orders were absolute: let the British come to them.

Oblivious as they were to the enemy that night, the British commanders had to find some way to sort out their trenches and to do so quickly. But how could they motivate men exhausted and disheartened from a day's desperate battle to perform the immense manual labor required to move the wounded and the dead? The answer was to condition the relief of these men on clearing the trenches. As Private G. S. Young, 1/6th North Staffs, explained, "We were told that if we could clear the trench of dead and wounded sufficiently, we would be relieved. We propped the dead in rows at the back of the trench and sat the wounded on the fire-step and we waited to be relieved." Who were "we"? "There were three of us left in my platoon."[8]

MORNING

The night of July 1 was hell—dark, delirious, and filled with pain. The morning brought light but no cheer. Two of Douglas Haig's grandest initiatives were summarily abandoned. The door was unceremoniously slammed on operations near Gommecourt, the diversion that Haig hoped would become an opportunity for a cavalry breakthrough. The pyrrhic victory Edmund Allenby had eked out in parts of his isolated northern sector shriveled into something even less, since the ground gained on July 1 was abandoned on July 2. Losses among the British at Gommecourt were 6,769 and among the Germans 1,241. Given the decision not to exploit the gains made, most historians categorize what had initially been a British pyrrhic victory as ultimately a German triumph.

Ill-conceived from the get-go, the Gommecourt fight accomplished nothing of enduring value. Despite temporary gains made, the engagement did not even achieve success as a diversion, since it failed to force General Fritz von Below to transfer his reserves from the main Somme front to meet the British threat here. Tactically, it was a win for the Germans, who inflicted six British casualties for every German one. If there is any value in the fight at Gommecourt it is as irrefutable evidence of the essential futility, stupidity, and waste of trench warfare.

The withdrawal from Gommecourt meant that Lieutenant General Sir Hubert Gough's planned attack toward Bapaume using two corps detached from Allenby's Third Army was instantly and forever shut down. As of July 2, Bapaume, a shining prize far into German-held territory, might as well have been on Mars.

In fact, on July 2, it almost looked as if the entire Somme campaign was heading toward shutdown. July 1 had seen fourteen British divisions committed to battle. On July 2, just three were fighting. The under-strength units that stormed, took, and held the Quadrilateral Redoubt, suffering heavy losses in repelling German efforts to retake the position, were all ordered to withdraw before July 2 even dawned. At Montauban, the easternmost prize of July 1, a position capable of being reinforced and becoming a forward base of operations, no orders to advance were received. Given the record of success in the southern portion of the British front, the absence of action seemed inexplicable as well as profoundly demoralizing to those occupying the front line at Montauban. Over the next several days, every man still living who had fought at the Somme on July 1 would be withdrawn and sent to the rear for rest.

The wee hours of July 2 belonged for the most part to the stretcher bearers. They trudged through no-man's-land until first light, when the Germans, many of them at least, were liable to shoot anyone, whether they carried a rifle or a stretcher. Despite the danger, however, some bearers could not abide waiting for the sun to go down before venturing out again. With or without permission from their commanders, they took their chances and, in the late afternoon of July 2, recommenced their mission of search and recovery. By ensuring that one more man did not die alone and abandoned, perhaps they hoped to salvage some good from this battle.

A rain shower broke out that afternoon near Thiepval. As it settled into a drizzle, sentries raised an alarm. Men, numbers of them, were crawling toward the frontline trenches! Local commanders got on their field telephones and called for an artillery barrage. Then, peering anxiously at the devastated ground on the other side of their wire, they gradually made out uniforms of khaki, not *Feldgrau* (the Germans' field gray). They got back on the phones to cancel the barrage. For what they saw approaching was an army of British wounded crawling back to their brothers in arms. The rain had revived them, brought them back from the dead, as it might a sere crop blasted by drought.

CHAPTER 13

All Summer Long

IT WOULD BE A LONG, HOT SUMMER ON THE CONGEALED BRITISH SEC-
tor of the Somme. At the end would be a cold, grim autumn. On November 18, 1916, the battle would be called off rather than ended. What had been planned as "the Big Push," the breakthrough that would end the war, became no more or less than the prelude to another two years of war—two years very nearly to the day.

The big push behind *the* Big Push was supposed to be the attacks of July 1. General Sir Douglas Haig had listed thirteen objectives to be taken by the BEF by the end of that day. Nominally, three were achieved. The German-held, German-fortified villages of Montauban, Mametz, and Fricourt were all occupied by British troops as of July 1. During the night of July 1–2, Fricourt was abandoned, so, in the end, just two objectives were held more than a few hours. In terms of the line separating Allied-controlled territory from German-held territory within France, there was measurable progress. At 7:30 on the morning of July 1, the front line descended from Foncquevillers in the north almost due south to a point just west of Fricourt before turning abruptly to the east past Mametz and to Maricourt, which was on the line separating the British portion of the Somme front from the French. Thus the line resembled a capital "L." The vertical portion of this "letter" separated French-held France from German-held France: the German rear. The horizontal portion separated French-held France not only from more of German-held France, but also from the rest of the German lines.

A TRAGIC BARGAIN

Let's put it another way. What the British gained on July 1 was about a mile of territory *north* of the starting position of the horizontal portion of the "L." With this gain came control of the villages of Mametz and Montauban.

Without question, the northward push was a territorial gain. But its strategic value was vanishingly small. Instead of pushing the Western Front *east*, against the German rear, the July 1 effort pushed perhaps three miles of the Western Front *north*, toward more German lines filled with more German troops. This meant that the front German line had been penetrated here, but the German second line—the main line in the enemy's defense in depth—had nowhere been breached. As it was, the Western Front extended some four hundred miles from the Belgian coast of the English Channel in the north to the Swiss border in the south. In strategic terms, pushing three miles of this line a single mile northward

Australia sent Frank Crozier to the Western Front as one of the army's "official war artists." He completed his oil painting *Mametz, Western Front: Men, Animals and Supplies in Snow Covered Valley* (30 by 50¼ inches) in 1919. It depicts a scene in the rear area of I Anzac Corps (Australia-New Zealand Army Corps) during the winter of 1916–1917 at the end of the Battle of the Somme. AUSTRALIAN WAR MEMORIAL

was infinitesimal progress. Besides, going north was going in the wrong direction. The war could be won only by moving east.

Infinitesimal in strategic terms, moving the horizontal portion of the "L" had cost the lives of 19,240 men, who were either killed in combat outright or died of their wounds. Officer deaths totaled 993 on July 1; other ranks, 18,247. Wounded totaled 36,493; missing, 2,152; prisoners, 585. The one-day casualty total, 57,470, was the worst single-day loss the British army had ever suffered. The grim record still stands.

Put another way, almost precisely half of the personnel of the 143 battalions that attacked on July 1, 1916, became casualties. For those who assume enlisted men always fare worse than officers, consider that three out of four officers became casualties on the first day of this battle. In the tradition of British military leaders throughout history (one thinks of Lord Nelson magnificently arrayed as he strode the decks of HMS *Victory* at Trafalgar), officers on the Somme front went into combat with a polished leather Sam Browne belt, possibly a helmet (though more often a soft cap), and a revolver or, perhaps, nothing more lethal than a cane or swagger stick. At least one, the adjutant of the 9th Devons, wore his sword into no-man's-land. Statistically, the most dangerous rank to hold that day was captain. The least dangerous was private. "For every yard of the sixteen-mile front from Gommecourt to Montauban there were two British casualties."[1]

The casualty figures generally accepted today took days for the British mortuary men to calculate. As usual, the senior commanders—Haig, Rawlinson, Allenby, and Gough—farthest to the rear, had the least accurate information. Fourth Army headquarters, as of July 2, was calculating a casualty rate that was fully 40 percent below the actual number. After they learned the true numbers, neither Haig nor Rawlinson ever made any official reference to their catastrophic level. Of human tragedy, there was not a hint, even in the deepest privacy of their own diaries.[2]

As for public accountability, Haig, Rawlinson, and Gough were immune. Edmund Allenby thought his failure to take and hold Gommecourt, combined with the heavy losses among his Third Army, would surely cost him his job. It did not, and he went on to lead the Third Army at the Battle of Arras (April 9–May 16, 1917), which suffered heavy casualties after making an initial breakthrough that quickly oozed into the customary bloody trench-war stalemate. It was then—at Arras in 1917, not the Somme in 1916—that Haig lost confidence in him. Instead of firing him, however, he approved his promotion to full general on June 3, 1917, just before replacing him, six days later, as Third Army commanding officer. Allenby would end his World War I career in command of British forces in Egypt and Palestine, achieving victory here—thanks in no small part to the unconventional genius of T. E. Lawrence ("of Arabia"). After the war, he was promoted to field marshal, created viscount, and named British high commissioner for Egypt and the Sudan.

Still, at the command level on the Somme, a few heads did roll. Lieutenant General Sir Thomas D'Oyly Snow, commanding VII Corps in Third Army, suffered the wrath of Edmund Allenby but nevertheless escaped the supreme censure of a trip back to England. As mentioned in chapter 11, Allenby did subject Major General Edward James Montagu-Stuart-Wortley to a formal court of inquiry, which Haig preempted by summarily consigning Montagu-Stuart-Wortley to backwater command in Ireland. Haig did not officially reprimand his quartermaster general, General Sir John Maxwell, who had furnished just three ambulance trains on July 1 when Haig had ordered eighteen. As for Lieutenant General Aylmer Hunter-Weston, whose VIII Corps had suffered the worst casualties of any unit between the River Ancre and the village of Serre, he and his entire staff were rusticated to a "quiet sector" far from the Somme.

Of all the field commanders, Major General Thomas Pilcher, commanding the 17th (Northern) Division, suffered the most unjust fate. On July 1, he was ordered to detach his 50th Brigade to another division in support of the attempted capture of Fricourt. The brigade incurred very heavy casualties before it was returned to Pilcher's division. On July 5, General Henry Horne, commanding XV Corps, of which the 17th Division was a part, ordered Pilcher to immediately attack the Quadrangle Support Trench in Mametz Wood. The division had just captured the main trench system there, and Pilcher defied Horne by ordering a pause to prepare properly for the assault on the Support Trench. Horne overruled him, forcing him to attack on the night of July 6. When this attack failed, he was

Lieutenant General Aylmer Hunter-Weston's VIII Corps suffered the heaviest casualties of any British unit deployed between the River Ancre and the village of Serre. After the Battle of the Somme, he and his staff were exiled to a "quiet sector" far from the Somme front. WIKIMEDIA

ordered to attack again on July 7. Pilcher protested, but complied—using, however, as few men as possible so as to obey the order without needlessly sacrificing a division that had already taken heavy casualties. Outraged, Horne accused Pilcher of lacking "initiative, drive, and readiness."[3] Unwilling to accuse a high-ranking officer of something approaching cowardice, Haig pronounced him less provocatively "unequal to the task" of divisional command and, on July 11, consigned him to preside over a reserve center in England. "It is very easy to sit a few miles in the rear and get credit for allowing men to be killed in an undertaking foredoomed to failure," Pilcher wrote after the war, "but the part did not appeal to me and my protests against these useless attacks were not well received."[4]

Thomas Pilcher had taken a principled stand against futile sacrifice and had paid the price. Some officers paid a price far higher. Lieutenant Colonel Edwin Thomas Falkiner Sandys, commanding the 2nd Middlesex Battalion, was severely wounded on July 1. Although he recovered from his physical injuries, he could find no surcease from the torment of having survived while so many of his command had died. To one of his subordinate officers—like him, on recuperative leave in England—he wrote a letter expressing regret that he had not fallen with his men. To another officer he wrote simply, "I have come to London to take my life. I have never had a moment's peace since July 1st."[5]

On September 6, 1916, with the Battle of the Somme still being fought across the Channel, Sandys closed the door to his room in the Cavendish Hotel, withdrew his service revolver from its holster, and sent a bullet through his head. He was forty.[6]

THE BATTLE OF ALBERT

Albert, with a population of about ten thousand, was the largest town on the Somme front. On January 15, 1915, the "Golden Virgin," a sculpture of Mary and the Infant Jesus by Albert-Dominique Roze that adorned the top of the town's chief structure, the Basilica of Notre Dame de Brebières, was hit by a German artillery shell. It fell over, nearly supine—but hung on, as it were, by its toes. Rupert Edward Inglis, a former rugby champion serving as an army chaplain, wrote to his wife in October 1915 as his unit passed through the town. "The statue was knocked over, but has never fallen. . . . It really is a wonderful sight. It is incomprehensible how it can have stayed there. . . . The Church and village are wrecked. . . ."[7] The numberless British troops who passed through the town told each other that whichever side finally toppled that holy statue would lose the war.

The top half of this montage shows a German trench at Delville Wood (left) beside a view of that trench as it exists today. The bottom two photographs show the gilded sculpture of the Virgin atop the Basilica Notre-Dame de Brebières after it was knocked over by a German shell (left) and in its restored condition today (right). HISTORICAL PHOTOGRAPHS, WIKIMEDIA; MODERN PHOTOGRAPHS, "FARAWAYMAN," PUBLISHED ON WIKIMEDIA

Three miles east of Albert were the front lines of the Battle of the Somme, the first thirteen days of which the official British military history refers to as the Battle of Albert.

By the end of the July 1 fighting, the British army had suffered the worst day in its history, and those units still at the front were unable to mount any new major offensive efforts until July 4, when the depleted divisions had been replenished or replaced. Operations, it was decided, were to be confined to the area south of the Albert-Bapaume road. Having achieved their few successes in the southern portion of the Somme front, British commanders hoped that they could build on their gains in this section. Besides, their intelligence sources were reporting that the German Second Army in this area was depleted and in a chaotic state.

Following the disasters of July 1, British command took a lesson from their French colleagues, piling on more artillery to support the infantry and making more, but smaller and shallower, attacks. This, it was believed, would reduce the risk of badly depleted attacking units getting flanked by the enemy, cut off, and isolated in the enemy's frontline trenches. The initial objective of this new phase of the battle was simply to keep jabbing at the enemy, always attacking toward the east, softening up the German defenses in preparation for a renewed general attack. Scheduled for July 10, this next "big push" would be postponed to July 14 thanks to disruptions in supply caused by intense fire from the German salient at Maricourt.

But the British were not alone in changing tactics. Instead of digging in and making a strictly defensive response to the modest jabbing attacks that began on July 4, the enemy ventured out of its trenches and dugouts to boldly counterattack. This shift in tactics initially proved costly to the Germans. After modest British gains during July 2–3, a major British effort on July 4 to take La Boisselle succeeded. At the same time, British units occupied Bernafay and Caterpillar woods, from which they launched attacks to capture Trônes Wood, Mametz Wood, and Contalmaison between July 4 and July 14.

Germany's top commander, Erich von Falkenhayn, chief of the German General Staff, had been greatly preoccupied with the Battle of Verdun. Now sensing the possibility of a crisis developing on the Somme front, he intervened, shifting reinforcements from Verdun to the Somme. But, uncharacteristically of the Germans, the newcomers to this sector were tossed into the battle, like logs into a fire, as soon as they marched in. The result was an absence of the kind of defensive coordination that had characterized the German effort on July 1. Both the British and the Germans took heavy losses, and by July 13, the Battle of Albert petered out indecisively.

Whereas the British attacks of July 1 had been aggressive, ambitious, but reckless, those of July 2–13 were numerous but tentative. The result was not as catastrophic as that of the first day on the Somme, but it was ghastly nevertheless. In the space of eleven days, roughly twenty-five thousand men were lost by the British and at least thirty thousand on the German side.

For his part, General Fritz von Below, commanding German forces on this front, was sufficiently alarmed to issue an order barring voluntary withdrawals. Like the departure from static defense to aggressive coun-terattack, this order was a significant departure from accepted German tactics. Central to the concept of defense in depth was the option to withdraw from a first to a second line of defense, drawing the enemy in and setting up the possibility of a flanking defense. Falkenhayn reduced the number of men at Verdun and accordingly ordered commanders in that sector to adopt a strictly defensive posture. The men thus released for duty on the Somme were to be used in a new strategy of counterattack.

THE BATTLES OF BAZENTIN RIDGE AND FROMELLES

The occupation of the Bernafay and Caterpillar woods and the capture of Trônes Wood, Mametz Wood, and Contalmaison between July 4 and July 14 put the British in position to fight the Battle of Bazentin Ridge from July 14 to July 17.

Denounced by one of General Rawlinson's French colleagues as "an attack organized for amateurs by amateurs,"[8] the Bazentin opera-tion, which began on July 14, shocked everyone—French, German, *and* British—by its success. Although Rawlinson prepared for the infantry assault using only about two-thirds of the guns he had used on July 1, the area they shelled was just 5 percent of that covered two weeks earlier,

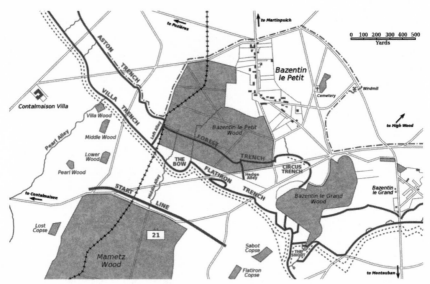

The British trenches before Bazentin-le-Petit. WIKIMEDIA

so that the front on which the attack focused was hit by 660 pounds of ordnance *per yard*. In addition, the artillery preparation was a so-called hurricane barrage that lasted a mere five minutes, beginning at 3:20 a.m., thereby preserving the element of surprise. Moreover, the infantry attack stepped off at 3:25, in the proverbial darkness before dawn, when the German machine-gunners could not see to aim. Although, in some places, the British infantry had to advance as much as twelve hundred yards, they did much of it stealthily, in the dark, before making the final rush.

As the infantry rushed in, the hurricane bombardment lifted, registering back to hit the second-line reserve trenches. These were fiercely bombarded for just two minutes. The first wave of the infantry assault consisted of "bombing parties"—hand grenade throwers—whose assignment was to push straight through the bombarded first-line trenches to attack the reserve trenches. It was the task of the second and subsequent waves to finish off the front line. In this way, the British hoped to avoid getting flanked, isolated, and cut off between the enemy's first- and second-line trenches.

An abandoned German trench in Delville Wood, near Longueval, September 1916.
WIKIMEDIA

The attack came both from the left and the right. On the left, the 21st Division charged in from Mametz Wood while the 7th Division, which had crept forward in the darkness to within a hundred yards of the enemy trenches, rushed in beside them. By mid-morning, the village of Bazentin-le-Petit was in British hands. On the right, the 3rd Division and the 9th (Scottish) Division (which included the South African Infantry Brigade) captured Longueval and reached the periphery of Delville Wood, but failed to capture the adjacent redoubt at Waterlot Farm.

While the left and right attacks were ongoing, the 3rd Division advanced from Montauban toward Bazentin-le-Grand, but suffered heavy losses from an unanticipated German defensive barrage. Still, the 18th (Eastern) Division, attacking from Bernafay Wood, captured Trônes Wood by late morning.

A German prisoner (second from left) helps British walking wounded make their way to a dressing station near Bernafay Wood after the fight at Bazentin Ridge on July 19, 1916. IMPERIAL WAR MUSEUM PHOTOGRAPHIC ARCHIVE

German general Friedrich Bertram Sixt von Armin had been assigned command of this portion of the Somme front just this very morning. He rose quickly to the task, shifting units from elsewhere on the front and bringing up his reserves. His plan was to arrest the British advance and hold it until it was possible to mount a counterattack, but he soon thought the better of it and ordered a defensive stand instead.

By 9:00 a.m., the situation looked promising to the British, who occupied the Bazentin villages and had possession of the high ground at Bazentin Ridge. From this elevated position, the troops and their officers beheld a vista of farmland relatively undamaged by shell fire, which meant that cavalry might at last have a chance to make a breakthrough here. But, presumably chastened by the consequences of moving too far too fast on July 1, orders were given to refrain from taking the High Wood and thereby clearing the way for a cavalry romp. Rawlinson did not want to risk the 2nd Indian Cavalry Division, which he decided to hold in reserve to oppose any counterattack.

It was seven in the evening of July 14 before a cavalry charge was finally authorized. At that time, the 7th Dragoon Guards and the 20th Deccan Horse, both belonging to the 2nd Indian Cavalry, charged against High Wood, lances anachronistically pointed forward like those of medieval knights in joust. By this time, however, German machine-gunners had been deployed throughout the wood. They took a heavy toll on man and horse. The cavalry troopers managed to take High Wood nevertheless, but, receiving no reinforcements, were soon forced to withdraw from their prize.

While the action unfolded in and around the Bazentin villages, the 33rd Division in the XV Corps reserve advanced toward Fricourt and attained the Bazentin Ridge just as the Indian cavalry was beginning its attack. The objective was for the 100th Brigade of the 33rd to continue the advance beyond the ridge and, on July 15, to carry the attack toward Martinpuich about a mile north of Bazentin-le-Petit. Noting however that contrary to reports, High Wood had not been captured, the CO of the 100th Brigade protested the order to attack. When the protests went unheeded, the attack stepped off at 9:00 a.m. Machine-gunners in the wood enfiladed the 100th, virtually wiping out a full company of its 16th Battalion, the King's Royal Rifle Corps (known as the "Church Lads Brigade Pals"), which had been sent to clear the wood in advance of the main attack. Of the two hundred men in the company, all but 67 were killed.

After the success of July 14, the failures of July 15 came as a heavy disappointment. After another two days of fighting, the Battle of Bazentin Ridge ended on July 17, and, on July 19, the focus turned toward Fromelles, near Armentieres, some fifty miles to the north. The objective here was to relieve pressure from the British Fourth Army by attacking German positions from their rear, descending upon them from the north.

It looked like a promising opportunity, especially since intelligence estimates reported that the enemy was weak here. Believing this proved to be the first mistake of the operation. The second was employing the 1st Australian Division (Australian Imperial Force), which was new to the

The Australian Imperial Force suffered some of the heaviest casualties of any UK unit—British, Colonial, or Dominion—at the Somme Front. Here infantrymen of the Australian 6th Brigade, 2nd Australian Division, march back to their billets after a stint on the front lines. Soldiers of the 2nd Brigade, who will soon head for a second tour at Pozières, look on. AUSTRALIAN WAR MEMORIAL

Western Front and completely inexperienced in trench warfare. Although the Germans suffered significant casualties during July 19–20—between sixteen hundred and two thousand killed and wounded—the BEF lost 7,080 killed and wounded, of which 5,533 were among the Australians, making this "the worst 24 hours in Australia's entire history." The losses were "equivalent to the total Australian casualties in the Boer War, Korean War and Vietnam War put together."[9]

BATTLES OF DELVILLE WOOD AND POZIÈRES RIDGE

Delville Wood is located just to the northwest of the village of Ginchy and to the southeast of High Wood. On July 14, the 9th (Scottish) Division, with the as-yet untested South African 1st Infantry Brigade

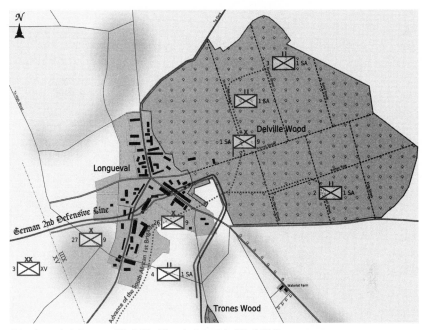

Attack and defense of Delville Wood, July 14–17, 1916. WIKIMEDIA

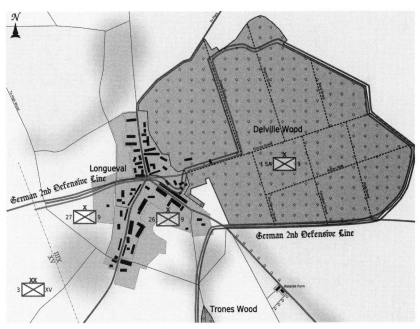

Attack and defense of Delville Wood, July 14–17, 1916. WIKIMEDIA

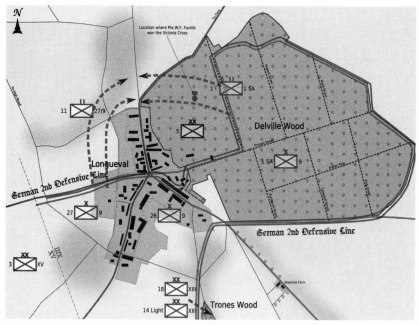

Attack and defense of Delville Wood, July 14–17, 1916. WIKIMEDIA

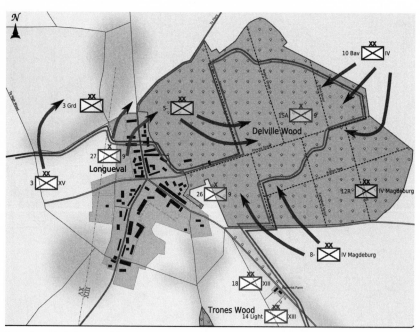

Attack and defense of Delville Wood, July 14–17, 1916. WIKIMEDIA

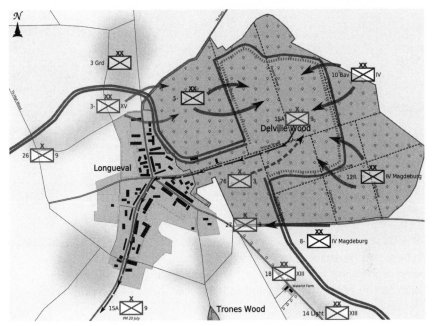

Attack and defense of Delville Wood, July 14–17, 1916. WIKIMEDIA

attached, advanced into the wood with the objective of securing the British right flank from attack. By July 15, the South African 1st Infantry successfully occupied Delville Wood—then spent the next six days fighting off repeated German attempts to retake it. On July 20, the brigade was relieved, and fighting continued here through September 3, during which the British, with some French aid, managed to hold Delville Wood. It remained a stubborn British salient in the German line, a sharp thorn in General Sixt von Armin's side. By September 15, the British had pushed that line back halfway to the point it would reach in November, when the Battle of the Somme ended in the mutual exhaustion of both sides.

Another Commonwealth unit, the battered 1st Australian Division (Australian Imperial Force), played a central role in the Battle of Pozières, beginning on July 22 when the Australians captured the village of Pozières, which lay roughly midway between Bazentin-le-Petit to the southeast and Thiepval to the northwest. The Germans replied on

An illustrated newspaper engraving depicts "Savage Hand-to-Hand Fighting with Bomb and Bayonet in Dellville Wood." The soldiers shown here belong to the South African Infantry Brigade, which was attached to the 9th (Scottish) Division. WIKIMEDIA

Infantry of the Wiltshire Regiment attack near Thiepval, August 7, 1916. IMPERIAL WAR MUSEUM PHOTOGRAPHIC ARCHIVE

July 23 with an artillery barrage followed by a series of counterattacks, which were made through August 7, when Lieutenant General Hubert Gough's Reserve Army, of which the 1st Australian Division was a part, captured the plateau-like ridge that ran north and east of Pozières. This put the British in position to threaten—from the rear—Thiepval, the elusive prize of July 1 and the strongly fortified bastion of the German presence on the Somme front.

CHAPTER 14

The Guns of Autumn

As the summer of 1916 began to chill and darken into the autumn of that year, Winston Churchill advised withdrawing from the Somme sector and mounting a new offensive elsewhere. "The open country towards which we are struggling by inches is capable of entrenched defence at every step, *and is utterly devoid of military significance.*"[1] But Churchill at this time was nothing more than a Member of Parliament for Dundee, having been forced to resign as first lord of the admiralty in 1915 for the role he played in the disastrous Gallipoli landings in the Dardanelles (April 25, 1915) and having stepped down as lieutenant colonel of 6th Battalion of the Royal Scots Fusiliers after six months on the Western Front. With him out of power, his opinions on the conduct of war were widely ignored. Future prime minister David Lloyd George believed that for Churchill, "national interests are completely overshadowed by . . . personal concern." It was, he scolded him, "the reason why you do not win trust even where you command admiration."[2]

Ears were shut, minds closed, and the Somme offensive continued. After the Australian 2nd Division made good progress north of Pozières on the night of August 4 and during the day of August 5, Joseph Joffre called on Douglas Haig at his headquarters chateau. Haig feared being taken on another trip to the woodshed for having advanced little more than a mile in six weeks. Instead, the French general-in-chief handed him a box of fifty Croix de Guerre. He asked Haig to distribute them as he thought fit. It was, in fact, a common enough French decoration for acts of heroism in action against the enemy and was often awarded to foreign allies.

"I managed to get together 10 officers," Haig noted in his diary, "who had rendered 'good service under fire' and [Joffre] presented the crosses to them himself."[3] He still had forty more left, undistributed, in the box.

THE ENEMY DESPAIRS

There was no joy in the château of Douglas Haig, but at least he could point to something of which Churchill's pessimism did not take account. To be sure, many Britons were dead, wounded, or maimed—and with little territorial gain to show for their sacrifice. But this war was now about attrition far more than conquest. Gaining ground was less significant than killing men. Victory? Victory would be measured in bodies—theirs versus ours—and by the fact that one side, however depleted, was still standing after the other had fallen or departed the field.

There is no question that the Germans were suffering. Despite their outstanding defensive fortifications, British artillery was finally taking a toll. A German officer recorded in his diary losses of at least half of his command due to artillery bombardment, and those "who survived are at this moment not men, but more or less finished beings. . . . Officers whom I once knew as very vigorous are openly sobbing."[4]

German prisoners of war captured during mid-August were described as despondent. "Attrition" is literally a wearing away. Haig crunched the numbers. His analysts calculated that the British had already fought twenty-three of the forty-one German divisions deployed on the Somme front. They were worn out, having been kept in the line for twenty brutal days. Rumors of German peace overtures were in the air. It was said that civil unrest was sweeping Berlin. Then came August 27 and the surprising entry of Romania into the war on the side of the Allies. It was a small country with a substantial army of 650,000, and its entry sent tremors of fear through the German people and their government. Upon the Allies, the effect came as a wave of new optimism. Add to this the dismissal of Erich von Falkenhayn as chief of the German General Staff just two days later, and the good feelings among the Allies intensified. Falkenhayn was a so-called Westerner, a member of the German military who believed the war would be won or lost on the Western Front, and he therefore devoted most of Germany's military resources to fighting the French

Paul von Hindenburg (left) and Erich Ludendorff (right) flank Kaiser Wilhelm II. The Hindenburg-Ludendorff team enjoyed tremendous success on the Eastern Front, a record Wilhelm II hoped they would duplicate on the Western Front. WIKIMEDIA

and British. Now he was being replaced by Field Marshal Paul von Hindenburg as chief of the General Staff, along with his military partner, General Erich Ludendorff, as first quartermaster general. This team had achieved smashing victories on the Eastern Front, and they were therefore assumed to be committed Easterners. Surely, they would transfer significant resources from the west to the east, providing just the opening Britain and France needed to end the Western Front stalemate at last.

BATTLES OF GUILLEMONT AND GINCHY

At the start of September, the German government published casualty lists for July. Seven of twelve German divisions engaged against the British on the Somme front reported losses of at least 50 percent. The Bavarian forces holding the village of Guillemont and its environs seemed especially vulnerable. Although not necessarily "despondent," these units had suffered very heavy losses and were inadequately served by reserve units.

Guillemont was close to the line separating the right flank of the British Fourth Army from the left of the French Sixth. The intention was to coordinate British and French forces here and use the capture of Guillemont and nearby Ginchy as the prelude to a new general offensive northward toward Courcelette.

It all began quite well on September 3. The British Fourth Army's 5th Division deployed one battalion of its 13th Brigade to capture trenches 400 yards from Falfemont Farm outside of Guillemont. The battalion attacked at 8:50 in the morning while German artillery pummeled the French 127th Regiment and also barraged the British.

While the 13th Brigade attacked Falfemont Farm, the British 95th Brigade was sent in to attack north of the farm and advance directly toward Guillemont. The brigade took the German first line, followed, at 12:50 p.m., by the second line. After a brief pause, the 13th Brigade renewed its attack and advanced against Wedge Wood, which harbored German machine guns. From the south, the French also reinitiated their attack on Wedge Wood. Supported by artillery, 95th Brigade renewed its advance on the farm and the village and, by mid-afternoon, entered Guillemont, taking 150 German prisoners.

To be sure, the British hold on Guillemont was precarious, but more British and French units soon joined the attack. By 3:30, another Fourth Army battalion and a company of pioneers entered Guillemont, from which they repulsed German counterattacks at 5:30 and at 6:30 p.m. In the meantime, elements of the 47th Brigade occupied the southwest corner of Ginchy. After German ground forces had been pushed out of Guillemont, German bomber aircraft flew over the village at dusk, dropping bombs on the new British positions.

With darkness came a lull in the fighting, but at dawn on September 4, the 5th Division began its advance on the German second line while the 15th Brigade, which relieved the exhausted 13th, prepared a new attack on Falfemont Farm. The failure of the French to coordinate with this new attack, however, exposed the British flank to punishing fire from machine guns deployed along Combles ravine. Nevertheless, a portion of Falfemont Farm was captured by 4:00 p.m. A follow-up frontal attack ninety minutes later failed with heavy losses, and so a battalion was assigned to "sap" (tunnel) forward under cover of darkness. In the meantime, elements of the 95th Brigade took Valley Trench and made it to the periphery of Leuze Wood by 7:30 p.m.

On September 5, the 20th Division was relieved by the 16th Division, and, by this time, new British trenches had been dug to link Guillemont with Leuze Wood. On September 6, the Germans counterattacked fiercely all day southwest of Leuze Wood. The counterattack was renewed at 10:30 p.m., but repulsed. The British 16th Division was now positioned to attack Ginchy, a bit less than a mile northeast of Guillemont. A small village, Ginchy nevertheless commanded the junction of six roads and was perched on high ground overlooking Combles, a German stronghold. The advance against the village had begun on September 3. Capture, by Fourth Army, came on September 9.

The loss of Ginchy was a blow to the Germans, who no longer had a position from which to observe a broad, big-picture swath of the Somme front. Although September 3–9 saw fierce German counterattacks, it was also a period during which the British and French at last coordinated quite well, and the French Sixth Army was set up for a series of attacks throughout the area through September 12. The Allies were now prepared to launch a final general offensive on this front.

FLERS-COURCELETTE: THE TANKS COME INTO THEIR OWN

By September 15, the British and French had pushed about three miles of the German line back a mile beyond where it had been on July 14. This, in turn, was a mile east of where it was on the first day of the Battle of the Somme. Again, much of the territorial gain was toward the north rather than the east, the more strategic direction, so it was more a tactical than a strategic gain for the Allies. In terms of attrition, the Anglo-French effort during September had exacted some 130,000 German casualties, killed, wounded, and captured.

The moment seemed auspicious for a third offensive on the Somme front. The Fourth Army's objective in this operation was to punch through the German line with artillery and infantry, and then, as Haig had hoped to do on the very first day of the Battle of the Somme, to exploit the breach in the line with cavalry, who would ride for the

German rear lines. The attack stepped off on September 15 from the Fourth Army salient across a broad seven-and-a-half-mile front. Twelve divisions were deployed in the attack, as was every tank the British army owned—forty-nine machines.

Early-twentieth-century industrial civilization created the Western Front deadlock by producing weapons better at killing than at conquering, suited perfectly to the needs of defenders and not so much to those of attackers. Back in January 1915, Winston Churchill held the office of first lord of the admiralty. Although he was a rib-rocked traditionalist in many respects, Churchill was also a great believer in modern science and technology applied to warfare. If technology had created the bloody stalemate on the Western Front, technology must be used to break it, Churchill reasoned. He wrote to Prime Minister H. H. Asquith early in January to recommend that a committee of engineering officers and other experts collaborate on developing machines to take trenches. Six months later, in June, a lieutenant colonel of engineers, Ernest D. Swinton, drew up a set of requirements for an armored fighting machine designed to overcome entrenched machine guns. He specified that the vehicle had to be capable of climbing a five-foot ledge and spanning a five-foot trench. It needed a range of twenty miles, could weigh no more than eight tons, and had to accommodate a ten-man crew to operate two machine guns and one field gun.

Churchill enthusiastically embraced Swinton's ideas, and although he was an army man, Swinton acquiesced in calling the machine what the first lord of the admiralty christened it, a "landship." Because the army had little faith in this innovation, the navy, goaded by Churchill, took charge of creating the world's first self-propelled fighting machines.

The navy's first landship, dubbed Little Willie, was cobbled together by the British firm of William Foster & Co. and made its appearance on September 19, 1915. It failed its initial tests, but, by this time, a new, larger design was in the works. Because of its naval sponsorship, the new tank was christened in ship fashion, HMS *Centipede*, but, more familiarly, it was known as Big Willie and, strangely enough, also as "Mother." The prototype worked reasonably well and went into mass production as the Mark I. It was this vehicle that was deployed to the Somme.

The Mark I was not only Britain's first heavy tank, it was the world's first tank to enter combat, doing so at the Battle of the Somme. WIKIMEDIA

Equipped with caterpillar-style tracks instead of wheels, Mark I could lumber across many obstacles and span most trenches. Those it could not span, it was usually capable of descending and climbing. The vehicle was more heavily armored and therefore much heavier than Swinton had specified—a staggering thirty tons rather than eight—which meant that it moved at a very slow meandering pace of about a half-mile per hour. Nevertheless, it was *almost* impervious to machine gun fire—unless a lucky (or unlucky) shot found its vulnerable fuel tanks.

Repeatedly foiled in his attempts to exploit the mobility of cavalry on the Somme front, Douglas Haig saw in the *tank* (this name came into use when early manufacturing drawings of the vehicle were labeled as self-propelled water carriers—"tanks"—to satisfy the curious and to thwart espionage) an alternate means of mobility suited to trench warfare. He therefore ordered a thousand to be built. What he got was forty-nine. It was a most disappointing number, but Haig resolved to make use of them nevertheless, even though he himself had earlier argued that the tanks were impractical unless employed in large numbers. In addition to being slow, the vehicles were notoriously unreliable and given to breakdowns. Visibility from inside the tank was extremely limited and radio communication out of the question. The first tank crews communicated via carrier pigeons.

Still, Haig wanted to give this new weapon every advantage, and he and Rawlinson agreed to employ a special artillery barrage that would leave unshelled designated "lanes" through no-man's-land, to facilitate movement of the tanks, which were put into their starting position on September 11. Of the forty-nine on hand, seventeen proved incapable of getting even as far as the front line. Another seven of the remaining twenty-two gathered at the front refused to work when zero hour came. The attack on Flers-Courcelette therefore began with just fifteen tanks.

As it turned out, they were quite sufficient to strike fear into the Germans—for a time, at least. Like most novel weapons of this war, such as flamethrowers and poison gas, the initial effect was terrifying, but it was also soon adjusted to and coped with. The combat debut of the tank was mostly anticlimactic. Perhaps this was just as well, since, instead of embracing the new technology, German commanders scoffed at it, and

The bodies of Canadian troops in no-man's-land a short distance in front of the Canadian lines at Courcelette. NETHERLANDS NATIONAAL ARCHIEF

the Germans, who would build some of the greatest tanks of World War II, developed almost none during World War I.

Even without much help from the Mark I tanks, the BEF, which fought alongside the Canadian Corps in this battle, pushed through to gain one and a quarter miles in the battle's first three days. The infantry followed the slow-moving tanks into Martinpuich, Flers, and Courcelette, all of which fell before the advance. High Wood, which had almost been captured earlier, finally succumbed as well.

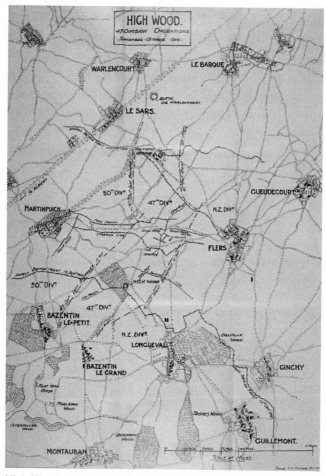

High Wood and surrounding objectives, September–October 1916. BRITISH ARMY MAP

Nature itself turned against the British on September 17. Stormy weather transformed no-man's-land into impassable mud, and the delays this imposed gave the enemy time to muster reinforcements, which arrested the advance of the combined British and Canadian forces. Bogged down, the Allies incurred heavy casualties, among whom was Raymond Asquith, the thirty-seven-year-old son of Prime Minister Herbert Asquith. The attack was aborted on September 22, having achieved a good tactical victory, even if it fell far short of the strategic victory that would have been a breakthrough to the German rear.

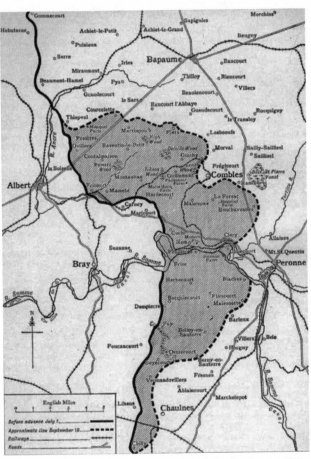

Territory gained by the British and French by September 18 (shaded area). WIKIMEDIA

Mud waged an undeclared war against both sides. Here, British troops improvise, pulling a heavy cannon over a makeshift narrow-gauge railway bed. The wheels of the gun carriage have been fitted with two homemade sets of caterpillar tracks. The men on the roadbed do the heavy pulling while those in the narrow ditch struggle to keep the gun traveling straight. NATIONAL LIBRARY OF SCOTLAND

BATTLE OF MORVAL

Three days after calling off the Battle of Flers–Courcelette, elements of the Fourth Army commenced the Battle of Morval, consisting of an attack on that village in addition to Gueudecourt and Lesboeufs, all held by the German First Army. Since these were the final tactical objectives of the Flers-Courcelette battle, Morval may be considered an extension of it.

The Morval operation was actually planned to begin earlier, but was postponed in order to coordinate with attacks on Combles by elements of the French Sixth Army. Stormy weather delayed these, creating great anxiety on the part of Allied commanders, who were eager to prevent the German units that were defending Thiepval from taking on reinforcements before September 26, when Gough's Reserve Army was to launch an attack on that German stronghold. Once the Morval operation got moving on September 25, the commanders pushed it hard.

The pressure paid off in the rapid capture of Combles, Morval, Lesboeufs, and Gueudecourt, one after the other. The Germans suffered heavily, but the full scope of the offensive was impeded by the tardiness of the French Sixth Army. Nevertheless, Rawlinson's Fourth Army moved swiftly on September 25, penetrating farther than it had since July 14. The German salient adjacent to Combles was left supremely vulnerable.

RENEWED OFFENSIVE AGAINST THIEPVAL RIDGE

Thiepval and the ridge adjacent to it had constituted a key German strongpoint since July 1. The position overlooked both Pozières and Courcelette and was capable of interdicting traffic on the Albert-Bapaume Road. It was both heavily fortified and defended by a fiercely determined garrison.

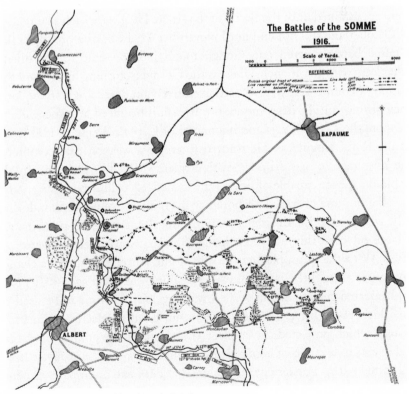

The Albert-Bapaume Road and vicinity. WIKIMEDIA

On September 26, in parallel with the Battle of Morval, General Hubert Gough launched an offensive against Thiepval. It was the first major operation of his Reserve Army. In addition to the formidable character of the German defenses here and the sheer grit of the troops who manned them, Thiepval ridge and environs were crisscrossed by a complex of trenches and shelters. This put some in mind of a garden maze, albeit one dug into the earth rather than rising in the form of hedge walls above it. The confusion was compounded by heavy shell damage inflicted on the trenches in many places and by the concentrated accumulation of shell craters that acted as a kind of detached moat around the German defenders.

Heavy fire from the Thiepval defenders combined with terrible weather and the sheer chaos of the surrounding terrain slowed Gough significantly. For this reason, some of the objectives assigned to this battle were not attained until the Battle of the Ancre Heights, which spanned all of October and did not end until November 11, a week before the entire Somme battle petered out. Gough found it impossible to coordinate effectively with the French, whereas the Germans, turning away from the notion of counterattack, refocused exclusively on defensive warfare, long their strong suit. In desperation, the British introduced an experimental weapon, the Livens Projector, brainchild of Captain William H. Livens of the Royal Engineers. He wanted to create a weapon that combined the advantages of gas cylinders with artillery shells. His idea was simply to build a device capable of firing fully loaded gas cylinders at the enemy.

The Somme provided a laboratory for military improvisation during July, when, near La Boisselle, toxic chemical agents were poured into a large oil can. This was then loaded into a twelve-inch-diameter oil drum. With the drum playing the role of gun barrel, an explosive charge fired ("projected") the large oil can containing chemical agents. A more sophisticated version of this system was developed in time to be used in the Thiepval offensive. The new weapon included an electric detonation system, which projected the canister, containing thirty pounds of chemical agent, to a range of about sixteen hundred yards. The canister itself was fitted with a burster charge designed to detonate on impact, dispers-

In 1916, Adolf Hitler was a corporal (left) at the Somme front, where he was seri-ously wounded in October. The photograph on the right shows him some twenty years later, as Germany's supreme leader during World War II. WIKIMEDIA

ing the agent over a wide area. The lethal load that was projected did not necessarily have to be poison "gas." The canisters could also be filled with flammable oil and used as incendiary ordnance. In addition to the Livens projector, the British tried what they called machine gun bombardment, using water-cooled heavy Vickers machine guns not as traditional direct-fire weapons—weapons aimed directly at a visible target—but as indi-rect-fire weapons that laid down a continuous barrage for hours on end, effectively transforming any area into a nonstop killing field.

This crew mans a British Vickers heavy machine gun, about fifty pounds in weight with a 28-inch barrel and a .303-caliber bore. Capable of firing five hundred rounds per minute to a muzzle velocity of 2,440 feet per second over an indirect fire range of forty-five hundred yards, the Vickers was perhaps the most formidable and versatile machine gun of the war. WIKIMEDIA

The most intriguing experimentation came in the formulation of methods of combining and coordinating tank and infantry operations, so that infantrymen were, in effect, provided with self-propelled artillery support. As the war progressed, this would shape British doctrine concerning the use of tanks less as weapons in their own right than as weapons to be used only to support the infantry.

The innovations all made for a formidable challenge to the Germans, who were significantly outnumbered during Gough's offensive, especially as the offensive was augmented by the French Sixth Army. Breaks forced in the German lines (northwest of Courcelette and east of Thiepval) on September 27 and 28 precipitated the defeat of the Germans here. Outflanked by the British 11th Division, they were at last forced to yield the village of Thiepval itself, with most of its garrison becoming prisoners of war. Once Thiepval and its adjacent ridge were in hand, the British continued over the next several days to attack the Stuff and Schwaben redoubts in what developed as the Battle of Le Transloy and the Battle of Ancre Heights, both beginning on October 1.

BATTLES OF LE TRANSLOY AND THE ANCRE HEIGHTS

When the Battle of Le Transloy began on October 1, the weather was fine, and the British captured Le Sars on October 7. This was a point six miles northeast on the Albert-Bapaume Road from where the British line had been on July 1. But, between October 8 and 11 severe downpours with thick fog immobilized both the British and the French. Rain, fog, and even mud troubled the Germans far less, since their eastward-lying supply routes were shorter and not cratered by shell holes. The Germans took advantage of the weather to concentrate artillery bombardment on roads passing through Allied-held territory, creating shell holes that filled with water and made them impassable at many points. This forced both the British Fourth Army and the French Sixth to reduce the scope of their attacks, refocusing them on localized objectives.

This is not to say that the deteriorating weather was easy on the typical German soldier. It was not. But German logistical problems were far less severe than those afflicting the Allies, and, in bad weather, fighting a defensive war was easier than trying to carry out an offensive campaign. It is true, however, that the British and French had more troops than the Germans, including a much larger pool of reserves. This enabled the Allies to rotate divisions in and out of the line at more frequent intervals. Still, the German Second and First Armies were able to recover from the reverses they had suffered in September. Fresh divisions were diverted from Verdun and sent to relieve the most seriously depleted divisions. Equally important was the arrival of more artillery and ammunition, as well as new airplanes, which were more advanced than anything the Allies had. The old German Air Service was also reconfigured as the *Luftstreitkräfte*, the German Air Force, with more efficiently centralized command. For the first time on the Somme front, German pilots posed a serious challenge to Anglo-French air superiority.

The cost to the Germans of the massive shift of men and materiel from Verdun to the Somme was heavy, however. In General Philippe Pétain's First Offensive Battle of Verdun (October 20–November 2), reduced German forces were badly defeated. In this sense, the Battle of the Somme accomplished at least one of its objectives, which was to relieve pressure on the French at Verdun.

No sooner did the Anglo-British forces recover from the weather delays of October 8–11 than they put off another infantry assault from October 13 to October 18 to give the Royal Artillery sufficient time to deliver a brutal bombardment of the German trenches at Le Transloy and the Ancre Heights. In contrast to July 1, Haig insisted on a very thorough reconnaissance to assess the effect of the bombardment. To his chagrin, he was forced to conclude that the enemy had largely rebuilt its defenses and had suffered minimally from the long bombardment. He therefore reduced the extent of what had been planned as a new Big Push, cancelling the participation of Allenby's Third Army entirely and limiting the attacks planned for Gough's Reserve Army and Rawlinson's Fourth Army. As if these reductions were not sufficient to sap momentum, the Allies were forced yet again to await the departure of foul weather. Fourth Army operations resumed on a limited scale on October 23, but the French Sixth Army suspended operations supporting Fourth Army attacks at Le Transloy until November 5, about two weeks before the Battle of the Somme was called off.

The Reserve Army (which would be renamed Fifth Army on October 29) conducted major attacks in the Ancre Heights area on October 1, 8, 21, and 25 and then, shortly before the Battle of the Somme ended, one more, during November 10–11. Between these main attacks, smaller, subsidiary attacks were launched continuously, except when bad weather intervened. The rain and the mud and the fog were enemies that could not be defeated.

The British objective now was to possess the Ancre Heights and rob the enemy of its ability to see to the west, to watch the British moving in and through Albert. Possession of the heights would give the Reserve Army—the newly renamed Fifth Army—a view of German positions in and around Beaumont-Hamel, Serre, and Beaucourt. For the Germans, the objective was to hold onto what it possessed on the Heights: the Regina Trench and those portions of the Schwaben Redoubt and the Stuff Redoubt that were north and northeast, respectively, of Thiepval village. They defended these positions relentlessly, not with a static defense alone, but also using multiple counterattacks and even some self-initiated attacks.

The British persisted—and persisted.

In his memoir of the Somme, Subaltern Max Plowman recorded what he termed the "Desolation of the Somme" during the late fall:

> *Not a sign of life is anywhere to be seen, but instead there appear, in countless succession, stretching as far as the eye can pierce the gloom, shell-holes filled with water. The sense of desolation these innumerable, silent, circular pools produce is horrible, so vividly do they remind me of a certain illustration by Doré to Dante's Inferno, that I begin to wonder whether I have not stepped out of life and entered one of the circles of the damned; and as I look upon these evil pools I half expect to see a head appearing from each one. Here and there the succession of pools is broken by what appear in the fading light to be deep yawning graves, and over these our duck-walk makes a frail and slippery bridge.[5]*

The fight wrested Stuff Redoubt from the enemy on October 9, and, five days later, the last piece of the Schwaben Redoubt still held by the Germans likewise fell. The loss of these remaining strongholds on the Ancre Heights instantly rendered vulnerable the 28th German Reserve Division, which was deployed in the Ancre valley below. Erich Ludendorff, who, with Paul von Hindenburg, had replaced Erich von Falkenhayn as one of the top commanders of the German army, proposed withdrawing from the salient centered on St. Pierre Divion and Beaumont on opposite banks of the River Ancre. The proposal was rejected because there were no better defensive positions to which to retreat. German First Army commander Fritz von Below proposed counterattacking instead. The recommendation was accepted—and it proved disastrous.

Each German counterattack failed. On October 21, advancing five hundred yards, the British captured all but the eastern portion of the Regina Trench. Compounding this defeat for the Germans, the French renewed their offensive at Verdun on October 24. This threat forced

German high command to halt the transfer of troops from Verdun to the Somme. Unfortunately for the British, however, bleak weather set in from the close of October to November 9, arresting the Allied movement of reinforcements to the Somme front.

Of the Germans and the mud, the mud became the more formidable enemy. "Rain, rain, rain! It has rained all day," Max Plowman lamented:

> We are all in the trench at last, though some of the men remained stuck on the way till long after daylight. While the trenches are in this condition we can neither get to the Germans nor they to us. Both sides are glued where they stand, so that Heaven alone knows what purpose we serve here, or whether we shall ever get out again. Like so many grotesque monuments, the men sit huddled under their ground-sheets at their places beneath the parapet. . . . To move fifty yards along the trench is, at present, half an hour's work.[6]

Even for the British, who now at last had the upper hand, the view from the Ancre Heights was bleak. Rain and fog cloaked the distant vista, rendering it opaque, and all Plowman saw were corpses lying

> along the parados, rotting in the wet: every now and then a booted foot appears jutting over the trench. The mud makes it all but impassable, and now, sunk in up to the knees, I have the momentary terror of never being able to pull myself out. Such horror gives frenzied energy, and I tear my legs free and go on. Turning sharply round a bend I come upon a fearsome sight. Deep water lies in a descending right-angle of the trench, and at arm's length from me a body has fallen face downward in the water, barring the way. Shall I push the body aside and wade, chancing the depth of the water, or shall I get out on top and double across the corner [risking a sniper's bullet]?[7]

WITH A WHIMPER

A break in the weather on November 11 allowed the Canadian Division to resume action, and the Fifth Army returned to the offensive starting on November 13. The Battle of Ancre Heights was now the Battle of Ancre proper. It would prove to be the last major British initiative of 1916.

Gough's Fifth Army advanced through the Ancre valley, intent on hitting the exhausted, exposed 28th German Reserve Division there. The worsening weather as winter approached would almost certainly impose a suspension of fighting in this sector of northern France. Acting on the visions evoked in the 1915 conferences at Chantilly, Sir Douglas Haig had commenced the Somme offensive on July 1, 1916, intent on achieving on the Western Front what the Italians proposed to achieve on the Austrian (southern) front and the Russians on the Eastern Front. He would break through. They would break through. Germany, overwhelmed by offensives on three fronts, unable to transfer troops from one front to the other, would be finished. The Great War itself would be finished. But now, five months later, with summer a distant dreamlike memory, all Gough proposed to achieve was a decent position on the high ground from which to take up the offensive again—in the spring weather of 1917. In other words, the best that now could be hoped was not to end the war, but to continue it—on the most favorable (or least unfavorable) terms that a victory at Ancre might eke out.

Gough's engineers reloaded a mine that had been dug under the German position at Hawthorn Ridge Redoubt. It was detonated on November 13, and the 51st (Highland) Division attacked the redoubt. Although a parallel attack on Serre quickly collapsed, Beaumont-Hamel and Beaucourt-sur-l'Ancre, both to the south of Serre, fell to the British. South of the River Ancre, St. Pierre Divion was also captured, and British troops occupied trenches just outside of German-held Grandcourt. The Canadian 4th Division targeted the remaining German-occupied portion of Regina Trench north of Courcelette. After capturing this, on November 18, they went on to clear the Desire Support Trench adjacent to it.

"Desire Support Trench"! It was hardly a name designed for posterity. None of the landmarks and tiny villages the British had paid for with so many lives had names that ever meant much of anything to anyone who did not live in Picardy. During the five months of the Battle of the Somme,

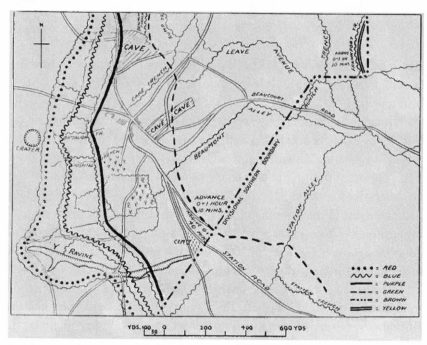

Beaumont-Hamel and vicinity, November 13, 1916. WIKIMEDIA

After capturing German trenches at St. Pierre Divion, a party of British soldiers sorts through the enemy's abandoned equipment. Note the three rifles slung on one Tommy's shoulder, and the two on another. Machine-gun ammunition was especially sought after, and the soldiers at the right foreground comb through ammunition belts. NATIONAL LIBRARY OF SCOTLAND

there had been slight territorial gains bought with exorbitant human losses. The German line along the Somme front—some sixteen miles of a four-hundred-mile-long Western Front—now bulged toward the north and, to a lesser extent, the east, six miles at its greatest extent. But that was six miles into eastern France, of which there was still much more that was held by German soldiers. Germany itself seemed in no danger of invasion.

Shortly before the British ended their offensive on November 18 and the Germans obliged by launching no counteroffensive, Max Plowman, the lowly subaltern who, like so many other young Englishmen had volunteered to fight for king and country, gazed at Le Transloy "1500 yards away. . . . How peaceful and calm it all looks in the sunshine! Gazing over here, who could imagine what a hell this place has been? Now there's no firing it seems absurd to stay here. Why don't we walk over the fields and explore the village that looks so inviting? You can bet the Germans are feeling the same. Why don't we all get out and walk away?"[8]

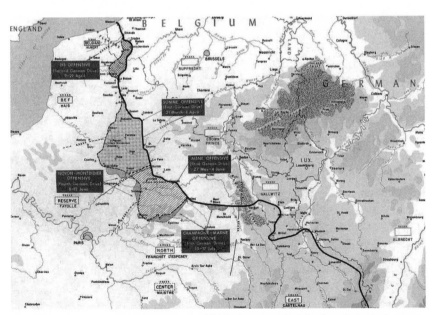

Battles fought in the Somme sector in 1918; the cross-hatched and shaded areas show the fighting during the German offensives of this year, in the course of which the German army retook (for a time) much that had been lost during the Battle of the Somme in 1916. UNITED STATES MILITARY ACADEMY

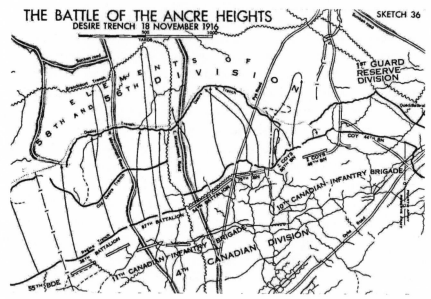

The Battle of Ancre Heights, showing "Desire Trench." WIKIMEDIA

Plowman answered his own question: "We seem to be here under the constraint of some malevolent idiot. . . . No doubt it's good to fight when indignation and hatred boil up as they did in 1914. But these passions have long since spent themselves." Then he asked the same question again: "Why are we fighting still?"[9]

"Machine-made," that's how Plowman described the war he had come to know. "If all the machinery of war were now suddenly taken from our hands, I am certain the war would stop at once."[10]

But what stopped it was the weather in a place where the climate at such a time of year inevitably produced such weather. The weather did not drive out the armies of the Somme. They remained, more or less inert throughout the winter. But the weather did stop most of the fighting—until . . . until, inevitably, the season turned again. With spring, troops could again move up to the front and airplanes could again spy out targets and gunsights could look out, again, on sunny fields of fire.

Endnotes

Chapter 1: Chantilly Visions

1   David F. Burg and L. Edward Purcell, *Almanac of World War I* (Lexington: University of Kentucky Press, 1998), "28 July 1914."
2   Burg and Purcell, "29 July 1914."
3   Barbara Tuchman, *The Guns of August* (1962; repr., New York: Ballantine, 1994), 17.
4   Steven Schlesser, *The Soldier, the Builder, and the Diplomat* (Seattle: Cune, 2005), 130.
5   Walter Lord, *The Good Years: From 1900 to the First World War* (New Brunswick, NJ: Transaction, 2011), 341.
6   G. K. Chesterton, *Collected Works* (San Francisco: Ignatius Press, 1987), 5: 268.
7   Bob Carruthers, *Images of War: The British at First and Second Ypres* (Barnsley, UK: Pen & Sword Military, 2015), 7.
8   Alan Clark, *The Donkeys* (London: Pimlico, 1991), 73.
9   Robin Prior and Trevor Wilson, *Command on the Western Front: The Military Career of Sir Henry Rawlinson 1914–1918* (Oxford: Blackwell, 1992), 25.

Chapter 2: Chantilly Revisions

1   Winston Churchill quoted in Martin Gilbert, *The Somme: Heroism and Horror in the First World War* (New York: Henry Holt, 2006), chapter 15; Kindle ed.
2   Churchill quoted in Gilbert, chapter 15; Kindle ed.
3   A. J. Balfour quoted in Gilbert, chapter 1; Kindle ed.
4   Lord Kitchener's rebuttal cited in Gilbert, chapter 1; Kindle ed.
5   General Douglas Haig quoted in Gilbert, chapter 1; Kindle ed.
6   General Douglas Haig quoted in Gilbert, chapter 1; Kindle ed.
7   Churchill quoted in Gilbert, chapter 9; Kindle ed.
8   Churchill quoted in Gilbert, chapter 9; Kindle ed. (italics added).
9   Erich von Falkenhayn, "Verdun," *Militär-Wochenblatt, Zeitschrift für die deutsche Wehrmacht* 104, no. 6 (July 12, 1919): 98–107.

10 Erich von Falkenhayn, "Christmas Memorandum" (December 1915), in Falken-hayn, *General Headquarters (German) 1914–1916 and Its Critical Decisions (Uckfield, UK: Naval & Military Press,* 2004), 176ff (emphasis added).
11 Haig quoted in Gilbert, chapter 1; Kindle ed.
12 Kitchener quoted in Gilbert, chapter 1; Kindle ed.

Chapter 3: The Men and Their Plans

1 General Henry Rawlinson quoted in Martin Middlebrook, *The First Day on the Somme* (Barnsley, UK: Sword & Pen Military, 2006), chapter 4; Kindle ed.
2 General Douglas Haig quoted in Denis Winter, *Death's Men: Soldiers of the Great War* (London: Penguin, 1979), 63.
3 Lieutenant-Colonel John Frederick Lucy, *There's a Devil in the Drum* (1936; reprt. ed., n.p.: Pickle Partners, 2015), chapter 13; Kindle ed.
4 Max Plowman, *Subaltern on the Somme: A Classic True Story of the First World War* (1928; reprt. ed., n.p: n. pub., 2014), "The C.O"; Kindle ed.
5 Plowman, "The C.O"; Kindle ed.
6 The British First Army would enter the action on the Somme in earnest at the Battle of Fromelles (July 19–20, 1916), considered "subsidiary" to the main Battle of the Somme. This "subsidiary" battle pitted between 10,000 and 15,000 First Army men against perhaps 30,000 Germans, resulting in catastrophic First Army casualties of more than 7,000 killed and wounded.
7 Tim Travers, *The Killing Ground* (London: Allen & Unwin, 1987), 105.

Chapter 4: Breaking Ground

1 Martin Middlebrook, *The First Day on the Somme* (1971; reprint ed., Barnsley, UK: Pen & Sword Military, 2006), chapter 5; Kindle ed.
2 Middlebrook, chapter 5; Kindle ed.
3 Max Plowman, *Subaltern on the Somme* (1928; n.p., Amazon Digital Services), "Still Alive"; Kindle ed.
4 Middlebrook, chapter 5; Kindle ed.
5 Henry Rawlinson, letter to Quartermaster General, June 14, 1916, quoted in Middlebrook, chapter 5; Kindle ed.
6 David R. Woodward, *Lloyd George and the Generals* (London and New York: Frank Cass, 2004), 37.

Chapter 5: Into the Fire

1 Quoted in Peter Hart, *The Somme: The Darkest Hour on the Western Front* (New York: Pegasus, 2008), 91.
2 Quoted in Hart, 91.
3 Quoted in Hart, 212.
4 Quoted in Martin Middlebrook, *The First Day on the Somme* (1971; reprint ed., Barnsley, UK: Pen & Sword Military, 2006), chapter 5; Kindle ed.

5   Quoted in Middlebrook, chapter 5; Kindle ed.
6   Max Plowman, *Subaltern on the Somme: A Classic True Story of the First World War* (1928; reprt. ed., n.p: n.pub., 2014), "Lieutenant Hardy"; Kindle ed.
7   Quoted in Middlebrook, chapter 5; Kindle ed.
8   Quoted in Middlebrook, chapter 5; Kindle ed.
9   Plowman, "Billets at Halloy"; Kindle ed.
10 Quoted in Middlebrook, chapter 6; Kindle ed.
11 Sir James Edward Edmonds, *History of the Great War Based on Official Documents by Direction of the Committee of Imperial Defence, Military Operations: France and Belgium, 1916*, vol. 1 (London: Public Records Office), 392.
12 Quoted in Middlebrook, chapter 6; Kindle ed.
13 Quoted in Middlebrook, chapter 6; Kindle ed.
14 Middlebrook, chapter 7; Kindle ed., and Hart, 104.
15 Quoted in Middlebrook, chapter 7.
16 Middlebrook, chapter 7.
17 Middlebrook, chapter 7.

Chapter 6: An Aptitude for Folly

1   Martin Middlebrook, *The First Day on the Somme* (1971; reprint ed., Barnsley, UK: Pen & Sword Military, 2006), chapter 7; Kindle ed.
2   Captain Sir Basil Liddell Hart, *Through the Fog of War* (New York: Random House, 1938), 342.
3   William Butler Yeats, "An Irish Airman foresees his Death" (1919), www.poetry foundation.org/poem/248416.
4   Middlebrook, chapter 7: Kindle ed.
5   Middlebrook, chapter 7; Kindle ed.
6   Middlebrook, chapter 7; Kindle ed.
7   Middlebrook, chapter 7; Kindle ed.
8   Middlebrook, chapter 7; Kindle ed.
9   Henry Williamson's *The Golden Virgin*, quoted in Gilbert, 1027.
10 Martin Gilbert, *The Somme: Heroism and Horror in the First World War* (New York: Henry Holt, 2006), chapter 3; Kindle ed.
11 Britain called upon the semi-independent Dominions of the British Common-wealth (Australia, Canada, Newfoundland, New Zealand, and South Africa) as well as its colonies (chiefly India) to assist in fighting on the Western Front.
12 Gilbert, chapter 3; Kindle ed.
13 Gilbert, chapter 3; Kindle ed.
14 Gilbert, chapter 3; Kindle ed.
15 Gilbert, chapter 3; Kindle ed.

Chapter 7: South of the Ancre

1   Quoted in Martin Gilbert, *The Somme: Heroism and Horror in the First World War* (New York: Henry Holt, 2006), chapter 3; Kindle ed.

2 Quoted in Gilbert, chapter 3; Kindle ed.
3 Quoted in Gilbert, chapter 3; Kindle ed.
4 Quoted in Gilbert, chapter 3; Kindle ed.
5 Quoted in Peter Hart, *The Somme: The Darkest Hour on the Western Front* (New York: Pegasus, 2008), 154.
6 Quoted in Hart, 154.
7 Quoted in Hart, 154.
8 R. H. Tawney, "The Attack," *Westminster Gazette* (London), August 1916; retrieved at http://leoklein.com/itp/somme/texts/tawney_1916.html.
9 Sir James Edward Edmonds, *History of the Great War Based on Official Documents by Direction of the Committee of Imperial Defence, Military Operations: France and Belgium, 1916*, vol. 1 (London: Public Records Office), 342.

Chapter 8: South of Bray: France's Fight on the Somme

1   Alan Seeger, *Letters and Diary of Alan Seeger* (New York: Charles Scribner's Sons, 1917), 206–7.
2   Seeger, 208.
3   Seeger, 211.
4   Seeger, 213.
5   Seeger, 213.
6   Seeger, 214–15.
7   Seeger, 215.
8   Seeger, 215–16.
9   Seeger, 216.
10 Seeger, 216–17.
11 Seeger, 217.
12 Seeger, 217.
13 Seeger, 218.
14 Seeger, 218.

Chapter 9: The British Follow Up

1   James M. Gavin, *War and Peace in the Space Age* (New York: Harper), 64.
2   Martin Middlebrook, *The First Day on the Somme* (Barnsley, UK: Pen & Sword Military, 2006), chapter 9; Kindle ed.
3   Middlebrook, chapter 11; Kindle ed.
4   Max Plowman, *Subaltern on the Somme* (1928; n.p., Amazon Digital Services), "Still Alive" and "Battle Instructions"; Kindle ed.
5   Plowman, "Battle Instructions"; Kindle ed.
6   Middlebrook, chapter 9; Kindle ed.
7   Middlebrook, chapter 9; Kindle ed.
8   Middlebrook, chapter 9; Kindle ed.
9   Middlebrook, chapter 9; Kindle ed.

10 Middlebrook, chapter 9; Kindle ed.
11 Middlebrook, chapter 10; Kindle ed.
12 Middlebrook, chapter 10; Kindle ed.
13 Middlebrook, chapter 10; Kindle ed.
14 Middlebrook, chapter 10; Kindle ed.

Chapter 10: Flyover

1 Thomas G. Bradbeer, *The British Air Campaign During the Battle of the Somme April–November, 1916: A Pyrrhic Victory* (PhD dissertation, University of Kansas, 2011), 390–92.
2 W. Alister Williams, *Against the Odds: The Life of Group Captain Lionel Rees, VC* (Wrexham, Clwyd, UK: Bridge Books, 1989), 90.
3 Gwilym H. Lewis, *Wings Over the Somme, 1916–1918* (Wrexham, Clwyd, UK: Bridge Books, 1994), 47–48.
4 Bradbeer, 194.
5 Bradbeer, 194.
6 Bradbeer, 194.
7 Quoted in Martin Middlebrook, *The First Day on the Somme* (1971; reprint ed., Barnsley, UK: Pen & Sword Military, 2006), chapter 10; Kindle ed.
8 *Douglas Haig: War Diaries and Letters, 1914–1918*, ed. Gary Sheffield and John Bourne (London: Weidenfeld & Nicholson, 2005), 197.
9 Tyrrell M. Hawker, *Hawker VC: The First RFC Ace* (Barnsley, UK: Pen & Sword Military, 2013), 185–86.
10 Middlebrook, chapter 15; Kindle ed.
11 Sir James Edward Edmonds, *History of the Great War Based on Official Documents by Direction of the Committee of Imperial Defence, Military Operations: France and Belgium, 1916*, vol. 1 (London: Public Records Office), 483.
12 Christopher Cole, ed. *Royal Flying Corps, 1915–1916* (London: Kimber, 1969), 173; Peter Hart, *Somme Success: The Royal Flying Corps and the Battle of the Somme, 1916* (Barnsley, UK: Pen & Sword Military, 2012), 100.
13 Quoted in Bradbeer, 196.
14 Quoted in Bradbeer, 200.
15 RFC Personnel Casualty Reports, AIR 1/844/204/5/369 through AIR 1/845/204/5/376, NA, reproduced in Bradbeer, 400–401.
16 Nicholls, Jonathon. *Cheerful Sacrifice: The Battle of Arras 1917* (Barnsley, UK: Pen & Sword Military, 2005), 36.
17 Nicholls, 36.

Chapter 11: Remains of the Day

1 Martin Middlebrook, *The First Day on the Somme* (1971; reprint ed., Barnsley, UK: Pen & Sword Military, 2006), chapter 11; Kindle ed.
2 Middlebrook, chapter 11; Kindle ed.

3 Middlebrook, chapter 11; Kindle ed.
4 Alan MacDonald, *A Lack of Offensive Spirit?* (Eastbourne, UK: Iona Books, 2008), 503.
5 Martin and Mary Middlebrook, *The Middlebrook Guide to the Somme Battlefields: A Comprehensive Coverage from Crécy to the World Wars* (1991; reprint ed., Barnsley, UK: Pen & Sword Military, 2007), 109.
6 Middlebrook, *First Day on the Somme*, chapter 11; Kindle ed.
7 Middlebrook, *First Day on the Somme*, chapter 11; Kindle ed.
8 Middlebrook, *First Day on the Somme*, chapter 11; Kindle ed.
9 Middlebrook, *First Day on the Somme*, chapter 11; Kindle ed.

Chapter 12: Armies of the Night

1 Martin Middlebrook, *The First Day on the Somme* (1971; reprint ed., Barnsley, UK: Pen & Sword Military, 2006), chapter 13; Kindle ed.
2 The War Poetry Website, Wilfred Owen, "Dulce et Decorum Est," www.war poetry.co.uk/owen1.html.
3 Middlebrook, chapter 13; Kindle ed.
4 Middlebrook, chapter 13; Kindle ed.
5 "Stretcher Bearers," Spartacus Educational, http://spartacus-educational.com/ FWWstretcher.htm.
6 "Stretcher-bearers on the Western Front," *New Zealand History*, www.nzhistory .net.nz/media/interactive/stretcher-bearers.
7 Middlebrook, chapter 13; Kindle ed.
8 Middlebrook, chapter 13; Kindle ed.

Chapter 13: All Summer Long

1 Martin Middlebrook, *The First Day on the Somme* (1971; reprint ed., Barnsley, UK: Pen & Sword Military, 2006), chapter 15; Kindle ed.
2 Middlebrook, chapter 14; Kindle ed.
3 University of Birmingham Centre for First World War Studies, "Lions Led by Donkeys, Thomas David Pilcher," https://web.archive.org/web/20070121124832/ http://www.firstworldwar.bham.ac.uk/donkey/pilcher.htm.
4 Thomas Pilcher quoted in Middlebrook, chapter 14; Kindle ed.
5 Sandys quoted in Middlebrook, chapter 14; Kindle ed.
6 "Death of Lt. Col. Sandys," www.militarian.com/threads/death-of-lt-col-sandys .7292/.
7 "Rupert Edward Inglis," www.inglis.uk.com/RUPERT%20EDWARD%20ING LIS%20thiepval.htm.
8 Gary Sheffield, *The Somme* (London: Orion Publishing Group, 2015), 184.
9 Ross McMullin, "Disaster at Fromelles, Australian War Memorial," https://www .awm.gov.au/wartime/36/article/.

Chapter 14: The Guns of Autumn

1 Churchill quoted in Martin Gilbert, *The Somme: Heroism and Horror in the First World War* (New York: Henry Holt, 2006), chapter 9; Kindle ed.

2 Kevin Meyers, "The Greatest 20th Century Beneficiary of Popular Mythology Has Been the Cad Churchill," *Irish Independent* (03/09/2009), www.independent .ie/opinion/columnists/kevin-myers/the-greatest-20th-century-beneficiary-of -popular-mythology-has-been-the-cad-churchill-26563434.html.

3 Haig diary quoted in Gilbert, chapter 9; Kindle ed.

4 Quoted in Gilbert, chapter 9; Kindle ed.

5 Max Plowman, *Subaltern on the Somme: A Classic True Story of the First World War* (1928; reprt. ed., n.p: n. pub., 2014), "Desolation on the Somme"; Kindle ed.

6 Plowman, *Subaltern on the Somme*, "Rain and Mud"; Kindle ed.

7 Plowman, *Subaltern on the Somme*, "Rain and Mud"; Kindle ed.

8 Plowman, *Subaltern on the Somme*, "In Front of le Transloy"; Kindle ed.

9 Plowman, *Subaltern on the Somme*, "In Front of le Transloy"; Kindle ed.

10 Plowman, *Subaltern on the Somme*, "In Front of le Transloy"; Kindle ed.

Index

About the Author

Alan Axelrod is the author or coauthor of more than 100 books on leadership, management, history, military history, corporate history, general business, and more. After receiving his PhD in English from the University of Iowa in 1979, Axelrod taught early American literature and culture at Lake Forest College (Lake Forest, Illinois) and at Furman University (Greenville, South Carolina). He then entered scholarly publishing in 1982 as associate editor and scholar with the Henry Francis du Pont Winterthur Museum (Winterthur, Delaware), an institution specializing in the history and material culture of America prior to 1832. Axelrod was a featured speaker at the 2004 Conference on Excellence in Government (Washington, DC), at the Leadership Institute of Columbia College (Columbia, South Carolina), at the 2005 Annual Conference of the Goizueta Business School, Emory University (Atlanta), and at the 2014 annual conference of Ecopetrol (Bogota, Colombia). He was creative consultant for *Bombing Hitler's Supergun,* a 2016 Nova/PBS documentary.